Undeterred

Undeterred

KKK Target, KKK Witness

TRACEY BRAME

Copyright © 2016 Tracey Brame
All rights reserved.

ISBN-13: 9780692822753
ISBN-10: 0692822755
Library of Congress Control Number: 2016920979
NB Bookshelf, Fishers, INDIANA

Dedication

I dedicate this book to veteran and civilian PTSD survivors.

For by grace are ye saved through faith; and that not of yourselves: it is the gift of God: Not of works, lest any man should boast.
  Ephesians 2:8–9

Acknowledgements

I am thankful for
Thomas Henry and Margaret Ellen Brown,
Nancy Ellen Brame,
the staff of the Richard L Roudebush VA Medical Center
Fred Black,
And JoAnn.

Preface

The events surrounding the 2016 election only make my story more relevant. My history demonstrates the Indiana Ku Klux Klan's inability to control themselves in the face of a diversifying America. The Klan is only the most recognizable arm of the white nationalist movement that rallied on President Donald Trump's behalf, and, as we have come to see in recent weeks, there are many who do not swear allegiance to a grand dragon, but still agree with the KKK's aims and goals. *Undeterred: KKK Target, KKK Witness* chronicles my life as touched by Hoosier hate that resides beneath the surface of "Midwestern Nice." It is a hate that has long resided within the psyche of America that many are only now awaking to.

History repeats itself. President Woodrow Wilson actively embraced the Ku Klux Klan, but in the 2016 election we witnessed the Ku Klux Klan embrace presidential candidate Trump, who maintained a cautious silence and public indifference to the Klan's fervent hug. Trump's KKK supporters rallied before and after the election with KKK zeal, hailing Trump with Nazi salutes, at times physically acting against those they hate. The Klan found an impassioned solace in Trump's candidacy based on inflammatory messages, often labeled by the more moderate as hate speech. As a candidate, Donald Trump made no overt acceptance of the Klan's endorsements, often claiming he was unfamiliar with the Klan supporters who hailed him the loudest.

In Indiana, as in the rest of the nation, KKK propaganda and hate-infused defacements of buildings and landmarks spiked in the wake of Trump's election, but Indiana law refuses to define, acknowledge, or punish hate crimes. Indiana legislation also declines to recognize gay, lesbian, bisexual, or transgender (GLBT) rights, allowing civil wrongs to persist in the tapestry and spirit of Hoosier law. Some citizens of Indiana, thanks to Klan influence, actually pride themselves in being anti-GLBT. "We hate you people!" spit the grand dragon at me when he barreled toward me disapprovingly in a filing station. I was trying to use the bathroom.

Bloomington, the home of the Indiana KKK and the site of my first hateful attacks by the KKK, is viewed by many as a liberal college town. Yet it awarded the grand dragon who targeted me with his own official 'celebratory day,' despite the fact that many of the town's residents knew of his and his son's hate-based crimes. Even if many did not agree with this behavior, the majority stayed silent, tacitly giving approval of the Klan's depredating treatment of others.

In the wake of President Trump's election, he has stepped away from his campaign rhetoric filled with hateful promises. Trump's denunciation of prejudice hints that the promises he made to win the election may not be the focus of his rule. Ultimately, what President Trump says and does on the issue of diversity in the coming months and years will write a history of exclusion or inclusion.

Awaken yourself. A nation asleep is a nation in danger.

Tracey Brame
December 2016
Fishers, Indiana

Contents

Dedication · v
Acknowledgements · vii
Preface · ix

Part One: Youth · 1
Part Two: Jayns and PTSD · · · · · · · · · · · · · · · · · · · 43
Part Three: KKK · 149
Part Four: Challenges · 341

Endnotes · 361

Part One: Youth

Monterey, Friday, Shocked

I woke up on my back–though I rarely sleep in that position–head angled back, legs slightly open, hands broadly outstretched like a crucifix. I stared at the ceiling, but my mind was blank, in a strange peace like when at the ocean, but there was no sound. I checked the windows on the right side of the room. Mannish opaque curtains covered the view. I looked left, and he sat there, waiting, angry. Lately, Jayns C. Jhomes Jr. always looked perturbed. His 1990 senior yearbook entry scowled and spit one word: BYE! I never understood his ire, except that he had not wanted to go to West Point. His father made him matriculate because West Point's free tuition beat Brown University's high price tag. He certainly did not want to serve. He despised his uniform and detested his parents for insisting he wear it. Still, he hated me with even less cause, though I'd yet to realize it.

I looked back at the ceiling, unmoving, as though nailed to the bed. I could already tell that stirring would prove a huge burden, but I hated to drag in the morning. I liked early starts. From the slit in the curtain I could tell that the sun already beamed down on Monterey, yet I did not know my specific location within the city. Nothing registered. I didn't even greet Jayns.

We were engaged. I had just begun my junior year at the United States Military Academy at West Point. He had recently graduated from West Point and *started Greek language training at the Defense Institute of Language Training in Monterey, destined for a field artillery post in Thessaloniki, Greece.*

I attempted to curl up and gave a slight wince. My belly and groin ached. I tried to assess why. I possessed that familiar feeling that announced to a woman she just had sex, that something foreign had entered her. That feeling lingers for some time, as if the male organ is still there. This morning though, it was much more painful than that, but it was the only answer my brain could conjure in my situation. I failed to register that it should not have lingered so intensely overnight.

My panties and jeans rested around my ankles, with one leg wrenched free. I took off my shoes and socks and stood, pulling my panties up. I felt dazed, as though my head had been wiped clean of thoughts and impressions. I stood there, getting my bearings, and then gingerly made my way to the bathroom. Things felt new. I removed my shirt and bra and stood in front of the mirror.

Jayns appeared instantly in the doorway. He was only 5'8", weighing in at 150 pounds, but still wore a well-sculpted body from playing light-weight football at West Point, in spite of his lack of current maintenance. He had a dark complexion, military crew cut, and a gap between his front teeth that may have caused some shame in younger years. One time I suggested that we could save for braces, but he answered, hunching his shoulders, "Forget it now." He appeared to brush off a lot verbally, always hunching his shoulders as he did so, but the secret to Jayns's demeanor, the reason for the furor in his motivations, was that nothing was ever forgotten and everything was worth getting even for. No matter how small.

"You need to take a shower," he reminded me.

"I know."

"Now." As if I would forget my morning routine, he started the shower.

Ignoring his sudden urgency for my cleanliness, I focused on the fibers of my washcloth, which seemed exquisitely new, white, and clean. I touched the dry fabric to my face. How long had I slept? I did not feel groggy. I marveled at how novel small items seemed. I felt myself experiencing everything in slow motion as I removed my panties. My belly and groin continued to remind me that something had transpired, but I continued to ignore the message.

Undeterred

He watched me as if supervising my progress. "Let's go," he coaxed, smiling, but I had known him long enough to recognize such fakeness. Never had my washing been so urgent. "We have to check out soon."

Why so early, I thought. Did I wake late? Why rush me? I suddenly noticed a small mass of tissue curling in the crotch of my panties. I stared at it for a long time, catching his attention. He walked over and looked at it too. The pale pink mass sitting inside my underwear lacked blood.

"I did that," he bragged. The idea seemed ridiculous: how could he land a piece of soft tissue not nearly the complexion of his dark skin inside my underwear? "You need to hurry," he ordered, dragging the shower curtain aside and making the hooks squeal along the metal shower curtain rod.

I used a piece of toilet paper to remove the curl of flesh and flush it down the toilet. Meanwhile, he stood there, staring, hurrying me to get me in the shower.

I got in, but he continued to observe. The water hit me, and that felt like a fresh experience as well. I tried to take it in and spread the wetness around my stomach and breasts with my fingers. "Are you just going to watch me?" I asked.

"Yes. I want to see you wash up well. I'm going to watch you do it."

"Why?"

"Can't a man watch his future wife shower?" He tried to make it a playful request, but the question fell flat.

"It's weird."

I believe that to have been the longest shower I ever took. I could not get myself together. When I touched between my legs, something soft rolled between my fingers and my left thigh. It startled me because it felt like a small caterpillar, and I jumped. I held it up and it proved to be pinkish as well. I handled it between my right thumb and pointer finger, perplexed as it rolled into a coil and unrolled to a thin sheet of torn membrane.

Jayns smirked, "I did that too."

I said, "It's skin. It looks like raw chicken." I could not understand it. I did not question why I had raw skin between my legs.

"Sorry about that," his words were flippant and he did not sound sorry at all.

"What?" I wondered.

He pointed to the skin, and I let it fall to the shower floor and muddle with the used water rushing towards the drain.

"Will you give me a break?" I asked. "Women lose a lot of skin when they come on their period. I must be about to come on my period."

I failed to realize how strange it was that I was standing in a shower in an unfamiliar room with Jayns supervising my cleaning. I also failed to recall that menstruation never shed flesh-toned skin; it dispelled red clots of blood and tissue. What I witnessed suggested no blood, just tiny, red, pin-sized dots in the tissue. I did not question it critically. I just made my own version of an explanation and continued showering.

I ached as I washed between my legs. The fibers of the cloth irritated the soreness, and it retarded my strokes. I had never been that sensitive before, but I did not note that at the time. I just washed slower so as not to disturb my obviously raw skin. Cleaning between my legs took almost as long as the rest of the shower. I just could not roughhouse so tender a spot.

He wanted me to brush my teeth twice because the toothpaste the hotel provided was off-brand. He watched and asked me to get into various crevices that were obviously bothering him. I tried to laugh off his concerns. He made no sense.

"No cavities this weekend," he joked. He got on my nerves. I went back to the bed with purposefully slower movements and sat down.

He had laid out my next outfit nearby, a detail he had never bothered with before. I reached for it, but had to stand and walk to it–more purposeful movements, more pain. I sat back down at the foot of the bed and listened to him running bath water. I heard scrubbing on the textured tub floor.

"What are you doing?" I called.

"Making sure all of you is out of the shower."

"Are you suddenly afraid of standing in the shower after me?" He didn't respond. More scrubbing. Wringing of the cloth. Scouring.

I looked at the wall in front of me as I sat on the bed and noticed that something was splattered on the wall. I willed myself to stand again to better observe my findings. More chicken. Three pieces randomly slammed against the wall. I sat down again. I could not comprehend it.

Undeterred

Jayns came back into the room and announced that we were losing time, that I moved too slowly. I finished dressing while he grabbed his backpack and headed to the door. As I followed him out, I stopped and touched one of the skin masses on the wall's surface. It was exactly like the ones in the bathroom except it had grown soft and sticky, drying in the air. Very odd, I thought but said nothing to Jayns, who failed to notice the remaining lumps at all.

It would be years before I knew he had raped me, brutally raped me, and that the skin strewn on the wall and my clothes hailed from the inside lining of my vagina, which had been purposely and forcibly ripped out and left to rot by the man who swore that he wanted to marry me.

PTSD

My brain, unable to process what happened that night, needed time to cope with my truth, and so I simply forgot it as if it had never happened. This memory lapse is part of a medical condition called "being in shock." It is an aspect of post-traumatic stress disorder (PTSD), a medically injured response to fear. In most people, fear triggers natural, involuntary reactions that include flight, fight, or freeze responses. With the "freeze" response, a person facing terror can go into shock, and may simply go numb and dismiss the incident. In my case, I froze and my brain involuntarily decided to forego facing a horrid truth, thus beginning a long era of PTSD for me.

Those of us with PTSD may have triggers that invite flashbacks to the terror we experienced. Many shock victims try to avoid similar situations to protect themselves. Unfortunately, if we cannot recall what sent us into shock in the first place, it is hard to avoid triggers.

My particular type of memory loss, called dissociative amnesia, is worse than simply forgetting. My brain still has the memory filed away, but it won't let me access it without time to adjust to the trauma. It's dangerous. It's like being punched in the gut, and by the time you stand up you cannot remember that the guy in front of you swung the blow. You know your belly aches, but are unsure as to why. It's that immediate. It's also involuntary. There is nothing wrong with your intellect. You are a smart or brilliant person who has been punched, but are unable to recall the slug. Imagine the danger you're in when your memory is suspended, when you are susceptible to more violence. While you try to make sense of your environment, the perpetrator is trying to make sense of you.

Our memory loss is not permanent. Doctors know this. Dissociative amnesia always allows for memory recall with time, the length of which may vary. The disease is the brain's way of saying, "Enough terror for now."

Shock victims linger in harm's way. We simply do not know to escape, nor can we remember to run. We feel no fear in the moment at all. Two percent of the nation wades through one such response to a tragic life event, but I have lived through many, many more.

Ours is a disease of memory, not of make-believe. If someone was not present, we do not recall him being a part of the events that sent us into shock, or conjure fictitious events about him. When we come out of shock, we remember what happened, and, as events take shape, there is often someone who confirms the truth, even if only by taunting.

Shock victims attract criminals like Jayns and the Ku Klux Klan (KKK). These kinds of people immediately sense that we are stricken, vulnerable, but the question remains: what does a psychopath or sociopath choose to do with the realization that his or her victim suffers shock? How does he or she weave a cloak of innocence? Saddled with shock, how does one gain strength to speak for herself and others? This is my story.

HOME

Chess

Castling is a king's move in chess. Essentially, the king dives for cover behind a row of pawns by trading places with a rook (also called a castle) and the castle assumes a fighting position on the king's behalf. From this vantage point, the king can relax and watch the battle for his life play out from relative safety.

My Uncle Ted taught me to play chess after he married my mother's sister, Aunt Joyce. He seemed smart and informative. He took an interest in my mind and declared me bright enough to give chess a shot. An ornate chess set sat on a glass shelving in the living room for display. I often stopped and eyed its beauty, but no one played at our house.

Though I saw my parents regularly when I was growing up, I lived with my grandparents, Mama and Papa. Mama did not work, and when at birth I suffered from convulsions and fevers, she declared that I needed more care than my mother, a working mom, could yield.

My grandparents knew nothing of chess. The fact that we had a game board and ornate pieces made me believe that we were rich. We had an elaborately decorative living room; Mama's touch on display. She traveled the country to places I had not been and brought back keepsakes; therefore, to my mind, we were rich.

Back in the '70s, many people used chess sets merely as an interesting display in their home, which is probably why there have always been more chess sets sold than games played. Most people do not even pretend to admire the game of thought anymore, but our lives may parallel chess more than we know.

Our classic black-and-white game with faux-marble cut pieces mesmerized me. The pieces in the back row with the minute facial expressions drew me closer. Uncle Ted began the process of unlocking that curiosity. Piece by piece, he explained their secret strengths in movement. It struck me that their strengths also determined their weaknesses. A piece that only moves in one manner cannot do other things by default.

Though the king is the central piece whose life determines the game, I fell in love with the queen. She makes almost every move the other pieces can make. She, to me, enjoyed the most accomplished activity on the board. I learned to abhor losing her in battle.

When Uncle Ted moved a pawn, I moved a pawn, excited to believe in myself, holding great confidence that I could maneuver with style. He coached me. Once we had scattered the pieces a bit, he showed me the king's defensive move, the castle. "It is a powerfully important move to make early so that the king is protected throughout your game."

I stared at the board, studying the king's cocoon. It seemed like a cowardly move to overcompensate for his inability to fight like a versatile queen.

"The knight and the bishop have to desert the king for him to hide like this," I observed.

"Right. There is no escape by horse or religion," instructed my uncle. "Castling is a relationship between the king and the institution. His is an act of self-preservation."

"Who protects the queen? She moves better than any piece on the board." I wanted to know the capabilities of all the pieces.

"Sometimes, no one. Sometimes, everyone. It's the preference of the player."

"Really?"

"When given the choice between the queen and the king, you have to remember that the king's life stops the game. The queen's life just keeps it interesting."

I have spent my life watching the decisions of others whether to protect the queen. Sometimes everyone does. Sometimes no one bothers. It really is the preference of society.

Family

My grandmother protected me. She was yellow-complexioned, her looks a blend of her full-blooded Native American mother and her blonde, blue-eyed father, leaving her beauty elegant, refined, and undeniable. I often suffered jokes in grade school that the white woman who picked me up on occasion had really adopted me. My earliest memory is of her face, smiling, hovering over me while I was sick.

Papa was a medium height, brown-skinned man, who in his youth looked a great deal like Martin Luther King, Jr. In the evenings he was a Pentecostal preacher. Mama was always the traditional Pentecostal preacher's wife.

There were five grandchildren living with Mama and Papa, three girls and two boys. I was the youngest, burdened by the others labeling me the geekiest, a tattletale. The truth be told, I was.

We had rules and more rules. If actively committed to the church, women could not wear pants, makeup, or strange hairstyles, and they could not be with men that weren't their husbands. No one drank, smoke, or frequented worldly pastimes. While the other grandchildren tended to bellyache about our restrictions, I did not. Rules made me safe.

I felt that Mama's rules were fair. My grandparents went on vacation one year and left my mother, whom I always called Mommy, in charge.

While they were away, Mommy had a boyfriend in the house and beer in the refrigerator, both things that were strictly on Mama's "no" list. When my grandparents returned from their vacation, I updated Mama on all of the frolicking that had transpired while she was gone before she could even walk to airport's baggage claim. My mother was reprimanded. I thought that she deserved it and that she should have followed the rules. I was probably eight years old.

Of course, this doesn't mean that I was always a perfect child myself, and Mama didn't hesitate to punish me when I misbehaved. One day, while playing outside in the yard, I delighted in chasing my cousin, Monique. She led me past a tree and around the utility shed as we circled the dogs' houses. Both German shepherds ignored us as we tore through the backyard shrieking. She ran past the sliding glass door, and I did too. She jumped on the seat of the picnic table, and so did I. She grabbed the umbrella pole and swung around; so did I. As I twirled around the umbrella pole, I actually caught her, which is when the creaking began.

Monique and I looked at each other and realized that the table was collapsing. There was a loud crack of wood and one of the benches caved in. All five of us cousins were crying and shouting as Monique and I crawled to safety. The entire picnic table never sat straight again.

Mama spanked us for tearing up an otherwise nice place to sit in the backyard and we were both sent inside as further punishment. Monique went to the family room. My banishment landed me in Mama and Papa's bedroom.

Mama kept her Estée Lauder perfumes on her dresser. Sometimes I played in her bedroom while waiting for my cartoons to begin after school. Her perfume impressed me as a least-favorite thing. I rarely liked the smell, but I did admire the tiny decorative bottles it came in. I took Mama's favorite brand into the tiny bathroom off the master bedroom and dumped out the contents into the sink, then filled the bottle with water. Voila—I had a new little canteen of sorts! To test it out, I tasted the water to find it bitter and rancid like the residue of the perfume it had contained. I choked and heaved. Mama, hearing my squeals, opened the door to discover me with my tiny tumbler in hand, indicating the end of her precious aromatic treasure. She assessed the situation quickly and realized that a lot of money had literally gone down the drain, earning me a second spanking that day.

There were consequences for behaviors growing up, but I honestly wanted to do the right thing. It won my grandmother's favor and I never lost that love of pleasing her. The love and attention that she granted me while I was doing homework taught me more than the lessons on the page ever did.

Mama had a tenth-grade education. She worked in a factory once, but had to give it up when a car crash caused by a sleeping driver left one leg unable to bend. She often referred to herself as a cripple when she banged into something while having to slightly swing that leg to the side while walking. I never knew her without her lopsided gait. After the factory job did not work out, she stayed at home, which proved to be a benefit when I came along. May life bless a stay-at-home parent who nurtures a young mind. I certainly felt blessed.

We studied at the dining room table every day without fail. I would come home from school, throw everything on the floor, and search for the makings of a peanut butter and jelly sandwich. Once I settled in with my homework, Mama joined me at the table and listened to our shared missions, whether it be math, English, or science. I usually did social studies alone. She liked to work through English and grammar first, since they were her strengths. She was my math and science answer-keeper, checking my work for accuracy.

I earned an A average through high school, graduating from North Central High School's Gifted and Talented Program. I still believe that the primary reason academics was so important to me was due to the importance my grandparents placed on doing well in school. With this mindset instilled at a young age, at nine years old I decided that I would attend a top ten university. I put the *US News & World Report* and *Newsweek* magazines listing the top ten universities under my mattress. They stayed there until decision time years later.

Papa quit school after the eighth grade to work. He eventually found employment at Eli Lilly. He told us once that when he interviewed there, they told him, "Boy, we don't have a lot for N-words. If you want to do something, you will have to mop the floors. That is all we have for y'all."

He took it. He worked for Eli Lilly for forty-six years, retired, and often bemoaned the younger generations that job-hopped too much for his liking.

"There is no good in moving and moving and moving," he said. "Get married to your job. Stay through thick and thin. Companies take care of the loyal, but you have to be theirs." He came from a day when that was the norm. "You cannot get stability without being stable yourself."

Papa worked two jobs. Upon leaving Eli Lilly each night, he exchanged his uniform for jeans and headed to the west side of town to clean a bank. I often accompanied him and helped polish those metal dividers in the customer line or wiped off desktops. I worked until I was exhausted, because when I did he would laugh and praise me, calling me a good little worker.

Papa captivated us with stories. He kept visitors in stitches with long tales that he set up and bowled over. He had no enemies on Earth, black or white. He knew every Pentecostal person in town, and they treasured him. We all did.

Everyone flocked to hear him preach. He taught scriptures better than any other Pentecostal preacher in town. Along with three boyhood friends, he even helped compose, write, and lead songs for the Gospel Chimes quartet.

I loved Papa. His word was golden, and his help was guaranteed if he could make the time. I sat on many riverbanks beside Papa catching fish after fish, sharing stories, and listening to his past and present life. He liked fishing early in the morning or late at night, but fishing was always a weekend activity. We ate everything we caught, save catfish and carp.

An old-fashioned man, Papa gladly let Mama rule the house. He earned as much as he could and she cared for the house and kids. He almost never set foot in the kitchen, except to cook his own breakfast from time to time. I usually joined him in the morning as he read the paper.

I could read earlier than most, thanks to my grandmother's help, so even at six or seven I would read some of *The Indianapolis Star* newspaper with him. The *Star* was written with the vocabulary of a fifth-grader, a teacher told us once, so I thought I could handle it. Papa only let me read those sections he had just read, so that I didn't read anything inappropriate for a child my age. He sipped coffee. I sipped hot chocolate. We were well-read people, Papa and I.

Eventually Aunt Joyce, my mother's sister, took her three kids away and raised them on her own, leaving my brother and I at Mama and Papa's house. Aunt Joyce worked at Eli Lilly over nights, which gave my cousins more freedom than they could handle.

Next, my brother moved away. Mommy, newly divorced from my father, got a good job and wanted us both to come live with her.

I refused to leave my grandmother though. My refusal lasted for a year, until my grandmother explained one day that she had no legal right to keep me. I had to move in with my mother. The schools demanded papers for legal guardianship. Even though I had lived with Mama nearly since birth, I did not have papers to stay in the suburbs with her. On a sad day before fourth grade, I found myself packed and transported to the inner city to live with my mother. It was not my choice.

Inner City

I stayed in my room a lot. Mommy's house had two bedrooms. She used one and we shared a bathroom between us. Willie, my brother, lived in the family room at the back of the house. I did not talk much at home or at school. In school, I performed a grade level higher than the other inner-city schoolchildren. Indianapolis public schools struggled with equality and performance when compared to the suburban schools.

Tracey Brame

We walked to Public School #40 every day. My brother refused to walk with me because I wasn't cool. The geek in me carried on alone. There were some boarded-up houses that looked interesting and I wanted to explore, but I did not dare. The walk took thirty minutes. My upper body often hurt at first because I took all my books home every night.

I had no friends. Everyone cursed and spit. They walked in groups and someone always managed to create a ruckus that halted the gaggle along the sidewalk. I feared going around them, since then they might notice me. I preferred to be unseen.

The street appeared filthy. I felt as if someone had urinated on every concrete section on the sidewalk. A foul smell, sometimes from burnt trash or Kentucky oysters, tainted the air. Besides the corner store, there were no other landmarks. I mostly watched the ground as I walked.

I longed daily for my grandmother. I knew that she prayed for me on my way to and from school, so that made the trip a little more manageable.

In class, no one else did the homework and the classrooms often sounded like a busy restaurant. There were days I forgot that I was in school because I learned nothing at all. In most of my classes, only the teacher and I talked about the lessons, her at the head of the class and me in my chair. I helped her finish statements and problems that she had put on the board. I really do not know what she would have done if I were not there, or what I would have done had she not been there.

Being smart had its dangers, though. Aletha, a round, very dark-skinned child in my class, told me in gym one day that she was tired of hearing me talk like a white girl. She informed me that she was going to beat me up after school. I had never noticed her before.

After school I traversed between the mobs of unruly kids to get home, as I always did. In front of the corner store stood a pack of kids backing Aletha. I wondered if this was real. Amazingly, it was. The mob of kids was not going to let me pass and repeatedly screamed, "Fight! Fight! Fight!"

"Put your books down, bitch!"

Undeterred

"Yeah!"

"Kick her butt, Aletha!"

"Yeah!"

The cheers grew.

I carefully put my books down out of the way, so they wouldn't get damaged. As I stood back up, Aletha pushed me to the ground.

"Get up. You got it comin'," she broadcasted.

I stood up. Remember who were our stars in those days: boxers like Sugar Ray Leonard and Muhammad Ali. Blacks revered them. I started shuffling like a boxer. I'd shake her punch off in front of her and then dance in the opposite direction. Whenever I stopped, I pummeled Aletha in the face with my tiny, God-given fist. Her nose bled. She was out of shape. I hurt her several times, and when she gave in, I turned to get my books.

A sixth-grader, who turned out to be Aletha's older cousin, took issue with the fight's result. Grabbing me, she threw me into the window of the store and started swinging.

When she stopped to celebrate her perceived victory with her crowd, I started shuffling again. My feet, decked out in special, fitted Buster Browns to correct my crooked ankles, shifted, carrying me one direction and then the other. I beat the living daylights out of that girl. When she took a knee, I circled my fist through the air like Ali, as if I were going to uppercut her. She lay down in concession. The bruises and the pain on her face compelled me to stop.

I picked up my books. No one in the city threatened to fight me again.

Fools

What comes first: the atrocious student or the atrocious administrator?

Every day at lunch, our principal, Ms. Barks, sashayed her corpulent, well-dressed frame through the aisles of the cafeteria and banged a yardstick against a lunch table if someone did not listen actively. No part of her was small, including her hair, which was permed and styled so often that I thought she was just born with 'good hair.' She often announced that the school was doing so poorly that we were not allowed to talk at all. No-good heathens like us, she scolded, needed to think more than speak.

WHACK, slammed the yardstick. Each time it came crashing down, we all froze in front of our meal, which resembled a lukewarm Lunchable.

"Listen up, fools!" Ms. Barks emphasized herself by beating the yardstick against whatever table she passed. It kept those on the end seats on edge in case she missed.

"It has come to my attention that the number of students who may not be passing this midterm is steadily increasing. I am sick," *WHACK*, "and tired of walking through the hallways seeing your hollow little heads and empty little eyes staring back at me when most of you are not doing your homework. Most of you don't know how to do your homework. You couldn't if you tried because you don't take your books home." She felt she had made a good point, and she took a moment to savor her own insults. She appreciated herself.

"I'll take that one step further," she continued. "Most of your sorry tails don't know how to read. Is that right, Mr. Winston?"

The art teacher nodded, because he knew who buttered his bread at our school, which resembled a concrete warehouse from the outside and offered as little to a child's mind on the inside. I had seen Mr. Winston's artwork; he needed the safety of his job.

"Mr. Winston," she said his name, but appeared to be calling to the other side of the cafeteria, "what do you suppose can happen to uneducated black children from the inner city that can't spell anything but their names?" She did not wait for his answer.

WHACK on another lunch table.

"Young man," Ms. Barks addressed a kid who probably had his head lowered in reverence but appeared to be asleep, "what happens to dumb, uneducated black people?" The boy did not appear to have the nerve to answer or even to look her in the eye. I failed to discern if he offered a nonverbal answer or just shook from fear.

"Who knows?" she demanded. I thought of volunteering something, but she usually did not want answers. She would go on until tired.

WHACK.

"None of you will find jobs. None of you will amount to anything, because none of you can read. Your tests prove that you cannot answer questions that you do not understand. You can't read because you are not trying to read. Most of your parents can't help you because they can't read either. They sat in school and learned nothing, exactly like you.

"You are all destined to fail. I'm going to read about you in a newspaper article–every single one of you–a statistic. You don't know what a statistic is. It's you, every last one of you." Worn out by her public rant, she turned to complain to Mr. Winston in private.

Standing Up

My grandmother always insisted that we speak proper English, and would tap our mouths with the back of her hand if we said things like "dis," "dat," or "dose." Mama insisted that we sound like we were not poor, even though we were. This largely contributed to why Aletha had complained of my "talking like a white girl." At this inner-city school, I ate lunch with a girl named BeeAnn Purcell. One of my fourth-grade classmates, she also spoke proper English. A burden had lifted when BeeAnn moved in, because I did not feel alone any more.

At this particular moment, I had had enough of Ms. Barks. I looked at BeeAnn and said, "I'm going to say something to her."

"What?!" exclaimed BeeAnn.

"For starters, I can read. I'm going to tell her that we are not all statistics." I immediately stood to accomplish my mission, and in an instant BeeAnn decided that she was no statistic either, so up she stood and away we went.

I walked right up to Ms. Barks, looked her in the eye, and said, "I can read."

"So can I," spouted off my wing-woman.

Ms. Barks looked me up and down. "Who are you?"

"I'm Tracey Brame. This is my friend, BeeAnn Purcell. We read and we do our homework. We are not statistics."

She called Mr. Winston's attention to us as well. "I heard it," he admitted.

"What makes you think you can read well?" Ms. Barks challenged me.

"I read *The Indianapolis Star* with my granddad when I was about six years old."

"You can't read Shakespeare," she touted.

"Sure, I can too," I lied.

"Have you ever read Shakespeare?"

"Of course," I lied again. "She has too." I was confident in both of our abilities.

"I want the two of you to report to my office at 3 p.m. Mr. Winston, give them passes."

"Yes, ma'am."

"Run along and don't be late. If you can't read a clock, you can't read."

We trotted back to our seats. I felt a bit excited, but BeeAnn was clearly nervous. It was a mystery to me why reading skills heaved students to the principal's office for judgment. I did not know my fate, but I held on to my pass, not knowing its worth.

At the appointed time, the receptionist ushered us in. We could hear Ms. Barks putting someone in his or her place on the phone, so we sat down and waited.

"Come in here, you two," she called us in when she was done with the phone. We obeyed. "Close the door."

Her office had framed papers and shelves of books. I had never seen such a collection. "Tell me about yourselves."

"My name is Tracey Brame. I am going to be a doctor when I grow up. I am going to save lives."

"Where did you come from?"

Undeterred

"I grew up on Sanwela Drive in Indianapolis with my grandparents. My granddad is a preacher, and he reads a lot too, in the Bible and the paper. My grandmother helped me learn to read and do my homework." I nodded to let her know I took everything seriously.

"And what does she do for a living?"

"She stays at home and helped me. I live with my mother now."

"Of course. That always helps," she nodded in approval. "Lucky you."

"And you?" BeeAnn took her turn with her own history.

"Okay. Today I am going to ask you to read for me. Tracey…" She paused, looking behind me at the shelf full of books. I moved slightly to let her see better. "Reach up to the third shelf, five books over from the left. Hand me that blue book."

I fetched it. She rummaged through it slowly until she felt she had the right page and handed it back to me. "This is Shakespeare. Have a seat. Take it from the top of the page."

I trembled from the start. I really did not know Shakespeare. Suddenly I second-guessed myself, but I plowed ahead, reading aloud:

"If it were done when 'tis done, then 'twere well It were done quickly. If the assassination

Could trammel up the consequence, and catch With his surcease success; that but this blow Might be the be-all and the end-all here,

But here, upon this bank and shoal of time, We'd jump the life to come."

She made me read several pages with word patterns I had never seen before. When she told me to stop, she handed me the Bible. Finally, I had something familiar to breeze through. BeeAnn tested as well, with similar results.

Ms. Barks stared at her desk for so long I feared she would conclude that I read inferiorly. Softly, she said, "You can read." She reflected more, "Both of you read very well. I checked your grades and talked to your teachers. You are not the people that I spoke to in the cafeteria. You're both smart."

"Thank you."

"From now on you will report to the sixth grade. You can't be learning anything where you are now. I will arrange for it. You start Monday."

We were excited. "Thank you!" we exclaimed. What a relief to actually be put somewhere where we would learn something. Part of me could not wait to tell my grandmother, to whom I told everything, that Shakespeare fancied the word "'twere." His excerpt helped me gain sixth-grade standing, but Shakespeare would not pass the grade with my grandmother using a word like "'twere." With a tap of his mouth he would have grown to write, "it were" or "there were" appropriately.

Bathroom

It happened after school. We were standing in line outside the school building, waiting to be dismissed, and I needed to go to the bathroom. I carried a load of books, unlike those around me. I thought of setting them down, but I feared someone would steal them. The books had a value to me that I assumed others shared. I was wrong in this assumption, but I didn't know it, so I toted the books back into the empty school.

A boy from my sixth-grade class followed me. I recognized his face but not his name. We were not friends. When I looked behind me, he was smiling. I walked faster. He did too. I ducked into the ladies' room, and immediately felt safe because only girls were allowed in there.

He entered. That may have been the point at which my fear took over. He forced me into the first stall, ripping my elastic pants down. A student from my old fourth-grade class came in, startling him. He ran.

My books were spread across the floor where they'd been thrown when he pushed me into the stall. I started to gather them up.

"Were you having sex?" the fourth-grader asked.

"No. I am not allowed to have sex."

"What was going on?"

"He went to the bathroom on me."

"You were having sex."

"That's a lie. I was not." I left feeling defensive, and forgot the experience completely once I exited the bathroom.

Sixth grade echoed fourth grade. BeeAnn and I were the only ones who knew the material, save the teacher. Teachers spoke only to us in class to keep from talking to themselves. I reported back to Ms. Barks. I cried because classes felt useless and I bemoaned being teased because that six grader entered the girl's restroom with me.

I hated school. Each day brought the same thing. Ms. Barks thought about what she could do for me, and decided that I would be better off in a gifted and talented program at a nearby school. It meant more walking on frostbitten toes in a different direction, but I didn't care.

I transferred. Many people with PTSD seek to change jobs or even locations after a trauma. The military accepts this as one of many signs that a significant event may have occurred. The victim often does not think twice about the desire to leave, but they are running from something in their subconscious when the new place very well may not prove to be any better.

86

At Public School #86, I was able to breathe. It was a striking contrast to Public School #40, despite also having a numbered name. It looked like a real suburban school with students who, having eaten breakfast, enjoyed having the energy to propel them to think in class. I felt better almost immediately when I walked inside.

One of my favorite classes was our writing class. We read our short stories and poems aloud to the class. It's a bit awkward to say this, but that time quickly became "The Tracey Brame Hour" by unanimous vote. Back in second grade, my teacher had told Mama to cut off my access to my birth mother's Stephen King novels. She scolded me for trying to move items on the playground with my eyes like *Carrie*. I thought I just needed practice. Mama forbade me from King's fright, but in sixth grade, living with my mother, no one remembered my restrictions.

I used poetry or prose to mesmerize my classmates in fear. This went on for a semester. It's easy to forget a small success like that, but it ceased only when the teacher asked me to stop scaring my classmates. Some of the parents were complaining about their children's poor sleep due to my terrifying stories. I dialed back my horror.

One day, during writing class, I waited my turn to read my work aloud, as usual. But when the teacher finally called on me, I heard her, but I couldn't answer. Other voices said my name, but I just stared at the seat in front of me. Kids moved to the door. I stayed. I didn't know why I was shutting down.

Years later, I would learn that many people who develop PTSD experience trauma and simply shut down like that. This could have lead a professional to conclude I had been raped in that bathroom back in P.S. #40, had they known of the incident.

As I sat unmoving in the writing classroom, the teacher pulled a chair close to me, but I do not know what she whispered. A stretcher soon moved me to the nurse's office. I lay on white sheets and thought of nothing in particular. I felt tired. A nurse asked someone, "Has she ever been raped?"

My mother leaned over me and kissed my cheek while answering, "No." I said nothing because I was not sure what raped meant. I certainly could not recall being raped.

People spoke to my mother of necessary medical attention. They thought I was in shock. The school excused me for a week, which turned into forever when my mother realized that what I needed was my grandmother.

Home Again

At Mama's I became an only child, her and Papa's legal ward. The other grandchildren visited on holidays, but they never stayed over as they had in the past. They moved on into habits of their own. I kept studying.

My grandparents sacrificed a lot to keep me clothed and fed. Sometimes I washed the same two pairs of jeans again and again. I felt

Undeterred

rich when I received a new article of clothing. It made me feel I was like everyone else.

I talked to my grandparents about almost everything. They always responded to my questions with advice. The one thing I did not tell them was that I wanted a wife some day. Even I had never heard of anything so outlandish at my young age. I wanted this long before I understood that the girls in class with me would grow up to be beautiful women.

I had played house as a child, where, with preschool logic, my imaginary wife would help me rustle up shredded paper potatoes, Play-Doh casseroles, and an older toy's legs or arms as chicken for my doll parties. I told no one this. I didn't want to feel like even more of an outcast.

The two people that I confided in the most worshipped a God that forbade women from marrying each other through "documented scripture." Hell awaited if I so much as touched a woman. I wondered why God castigated me this way, but I believed in my grandparents at the time and tried to not think about myself so much. My priority was to make Mama and Papa happy, to make them proud. I did not want their helping me to be a waste. I wanted to deserve their love.

God gifted me with a talent for public speaking. It started with simple homework presentations or projects in class. Everyone wanted me in his or her group so I could deliver the grade. Without preparation, I could deliver a speech on any topic for a speech competition. If given time to prepare, the chances that I'd win compounded. My forensics skills impressed everyone but me.

My speech teacher found himself transporting me to regional and national competitions. Even when I was elected president at Indiana Girl's State, I kept wondering what I might do with this. My acceptance speech in front of hundreds of people convinced me that I should pursue a career in politics, but I knew nothing of politics. Mama spoke of preaching, but I did not feel a call to that either.

In my junior year, I lifted the mattress on my bed, hoping Mama had not tossed the collegiate listings I had placed there years earlier. Thankfully, they were still there. I compared them to the new lists that she bought at the store. There were shifts in the rankings, but many names were the same. I defaulted to the new list and carried it to school.

Jodi

Jodi was the guidance officer for the newly inaugurated Gifted and Talented Program at North Central High School. She called us her "babies" or "kiddies." She had blond hair with bangs and a wide, warm smile, and she was always dressed fashionably. She was the first woman outside of a magazine that I witnessed wearing a poncho and I lost count of her color-coordinated boots. I assumed she was wealthy. I admired that she was rich with no husband.

Her office was a refuge for the school's geeks who were in the program. She helped us all with academic and personal matters to keep us on track. She seemed to know our special set of woes as nerds. Most of us celebrated our differences. You could learn as much from your classmate's questions as from your own.

I showed Jodi my list of schools and she asked, "Which one are you thinking about applying to?"

"All of them," I said, not knowing what that would entail.

She laughed, "Tracey, there is an application fee with all of these. Your grandparents would struggle to pay it. However," she thought aloud, "given your financial need and situation, I think that we can get the fees waived."

I had never talked to Jodi about the depth of my financial situation. She just guessed, based my clothes. I looked poor compared to her mostly wealthy student group. I knew it. I just didn't care. Pork and beans and wieners can still fuel a mind.

"Tracey," she said as I exited, "get ready to write essay after essay. There will be several for each school, and they are all different." She smiled. I appreciated her smile always.

As my applications came in one at a time, I began writing my essays. I tried to reuse material where I could, but Jodi warned me that I ought to answer all of the questions as specifically as possible, so after doing my homework every day, I edited my essays for delivery to Jodi.

Still, you don't sit around and languish in the waiting game when you have lots of things to do. I was the president of Speech and Debate and of the Black Student Council. I worked at a fast food restaurant to help pay for odds and ends.

I excelled at a lot, but by my grandparents' standards, I would never find love or marry. Everything was up in the air and college decisions loomed.

Failure

In addition to the top ten schools I discussed with Jodi, I also decided to apply to West Point. My high school boyfriend's family was grounded in army traditions, and I liked their attitude and outlook. My grandmother hated the idea of me joining the army, but Papa supported me. He had served in World War II and thought it was a worthwhile experience.

I researched West Point. Always doing the right thing was important to the Academy. I liked the army's "Be All You Can Be" slogan. *Top Gun* convinced many eligible service recruits in my generation to suit up. I could serve, I thought. Though the army's business was to fight, as a group it seemed safe, united, and purposeful. I yearned to go to West Point. I did not care if I died serving in the military. I wanted the mission. I became obsessed.

I read up on the physical entrance test and started practicing. I knocked out countless push-ups and sit-ups. Mama drove around the neighborhood to help me understand where two miles began and ended, and I ran that route daily. I failed badly at first, but everything I read dictated patience. I kept at it. I thought that if others could get good at these moves, so could I.

Unfortunately, I soon learned that the West Point physical entrance test for women was different from what I had practiced. I practiced for the Army Physical Fitness Test that every soldier took, consisting of sit-ups, push-ups, and a run. The women's admissions tests for West Point included a flex arm hang instead of push-ups. Women had to pull their chins above a bar and suspend their weight until failure. I thought that push-ups would prepare me for the flex arm hang, but when I periodically tried it after gym, I found that I was wrong. I could do push-ups forever, but I, bulky with new muscles, could not hang. When it came time for the West Point physical entrance test, I failed the flex arm hang.

The top ten schools' responses rolled in one or two at a time. Every one of them accepted me, but my attention remained on West Point, which rejected me because of my physical. It hurt. I cried, and then I stopped. I knew what I had to do.

I engaged the top ten schools to see who would give me the most money, so that my family could afford it. Stanford would cost me the most; Harvard ranked second. The others did not weigh in immediately or would cost less. Duke invited me to visit, as did many others. Papa consulted my birth father for transportation help.

Daddy

My birth father showed up religiously on Christmas and on my birthday to visit me at my grandparents' house. They always prayed for him. He needed a lot of prayers, from what I remember. My mother came with him when I was younger, but once she got her own place and divorced him, he came alone. Still, he came.

"How you doing, Brat?" Daddy greeted me. He was tall. When I was little, he would pick me up and I could see over shelves and trees that I could not normally. He always had a sweet smell to his breath that, years later, I would identify as liquor. His love of motorcycles created a love/hate relationship with bikes for me. Some of his friends had died on a 'cycle'.

Sometimes I felt that Daddy was mean. I remember him occasionally joking and shaking his fist at someone. I don't think he ever laid a hand

Undeterred

on me, but I felt certain that he laid his hands on many others. I always greeted him with love, but I lingered near him with caution.

"Hi, Daddy." I kissed him.

"I hear you got my smarts," he observed. Daddy had skipped from the fourth grade to the sixth, as I had, and then from the eighth grade to the tenth. He became so bored in school that he took to drinking and never stopped, which compounded many of his problems. My family did not tell me this, but I knew. Daddy was someone whom it was best not to cross. Until I gained years of experience, no matter how nice he was to me, I always moved closer to my grandmother when Daddy was around. I instinctively knew that the things I did not see between my mother and father were things that I did not need to see.

I sat across the room from him in Mama's living room, silent. "The bigwigs want your brain?" he asked.

"I've been accepted to college."

"Listen, Brat, I am interested and shocked that someone who came from me can do such a thing as go to college. Congrats, baby." His eyes hid behind sunglasses; he probably thought they hid his drink as much his eyes. "This Duke place, where is that?"

"It's in North Carolina."

"Lord, that's Ku Klux Klan land, isn't it?" He shook when he laughed. His shoulders bounced up and down when he was tickled.

I didn't know. Mama and Papa said that the Ku Klux Klan was headquartered right here in Indiana, in a town called Martinsville. All black people knew not to be there at night. Sometimes we drove through Martinsville to go to fishing spots. You couldn't see the KKK during the day, even if you squinted. That's what I thought, anyway.

"How much is the ticket?" Daddy looked at Papa, who cleared his throat and gave a figure.

Daddy rose to his feet. He wore a purple suede biker jacket with fringes that caught the wind when he rode his Kawasaki. He loved that bike more than most women he'd ever touched. The danger did not scare him; he welcomed it. "The good ones die young," he often chuckled.

He unrolled a wad of bills, removing his shades to count. He handed me several hundred dollars.

I thanked him. It was a lot of money.

"Buy the ticket, and also get yourself a nice outfit so that you look the level of your speech." He stood me up, so that we were eye level. "You are a brilliant little talker, Brat. Look the part." He glanced at my grandparents, adding, "Shoot, she has taken this family across all of the United States in these speech competitions." Then, with a point and nod in my direction, "Take us all to Duke. We can all go through you."

Monterey, Saturday

On Saturday mornings, the cadets at West Point parade for the public. They rarely know who is in the audience, and it never matters. The drum resounds deep and regular, like a heartbeat, and the flutes and trumpets pick up the melody over the percussion. It cheers you up. It moves your feet. Cadets are often miserable in the sun in their heavy dress uniforms, waiting for the parade to end so they can get on with their Saturday, but the music entices the listener to honor military pomp and circumstance or even previous days in uniform. Nostalgia abounds whenever the drum beats that bass note.

This particular Saturday morning, I was three thousand miles away from the United States Military Academy in Monterey, California. Less than twenty-four hours after my rape, Jayns and I had relocated to his one-bedroom apartment, never to return to the crime scene. As I sat on his couch, the only beat that I heard was that of my own heart.

We went out for a quick lunch in his neighborhood and then made our way on foot to see the sea lions on a rock in the bay. As we walked, I could hear people murmuring around me. Cars passed by. I was in a fog, and I let Jayns pull me along. I generally left logistics up to Jayns when we were out together, and he was always more than happy to take charge of these details. Today was no different.

On this afternoon, Monterey was pleasant, with sunny, clear skies and people out and about looking for entertainment. I felt shaky, like some part of me sensed that something was wrong. I willed myself to walk. We stopped to get sanitary napkins at one point because I had started spotting. I had an irregular cycle, but spotting seemed impossible given my last period's date. This did not worry me; it was more of a nuisance.

Jayns literally pulled me along the sidewalk. "Not so fast," I told him. I needed time to collect myself, to collect my thoughts. Hours after waking up from a night of sex with him, I could still feel him inside of me. I failed to realize that such a feeling is neither normal nor is it usually painful. I hurt. I ached.

He kept pulling. "Jayns, I am not in a hurry to see these sea creatures. If they are moving out to the ocean, we can catch them some other time. I am not in a hurry," I firmly told him. I just did not care.

"Well, can you at least walk? West Point teaches people to march and run. I'm asking you to walk, and you cannot make it." He smiled, but it was not a genuine, friendly smile. He sometimes said things to be a smart-butt or to amuse himself at the expense of others. I granted him a lot of latitude because I knew he was an awkward, smart person. In truth I would later learn, he was never jesting--the humor always covered a deep-seated irritation.

I looked up and saw the beaming sunlight reflecting off of street signs and festive flags and banners hanging from light posts. Concentric circles danced and darted. For some reason, I felt like I might faint. I had also lost track of time, and had no idea how long we had been walking since we had eaten. At that moment, I realized that I had no idea where we were. I was completely dependent on him.

"Don't even think about it," his voice broke through the fog I was in, low and purposeful. He stopped me and moved to the street-side of the sidewalk to block my view of what lay ahead. He stared deep into my eyes with that monster gaze of his that, until then, I had only seen him give others. As it leveled at me, I looked to both sides, seeing nothing and not knowing what he referenced.

I asked, "What are you talking about?"

"You're smart. You had better think it through."

"Think what through?"

Undeterred

"You're pretending to get away. You want me to take you out in public. You are looking all around. You are looking for an out. Let me paint the picture for you. You are poor. I am not. We are not at West Point. We are not at a government post. You can't afford the legal process. If I were you, I would be smart."

I couldn't understand why he was talking about money. Cadets are paid at West Point, but it is for subsistence, not luxury, and we received small deposits for sundry items. Jayns, having already graduated, received regular army pay for a lieutenant. Since I had little money compared to him, he often paid for dates and outings, but what did that have to do with going to see the sea lions in public?

"You sound like a mad man." Shock prevented me from even understanding why I might need a legal process. "What does my family have to do with seeing sea lions in Monterey? If I need an out from you I will just stop seeing you. Sometimes your personality makes you look uglier than you really are."

We were at a standoff. I certainly did not feel great, but logic kept me able to fight. When you feel lousy, even when you are in shock, logic can be called upon to keep you fighting. After all, my brain did not feel bad; my body did. Just like with exercise, when you overcome your body, you can go on forever.

After a long pause, Jayns gave in, smiling a sheepish, boyish grin. "Maybe I shocked you."

He took my hand and we continued on, with him staying between the road and me. The heavy foot traffic around the sea lions slowly came into view. Just past Jayns, on the other side of the street, I noticed a sea of blue uniforms. Jayns's lips grew taut and I could see him breathing heavily. There were several police cars parked nearby, while some officers rode bicycles or jockeyed horses. There were dozens of police officers just standing around, waiting for something to do. I gawked, wondering what had prompted the display of force.

Jayns cut me off again, then tugged me by my arm. "You act like you have never seen a cop before."

Seeing cops was a crime? I couldn't understand his reaction.

The sea lions were just okay. The cops beside cops, near cops, just waiting around to help someone–that was the circus. I remembered that. I forgot the rape.

College, 1987

Leaving Home

My grandparents listened to the AAA representative lay out the directions to Durham, North Carolina. Long before map icons on smartphones, AAA disseminated personalized flip-chart booklets to guide drivers, highlighting places to stay, gas up, and relax. While Papa drove, Mama read the map as shotgun.

Mama packed my luggage as well as hers and Papa's. She made sandwiches and filled coolers to make sure we could keep the cost down along the road. She exuded relief that I was not going to West Point, and her lack of support really hurt me.

"The army is full of dykes," she had said over dinner one night. "You don't want to be associated with that. You will go to hell." She intently made her point and her expression told me not to challenge her.

Dyke–I had never heard that word until Mama introduced it. At that point in my life, I thought a 'dyke' was a waterway. I assured Mama that I would get a different job, as working with pipes failed to interest me.

She did not want me to do any job in a service uniform. Duke was a better choice for her, and it happened to be the only choice for me from a financial prospective. I was glad that Mama was no longer harping on her disapproval of my joining the military, now that I was going to Duke instead, but my misery over not getting into West Point festered.

When poor kids arrive at big colleges, they are immediately reminded that they are poor: their rooms scream it. Mama and Papa carried my scant belongings, which fit into three pieces of Mama's good luggage, to my room. There were two beds, two dressers, and two desks. She and I emptied them, and I stored them under the bunk bed nearest the door, promising to treat them with care. She in turn promised to send me sheets, because we had not known they were not included.

"Thomas, pray for her in this room. Please pray," Mama said, studying the locks on the doors and listening to the other people moving around outside in the hallway.

The three of us gathered close together and prayed. "Father in heaven, thank you for your many blessings. Thank you for this day. Thank you so much for the joy of this, our granddaughter. We ask you to watch over her..."

We ate sandwiches in the car together and then just waited until it did not make sense any longer to not say goodbye. They drove away, and I prayed they would be safe.

When I arrived at Duke, people thought me muscular. I never stopped exercising. One of the things I had learned about exercising was that it made things disappear: a "B" on a test, a disapproval of my choices, a wish that I were not poor, it all dissolved with the burn and sweat of the last mile or the last rep of exercise. Cranking out one more push-up granted me freedom. So once my grandparents' car drove out of sight, I returned to my room, changed into running clothes, and began to erase the fact that life had temporarily removed my grandparents. That day I adopted the trek between Duke's two main campuses as a daily running ritual.

A Friend

Not long after my grandparents left, I began to realize that I was not like most of the people at Duke. They were mostly white, no one wanted to serve in the military, and the vast majority had discretionary allowances. Kylie, my neighbor, was short, energetic, and mixed racially. Her curly hair was a source of ire to her sometimes, but I thought she was beautiful. Kylie was not rich, but her father was an executive officer in the Marines. In her, I saw a buffer zone between all the rich girls in the hallway with whom I shared no commonalities and myself.

She burst into my barren room with only one knock on my first day after I had showered from my run. "Wow! You are scary fit," was the first thing she said to me.

"Hi," I greeted her back.

The liveliness with which she spoke and stood and walked and breathed and lived set her up as my polar opposite. She was more excited to be in my room than I ever was. She was more enthusiastic about the ceiling, windowsill, dust, everything. She was a girlie-girl unlike any I had met. I barely understood her animation, but it didn't hurt me, so I went with it.

"Come see my room," she demanded.

When I walked into Kylie's aromatic room, I immediately noticed a rug, furnishings, and dainty wall hangings, all well-placed. Her space was more comfortable than mine, because it looked lived-in, while mine favored a prison cell.

"It's really . . . normal . . . homey even." I tried to compliment her tastes and touch.

"I have arrived at normalcy!" she announced.

We both laughed, and then she did it: she broke out into a spontaneous cheer. "Go Team! Go Team!" Her hands moved through the air in sharp poses. "Who do we mean? We'll say it loud! We'll say it proud!" Hands, hands, and more hands.

I was speechless. I had not gone to sporting events in high school, because Pentecostals shunned such worldly activities. Now, here I was in a small room at Duke University, preparing for a simulated kickoff with a total stranger who, I would soon learn, often unexpectedly broke into a cheer.

Undeterred

Kylie smiled. I felt perplexed. We faced each other, and it seemed best to respond with, "Great."

"You and I are a *little* different." She smiled though, nodded her head, and walked to her desk.

I liked Kylie, and we ended up getting along. Mixed-raced and gorgeous, she fought off men of both races. She introduced me to many rhythm and blues musicians instead of just the pop-rock I listened to in high school. I hummed Luther Vandross thanks to her, but constantly dropped into her room to ask, "How's the song go after this part?"

Ideas and issues stirred her or made her steaming mad. Kylie had opinions and more opinions. I listened to her because I actually learned from her. She was perceptive and recognized my unspoken pain. She understood that Duke confused me. As with everywhere else, at Duke, growing up with love mattered less than it did growing up with money. Money permitted access to school and all of its amenities. Love comforted you when you lacked both. Duke had far more people who grew up with money, and thus they didn't fully appreciate the doors it opened for them; doors I had to fight my way through. For fun, people trashed the campus, drank, and acted out. I gravitated to ROTC. With no scholarship, I volunteered because everyone else there seemed focused.

I shared with Kylie that I simply could not afford Duke without substantial financial aid, and I could not afford to buy anything other than the bare essentials. My feet and ankles begged for a new pair of running shoes, but I did not dare burden my grandparents. I just kept running in pain. She, noting that ROTC was a strength for me, suggested that I lean on the ROTC program for a scholarship.

Major Earkle

I had a better idea. I spent a lot of time with my ROTC mentor, Major Earkle, a serious man that favored an accountant or engineer, right down to his thin-rimmed glasses and overly tidy office. With him I admitted frustration at being one of the poorer kids enrolled at Duke.

"You need to be at West Point, Tracey," Major Earkle agreed. "Our students are not wrong. You are not wrong either. You are different, Tracey. Your discipline will make a normally tough life at West Point relatively easy. You will love it."

Major Earkle also thought West Point would help me decide if I wanted to pursue a career in politics or public service. My freshman political science teacher at Duke travelled the world with international relations assisting governments. Every time I walked into his office, I found a different souvenir from a different country to claim as my favorite. I could present lectures like him, I thought. I knew I could do it.

Duke granted me a collegiate nomination to West Point, and I obtained a new congressional one from home. With two nominations and the body of a chiseled wolf, I left Duke after one year to join the class of 1992 at the United States Military Academy. I joined the rank and file in the Long Grey Line.

Monterey, Sunday

I castle. I leave a scene of fear, escaping what may not be pleasant to live through. I castle the experience of the rape deep in the recesses of my brain until I can reassess it in the future, in safer circumstances. Not dealing with the trauma at the time allowed me to cope in the present. I became my own rook, my own institution. I saved myself.

The medical world calls this post-traumatic stress disorder, and the army overflows with victims. But perpetrators can castle, too. Military rape victims and PTSD sufferers often find that repressed crimes dissuade the Department of Defense from helping them. Perpetrators can hide behind institutions like the law and courts. During the perpetrator's castle, the institution trades places with the king, fighting for his ease of evading the law.

Jayns liked his odds of getting away with rape. As I slept, deeply exhausted, on the bed in his tiny Monterey apartment, Jayns woke me to reveal that he had bought a woman's douche at the drug store. He suggested that it would make me feel better.

"I am spotting," I told him sleepily.

"It may help you stop."

"Give me a break. You are acting like a nuisance this weekend."

Drowsy, I slept.

He watched me like a hawk. I felt him study my eyes to see if I faked sleeping. I did not care, because I was too tired to open my eyes and see him breathing in my face. I lay enervated.

When a person "puts something away" through PTSD, there is a good reason for it. Only recently, I had told Jayns about a recent memory of the bathroom experience that I had had in with the boy in fourth grade. Even then, Jayns seemed to be taking keen mental notes.

Why did I go in the bathroom? Why didn't I keep going to find help? How has West Point prepared you to handle rape differently? He questioned me closely on these topics.

"Jayns, there is no way to know that he raped me. I think that he went to the bathroom on me. How can we assume that a sixth-grader is capable of reaching a girl who is standing up? I'm no expert, but I will not say that he raped me. I am, however, convinced that he was preparing for his life as one of America's most wanted perverts," I explained to him.

"Teach me the moves that West Point has taught you to avoid rape. What do they teach you to say or do?"

"Why?" I asked, almost annoyed.

"Men are raped, too, in the army. Don't you want me to be protected?" We were talking on the phone right before my trip to Monterey. I took some time and described West Point's prescriptive moves that we were taught to do when standing. "Interesting," he said. "This knowledge is really helpful. Very helpful indeed."

I slept endlessly in Monterey. He took pictures of me in my shorts as I lay on the bed. He ate. He waited. I slept for the rest of the weekend, never going out to eat or drink after the sea lion and cop incident. Jayns wanted me to have as little contact with the outside world as possible.

If only he could predict the future. While I slept, he sat in that one-bedroom apartment, debating my prospect to live. If I were bleeding internally and dying before his eyes, his only worry was that of timing; depending on whether I died in Monterey or West Point, he needed a story to show himself blameless, to duck behind legal pawns–a castle to save himself.

I was his first victim, and the extent of his knowledge led him to conclude that a douche would erase all evidence of a rape and keep his name clear.

Undeterred

He woke me. It took magnificent coercion, but he finally dragged me to the toilet and propped me up. "Let's get this done," he said. Never having given a douche, he followed the instructions he had read during my slumber. Thinking he could erase culpability, he administered the douche while I was nearly comatose. Now the only thing he had to do was hope for my silence.

In chess, the queen finds protection among those on the board who fear fighting without her. Her ability to execute moves that others cannot compels all other pieces to crave her presence in battle. Likewise, most fear the opposition's queen. It is her feminine fighting prowess they value most, but if the price for saving the king is shooting her, a player will have her take a bullet without second thought.

Part Two: Jayns and PTSD

West Point, 1988

AAA's directions put us into West Point precisely fourteen hours after leaving Indiana. Mama and Papa drove because I lacked a license; adding me to the insurance would cost too much. Unlike Duke, of which they seemed vaguely fearful, they were in awe of West Point.

Everything seemed more distinguished, more revered, and more official. The campus lay along the western bank of the snaking Hudson River, with architecture and grounds that had the distinction of being part of a National Historic Landmark, thanks to their Revolutionary War history. We parked and walked with other cadets and their families to the stadium to learn our next steps.

Mama immediately noticed an important difference between Duke and West Point. At Duke, I had called home many nights crying, the phone bills almost causing Papa to go broke. At Duke, I felt unsafe around campus and at night. University officials warned us about crime both on and off campus, and advised female students to travel in pairs. Given my conservative background, I avoided parties, wildness, and mayhem–all concerns at any college. Still, I never really felt safe at Duke.

West Point promised to be different. Rules protected us. I followed rules easily. Those who did not comply had to leave.

In that first briefing, the speaker in a green dress uniform assured our parents that we rested in professional hands: "Fear not. We will return soldiers, and then officers to you." With that confirmation, my grandparents were encouraged to say goodbye. With kisses and hugs, they left, my grandmother sobbing.

Once our parents vacated, we all took an oath to serve with one hand raised to God. I felt like I had promised my life. I gladly promised, willing to do what it took.

The traditional yelling, hazing, and humiliation were easier for me than for others, mostly because I did not believe it. I ignored accusations that I was good for nothing because I knew better. Upperclassmen found reasons to try us, just to see if they could break us. Many do break during that first, vulnerable year.

On the first or second day, we were taken through various stations at the gym where we had to sit down, fill out papers, and answer questions. At one station, a man in a green uniform asked me if I were a lesbian.

"Sir, I do not understand."

"Are you a lesbian?" he repeated.

Not understanding the question, I tried to think it through. "Lesbian" sounded like a food choice, like vegetarian or something, just more specific. I was not sure we grew that food in Indiana. No one in my family used that term, so I kept thinking.

"This is a simple yes or no question, New Cadet. Do you like women or not?"

"Yes, sir." It was not a lie. I liked everyone, but his question about liking women did not define lesbianism to me. I thought his question random. I was still mauling over lesbian as a food choice. I didn't know if anyone in my family was lesbian or not. We had reunions, but no one brought anything lesbian.

Perhaps, I thought, lesbianism was a religion. I told him that I was Pentecostal, and he wanted to know what that meant. I explained that we had more rules than some people and did things a bit differently.

Undeterred

The officer insisted that I follow him. He walked me over to a woman in a physical training uniform. She looked meaner than he did. "Tell her what you told me," he ordered me.

"I simply asked if she was a lesbian," he said to the female instructor before returning to his station, leaving me staring at my new inquisitor. She waited to pounce on my answer, so I told her that I didn't know if I was a lesbian.

"What does that mean?" She was a captain, feminine by most standards, but her countenance scowled so easily I assumed she wore that face often. "Are you trying to file a lawsuit?"

"Ma'am, I just don't understand the question."

"You don't know what a lesbian is?" she asked, surprised.

"Ma'am, I have never seen or read that term before."

"Do you date women?"

"No, ma'am."

"Do you sleep with women? Have you ever?"

"Ma'am, Andy is my friend from Girl's State back home. We slept in her bed once when her dad let me spend the night."

"What happened?" She was losing her patience.

"Ma'am, we slept in her bed and cooked breakfast the next morning before I went home." I thought that next she was going to ask what we cooked, but she didn't.

"Cadet," she asked me squarely, "do you have sex with women?"

"Ma'am, I don't understand how that would be possible." I truly didn't. The video in fifth grade hadn't shown that.

She stood there staring at me for a long time. Slight disgust faded to exhaustion, "Where are you from, Cadet Brame?" Her voice took on a more conversational tone.

"Ma'am, I'm from Indiana." I was proud to be from Indiana, but I was afraid I was trying her nerves. Maybe we didn't even have lesbians in Indiana. Did anyone think of that?

She looked back at the gentlemen who had escorted me to her and shook her head. "Your answer to that question, New Cadet Brame, is 'no.' Finish your station."

I answered no. Every time I saw her, I thought of that moment, but the word *lesbian* was not important to me then, so I did not retain it. I just thought her a tough instructor, and I hoped to not have her in class.

The military no longer asks that question of new recruits.

Formation

The hardest part about drilling in a New York summer was the long, hot, uncomfortable days. The actual physical training was surprisingly easy for me. Dropping to the ground to knock out push-ups was unfairly easy. When the upperclassmen found out that I failed to break a sweat, they turned up the heat on me verbally. Guys fall on swords to get into West Point. Some may have been on their last leg academically, but they were not going to let anyone, let alone a woman, casually walk through. A West Point degree deserves a good sweat, both metaphorically and literally.

We stood in formation and an upperclassman ordered us to say what we wanted to be when our tiny, innocent, Kool-Aid- pumping hearts grew up. Every guy in the queue before me popped off with an answer, but I still did not fully know what I wanted to be after graduation. As a child, I had wanted to be a doctor. As my good public speaking abilities came to the fore, I had considered a career in politics, but I still wasn't settled on that. Joining West Point, instead of staying at Duke, was a step toward some form of service, whether that be military or public. *What should I answer?* I wondered, just as the upperclassman appeared directly in front of me.

"What did you say, Brame?"

"Sir, I want to be president," I answered, a bit surprised at myself.

"Are you kidding me?" He looked from left to right incredulously.

"No, sir."

"Hey, upperclassmen, step to the front of my line and listen to little Miss Brame sing her personal desires in life." Then, to me he said, "Turn and tell them."

Undeterred

I looked at the junior cadets who were in charge of our formation, two white males and a black female named Cadet Twig. They waited for my answer.

"Tell them!"

"Sir, ma'am, I said that I wanted to be president."

"Of what, the Rotary?" asked one of the males incredulously. The two men chuckled.

"No, sir," I responded.

"Then of what?" he demanded impatiently.

"Sir, I want to be president of the United States."

"Someone give me a break," said one, dropping his head and turning his back to me. Cadet Twig had large eyes like Diana Ross. If she raised her eyebrows at you, something was about to explode. Right now, she looked at me as if I was beyond help and walked away.

"Get back in formation, you maggot. I will move from this country the day we trust more than a wet rag to you. Flipping retard. Hey, freshmen, raise your hand if you'll live in a land led by the likes of Cadet Brame?" my original questioner asked. The unit remained at attention.

"That's your vote, Brame." He got close to my face and nodded. "*That* is your vote."

This kind of hazing was actually pretty standard, because upperclassmen generally preferred that freshmen stay invisible, hidden in the woodwork. I would have been better off if I had simply said that I wanted to be a colonel. Unfortunately for me, that had not come to my mind in the moment. I realized that my admission in formation might be a lofty dream, and that I didn't truly know what I wanted to be in life.

I soon wished that I had not shared my thoughts at all, because it would almost cost me my life within the next few years.

Cadet Twig

That evening, Cadet Twig entered my room. Our rooms were built for two people: two beds, two dressers, two closets, and two gun racks. I popped to attention when she entered.

"Sit down," she ordered me and closed the door with her foot. She was taller than me, and had caramel skin, a toothy grin, and sometimes-bulging eyes. I sat back down at my desk while she took a seat on the bed, crossing her legs femininely. "How are you doing?" she asked.

I told her that I was fine.

"No, you are not fine," she informed me. "Listen to me. I cannot step out of my role as a cadet leader and be your friend as long as you are freshmen. That is why you may feel that I yell at you more than the others. I am constantly in your face, right?"

"Yes."

"No. 'Yes, ma'am,'" she reminded me.

"Yes, ma'am."

"I am not your buddy, but I know you are having a rough time. You do everything perfectly, and we rip you up harder than the guy next to you who did not do as well. Do you have any idea why?"

"No, ma'am."

"But you have noticed, right?"

"Yes, ma'am."

"Tracey–and know that when that door opens you are nothing more than Brame again–you have a serious problem with over-achieving. West Point is not a place where you want to stand out. You want to do the exact opposite and fit in. The cadets that have the easiest time are the average ones. You run faster than the guys, you do more sit-ups and even push-ups than most of the guys. We cannot tire you of doing push-ups. I, for one, won't drop you for push-ups because you'll wear me out."

She cleared her throat. "Everyone knows that you are fitter than many of your peers right now. Some of them will catch up. Others may never. But you also are the loudest, most motivated, hoorah cadet we have. So what's the problem?"

"Ma'am, I don't know," I confided.

"The guys hate women like you. You make them feel smaller, shorter. It will cut your throat here. Keep trying, but be aware of what is happening, or else your easy road will be made nearly impossible."

She paused for a moment, to make sure her words sank in. Then she asked more conversationally, "Where are you from?"

"Indiana."

"Lord!" she howled. "Are there black people there?" We both laughed. "You were surrounded by whites, so I am surprised that I had to tell you this. The trick for when men and whites come down on you is to watch what you believe. It's like acting improv. If they lay on you that you're dumb or inferior, you have to know not to accept the role. They will always want you to serve them as if they are kings. You have to play your own game."

"As if you are the queen," I said, making sense of her words.

"Right. Sometimes we are on the same team and sometimes we are not, but they cannot make you a pawn when you are really a queen, unless you let them. Play a better game. How did you do on the academic placement tests last week?"

"I tested into harder classes," I confessed.

"Oh no. Really? What?"

"Spanish and math."

"I wish I had talked to you earlier. I am sorry that I did not come to you sooner. I cannot show favoritism because you're black. You *do not* want to test into harder classes here. Extra burdens and being gung-ho will only make your life miserable your first year. I am sorry that I did not warn you. Your first two years may prove harder now."

She moved to the door, then stopped and turned towards me. "Hey," she said. I had never stopped looking at her. "This talk never happened. It's always business as usual." She smiled.

"Yes, ma'am."

Cadet Life

Moving into the school year took some of the heat off. The upperclassmen could not focus solely on the freshmen or none of them would graduate. At some point West Point does approximate a normal college, because we had to both get to and through classes. Sports and extracurricular activities aside, academic endeavors became the business of the day.

Rituals broke up the days. We went to formations before all meals, classes all day, extracurricular practices and parades. Mandatory activities were constants.

The freshmen always walked just under a running pace and maneuvered along the outside walls of the barracks to avoid the upperclassmen sauntering through the halls. We could only say four sentences when questioned by a superior, unless expressly permitted to do otherwise: (1) Yes, sir, (2) No, sir, (3) No excuse, sir, and (4) Sir, I do not understand. Most West Pointers dismiss windy, verbal excuses for this reason. We were not allowed to communicate an excuse for not doing, thinking, or being. Freshmen performed all chores, such as trash, can, or bottle pick up. The only place in the barracks that we were able to relax was in our bedrooms.

I stayed in my room whenever possible. One black classmate outside of my company called me "Ghost" because I rarely attended social events, preferring to study in my room. The thing that I appreciated the most was quiet. Horseplay ruled the evenings, but no one ran through the barracks drunk, crying, or bellowing because Duke had lost a basketball game, as I often experienced in dorms. Likewise, no one toilet-papered the post because the Duke basketball team won. Only seniors consumed alcohol, and only in a bar distant from the barracks. I never hung out there, because I never drank. I felt safer at West Point. Major Earkle proved right: Pentecostal rules had prepared me well for West Point. I felt at home.

Company Cadets

The upperclassmen hated me. As Twig had foreseen, they singled me out at every opportunity. They even talked to my classmates about how much they would like to see me gone. I just focused on my classes.

Undeterred

One cadet among the upperclassmen was particularly gruff to my classmates, but was rather aloof with me. Everyone hated him because he spoke ruthlessly to all. His name was Jayns C. Johns, Jr. He was a dark-skinned, scowling, thin man who was a great football player in his mind, but he failed to make the "the big boys' team."

West Point had two football teams, a regular team and a smaller, lower-weight team for those who did not make the big boys' team. Cadet Jhomes played on the little team, but he wore the ego of the captain of the big team. All cadets were required to go watch the big boys play, but no one had to go see Jayns. It simply was not the same.

He overcompensated for what he deemed the inferiority of his team placement with a massive superiority complex. When he corrected my classmates, he cut deep, as if he enjoyed trying to hurt them. The first time I heard him speak, I was repulsed and overcome with pity. Though he clearly aimed to hurt people, he did not speak well and he seemed like someone who could use help. I was really shocked that Twig was by his side constantly, and I came to believe that they were dating.

Cadet Tanner

I had two roommates my freshman year, because women were sometimes paired three to a room. One night, one of my roommates, Cadet Tanner, invited two upperclassmen to our room because she needed help with homework. When they arrived, there were sharp knocks at the door. Both of my roommates and I stood at attention and said, "Come in, sir."

Two of Jayns and Twig's classmates walked into our room. I often relaxed in our room with some article of clothing missing or open. I mostly did this, thinking that an upperclassman could not enter a room and scream at an undressed female. I often pondered refusing to put clothes on, just to have some nighttime peace.

The door slammed open against the wall and stopped. "At ease!" screamed one of the upperclassmen.

We stood a little looser but were still tense. "Relax!" His face turned red. That didn't induce calmness in any of us.

We waited. He looked at his counterpart and then at me. "Brame, what is your GPA?"

"Sir, I do not know."

"Are you getting As or not?" he asked.

"Yes, sir."

"Murtus, what are you making?"

Murtus was the tallest woman that I had ever seen and was a giant in my eyes: she was six foot two, blond, and unable to run well. She gasped when she ran. With no medical explanation for this and, of course, her health not being my business, I rationalized that she was mechanically too tall to run well. Perhaps oxygen simply couldn't get to all parts of her. Having never seen anyone like Murtus before, I worried that she would not make it, that one day we would find her collapsed, dead from a lack of oxygen in her bed. "Sir, I get Cs," Murtus offered.

Our questioner made his way past my roommates and behind my desk to me. Standing nose to nose with me, he asked my other roommate, "Tanner, what are your grades?"

"Sir, I have some Cs, Ds, and Fs," she informed him from outside his line of sight.

He continued to eyeball me, and I held his gaze. "Maybe you can tell me why you sit in a room with two other women and you have As for your classes and one of them is flunking out," he demanded.

I said nothing. After all, how was I supposed to know? My thoughts picked through Tanner's history. She rarely studied, she was never in the room, and she made comments that hinted that she wanted to find a husband more than she wanted to stay at West Point. What kind of answer was he expecting? I surely lacked an appropriate one.

"Why?" he ramped up. "Why is your roommate failing?"

"Sir, I do not know."

"When is the last time you helped her study?"

Undeterred

Never, I thought. You cannot force a horse to drink. Some students were uninterested in studying. They just want to graduate.

"We are entering final exams in two weeks. Next week is prep. You had better hope that her grades get better. If she flunks out, I am going to hold you personally responsible."

He didn't ask me if I understood. He assumed it, and both upperclassmen headed for the door. His back to us, he said, "Cadet Tanner, tell Brame what classes she will be ensuring you pass."

To the floor, Tanner murmured math and some other subject. The only thing I heard was math, which made me wonder how I was going to help her study when I had tested into and was taking another math class altogether. I wished I had been nude when they'd knocked. Maybe the entire conversation could have been averted.

The thing that tired me about helping Tanner study was that she had given up. She would start out trying, but for no reason she would pool spit to the front of her lips and say, "Look," then giggle. I just couldn't see the humor. If Tanner wanted to quit, I invited her to just do it–take charge of her decision and quit.

Instead, she worked the problems that I walked her through, and I taught her easier ways to think about them. I convinced her that these classes were not the right reason to go home. I helped her more than I studied myself for that semester's exams, but the ultimate decision was hers.

When she passed at the end of our freshman year, I felt no relief as I had probably sacrificed some part of my own potential grade point average helping her. I just congratulated her for saving herself. I would have ample opportunities to save myself.

Jayns

I went to the bathroom one night before our final freshman semester ended. When I came out, Cadet Jayns Jhomes was waiting for me.

"Brame, I have been watching you." There really was no answer for that, so I remained standing at attention. "At ease. Cadet Twig says you think you want to be president."

"Sir, I think I would be a good politician. I can look out for people," I told him.

"But a president who's black and female? You see that as possible?"

"Yes, sir." My family mixed white, brown, and black on a color palette. I lacked the racial prejudice that others around me knew, because I had always been around a lot of people who looked different.

He nodded, staring at me so long that I started to feel uncomfortable. "We'll see about that," he said. Then he nodded and winked with a smile. "Carry on." As I continued down the hall, he said it again: "We'll see about that."

Upperclassman, 1989-1990

Sophomore, 1989

My sophomore year at West Point met me with a rude awakening: the grudge that others felt against me during my first year did not instantly disappear. My classmates and I gained upperclassman privileges, but many of the juniors, now seniors, remained resentful that I did not break during my freshman year. The other freshman females in my company wet themselves, nearly flunked out, or in some way demonstrated that they were at the end of their rope. I did everything asked of me and gave a little more. For me, that was good enough. For the upperclassmen, it flaunted abilities they despised in a woman.

Tanner never showed any gratitude for my helping her make it to her sophomore year. Instead, she acted as though *I* owed *her* a favor. In her mind, anyone owed her a favor if she needed one.

She preferred to flirt with a specific classmate, rather than study. When he failed to profess anything serious for her, she turned her attention to various other male classmates, in an effort to make him jealous. Some nights she visited all of them, but when she lingered in our room, they came to linger too. She paraded guys in and out of our room, until one night I said something and an argument ensued. I wanted to be able to relax in my room without guy after guy parking his boots. After our argument, Tanner moved to another room, which worked out better for both of us.

During the next morning formation after her move, Jayns pulled me away from formation. "What happened?" he asked.

I told him, and he assured me, "She will not last in the real army. You will. Don't waste time on someone like her. She is here to find a husband. You're here to be my president, right?"

His humor was a bit sarcastic and I felt far from such thoughts at this point. "To be honest," I admitted, "right now I just want to survive."

"They are not going to make it easy on you. Don't cave. I am going to New York City for the weekend. Come with me."

I did not think my answer through. Involuntarily, I said, "Okay."

We had a blast. He held my hand and smiled constantly. Few saw him smile, save a sarcastic smirk. He appeared less threatening than he usually did. Joking constantly and teasing me, he was surprisingly likable.

Broadway offered Kathleen Turner in *Cat on a Hot Tin Roof*, my selection because I had seen her in several movies. On stage, she mesmerized. Jayns showed me that reading books and more books was not the only pastime in New York. I enjoyed the city, though I was a long way from home.

I ran into Twig upon returning from the weekend with Jayns. She smiled and said, "He is trying to make me jealous."

"Are you still dating?" I asked. I hadn't seen them together much any more and he had denied they were a couple, but I needed to hear her say it too.

"We were *never* dating. We were freshmen together. We've been through some things. He had a ridiculously hard freshman year because of the way he naturally is. We became the four musketeers: Riana, her boyfriend, Jayns, and me. Jayns wanted us to have the kind of relationship that Riana and her boyfriend have, but he is not my type."

"I see," I said, relieved.

"If you like him, great. He comes across as having a mean streak, but he breaks that to show his nice side. I am glad that you saw that over the

Undeterred

weekend. He really is harmless." She smiled and I felt better. Given that a real, commissioned Army officer hounded Twig for attention, Jayns may have been out of her league.

As I walked away, Riana joined her, calling, "Tracey, come back!" I turned. "There is one more thing you should know. I don't want to be the one to tell you this, but Jayns tried drugs, specifically crack, in the city–"

"What?" I interrupted her. "He's brilliant!"

"I did not say that he wasn't brilliant. We were all in New York City and he tried crack on a dare to impress the rest of us...well, to impress Twig."

"I didn't ask him to. He just did it," Twig defended herself.

"He went crazy," continued Riana. "We barely got him back to post on time. I believe he's looked for it again. Be aware if he develops a habit. He may not, but at least you know now."

"I did not see anything like that this weekend," I assured them. Surely I would have noticed; people notice such vices.

"Good. Maybe it was a passing thing," Riana said. I looked at Twig, waiting for her to contradict her friend, but she said nothing.

I wasn't sure what to do with this information. Jayns was the smartest cadet in our company. He had a lot of potential.

The next day I confronted him and, of course, he denied everything. He tried to convince me that Riana was just making things up, trying to sway our potential relationship. My upbringing did not include examples of academically brilliant people who made the choice to do drugs. My cousins smoked marijuana all the time while I was at West Point, but they were prone to doing things just for the fun of it. With no one else in the area to consult, and phone calls being so expensive, I decided to go with what I saw and thought I knew. Drugs were not in the picture.

I slowly started confiding in Jayns over the course of my sophomore year, as we studied and talked together regularly. Aside from his gruff behavior with others, the only thing that I really disliked about him was the disrespectful way he spoke of his mother. From him, I learned to be cautious of guys who do not treat their mothers well.

Jayns advised me to choose systems engineering and civil engineering as my major and minor, like him, because then I could always get a "real job" outside of the army. Cadet Twig also chose those disciplines, which is why they studied together so much before I came into the picture. My family had little advice for me, so I chose the same engineering route that he and Cadet Twig had, but held no love for the prospective courses. I wouldn't learn just how little I loved my classes until my junior year, though.

The best part of being friends with Jayns was that I was not alone all the time anymore. He understood that I wanted to spend my time studying, since he did as well. His stony look silenced our company unit in general for which I was grateful.

I often pondered the prospects of single black females in the United States. We are either ignored for life or, as in my case, we can receive escalated, unwanted attention, with or without a man in the picture. The determining factor seems to be whether or not our presence is found to be threatening by those around us.

Some males seem to think they are and should be better than women. As much as we want to believe that this is no longer the case, for many men, it is still true. When they sense that there is a woman who can best them in some capacity, they despise that woman. This is even heightened when the female is a minority. After all, a male thinks, he should definitely be better than her. When reality contradicts him, he tries to respond with aggressive proof to the contrary.

Jayns's presence at my side finally quieted the ratcheting talk that surrounded me throughout my freshman year. The resentment still persisted, but his fierce reputation stifled them, for which I felt grateful during my sophomore year.

Mrs. Angel, 1989

I carried the weight of West Point home after the first semester of my sophomore year, where seeing my grandparents sufficed to bring a

Undeterred

smile to my face, but another person lifted my spirits and reminded me that I was strong enough to weather the storms. Her name was Mrs. Angel, a tall, brown-skinned Louisiana native with a high-pitched voice. To me, she defined femininity and beauty in a regal way from her demeanor, dress, and speech. I examined every poster or picture in her office just to know more about her. I listened to her advice, but feared I could not hold it all in my head. At times I asked her to simply repeat herself.

Mrs. Angel became my guidance counselor in sixth grade. I rarely saw her until seventh grade though, when my social studies teacher began our unit on slavery. At this point, I was living with my grandparents again, and going to a suburban school, predominantly filled with white students.

There was no reading assignment for this lesson on slavery and our teacher just began the lecture from hand-written notes. Confused, I glanced through the book. There was an old, square photo of men wearing masks with burning crosses in the background. The text had words like "blacks" and fractions like "three-fifths of a person."

I listened to the lecture and quickly gleaned that slavery was a way of debasing black people. Not all churches were burning in the lessons, just black churches. Not all people were being lynched in the lecture, just black people. Not all people were picking cotton, just black people. I grew angry with my teacher.

"You are trying to stir the class up against me, aren't you?" I demanded, when he asked if there were any questions.

He denied my accusation while standing at a chalkboard covered with notes. There were pictures of Harriet Tubman, Frederick Douglass, Jr., and Abraham Lincoln stapled to the walls. But there were also pictures of black people outside working and white people standing around looking angry.

"Are you trying to convince them to hurt me?" I asked.

He assured me that that was not true. He was trying to teach history, but I was trying to pick apart his true motives. With the anti-black theories swirling through the lesson, I struggled to separate him from the lecture.

"How can I be lower than them because I am black?" I demanded angrily.

Class stopped. People started putting their hands down.

"I have the highest grade in your class. You told me."

"This is history, only history. No one believes that you are inferior because you are black. I am only trying to teach that people used to believe that."

We headed for the hallway to talk. I had frequently won essay contests around the nation for work I did in his class, but the illogic of slavery and its brutality arrested my conscious. "They will have better grades than me in this class if they write that I am inferior," I argued, indicated my classmates. "I can't write that. How can I pass the test?" If need be, I would skip the test on this unit. I absolutely refused to write that African Americans were inferior.

My teacher calmed me. "There will be several essays in the test on this unit, one of which will be about slavery. If you can discuss economics, politics, the war, and Abraham Lincoln without saying that African Americans inferior, you win." I felt better. I could win, keep my top grade, and still not have to write something that I absolutely disagreed with.

That afternoon, Mrs. Angel descended in my life like the Good Witch from the administration office. I cried inconsolably about our slavery lessons in her office. She asked if anyone at home had ever mentioned race relations, and I confided that my grandmother had some choice words for whites, but that was only because her father was white and had taken a lot of abuse for marrying an American Indian woman.

Mrs. Angel leaned back in her chair with an apple and began to pick apart my life, household, and beliefs. She would later tell me in her high-pitched song of a voice that I ranked as one of the most naive students in her career. She called me "Darling."

I became her counselor's assistant so that she could monitor those parts of me that understood so little about the world outside of books. I

Undeterred

grew to love her, eating at her house, being chaperoned to the doctor, laughing endlessly. I brought the subjects or issues that I didn't understand to her, which she mixed with her slew of knowledge, and then returned to me with a different common sense than was available at home. I was a piece of work for Mrs. Angel

My grandmother disliked her: a meddling school official. Pentecostalism got by just fine on its own without Mrs. Angel's Baptist God being friendlier than Mama's. I routinely returned to Mrs. Angel for advice and counsel throughout life.

On the day I visited her in 1989, I told her what was happening at the Academy with the upperclassmen. In turn, she told me that I was more than ready to face such people.

"We are defensive creatures. When we are offended, we swirl around looking for a lot of others to back us up. That's the story behind what those upperclassmen are doing. That is not scripture. I did not teach you that nor did your grandparents and, yet it is the way of the world."

I told her that I had started sleeping with my bayonet this year because the juniors were threatening to beat me up, even though I had helped my roommate. Those early feelings of being safe at West Point were definitely a thing of the past. Mrs. Angel asked if there was any adult supervision over each company, and suggested that I visit our supervisor.

"Darling, imagine two men lining up for a race. Now, most people would assume that both men prepared for the race as best they could and were evenly matched. When the starting gun fires, both take off running. But, in this case, imagine that one has paid others to beat his opponent with sticks as soon as the race starts. The one who has paid for help runs the race and throws his hands above his head in victory. Was he the best man in the race? Is he the best man after the race?"

I did not answer.

"You are talented–so much so that you draw out that part of other people that just want to beat you at any cost."

"I don't feel that way about anyone," I told her, confused.

"That's not you. You expect a fair race. You don't see the attack coming until its too late because you are not paying attention. You will continue to run into people who feel that way about you."

"That's sort of like hunting someone."

She loudly bit her apple with a smile. "Hunting is a pastime for some Americans."

Psychology, 1990

The academic class I struggled with the most my second year at West Point was psychology. It's a mandatory sophomore class grounded in case studies. After reading the case, we were expected to diagnose the soldier and prescribe some remedy for his situation. I worried about the final exam because I couldn't relate to the essence of the cases. I was stuck on why the soldiers behaved the way they did.

For post-traumatic stress disorder, we learned that soldiers underwent a traumatic incident like rape or attempted murder, the effects of which disrupted their life and daily function. I talked to Jayns about it in our study sessions. Since I had never knowingly been through a traumatic incident, I wondered why the soldier would dwell on such a negative event.

"PTSD people are weak," Jayns said.

We were in his room. A male and female cadet can be alone together in a dormitory room so long as both are clothed and the door is propped open. We both had on class uniforms–grey pants and a black shirt. I was nursing a cold and lay on his bed with my books open, trying to make sense of my psychology notes for the upcoming final. Jayns was meticulously neat, and sat at his desk detailing trusses for a bridge in an engineering class. "Everyone they teach us about in psychology is weak. They cannot help themselves," he continued.

"What does it mean to not be able to help yourself?" I stood and grabbed a throat lozenge off his desk for my sore throat. People helped themselves all day long, I thought.

Undeterred

He stared three floors down out his window at the cadets walking to and from class. Resting his chin in one hand, he explained, "First, they relive the horror over and over in their mind. Think of it like a video playing again and again. They don't turn away. They can't turn it off. They just keep watching themselves get hurt." He chuckled. "Stupid, if you ask me."

Jayns twirled his mechanical pencil in his left hand like a drumstick. "Anything can trigger their brain to flash back to that video or haunt them in their nightmares," he continued.

"I just can't relate to that," I told him. "I don't even dream, let alone have nightmares."

"Second, they act like wimps and start avoiding things. They avoid people, places." He shook his head as if such people made him sick.

"I avoid coconut," I ventured. I was still confused.

"No, no. People with PTSD avoid their wives, other soldiers, vehicles that go boom in a crash. It's ridiculous."

I reasoned that anyone might avoid his wife. Papa didn't, but Daddy did. Couldn't a soldier get tired of being around other soldiers? Military humor alone might make a gay soldier want to desert. *These people were fine*, I thought. I empathized to the point of rationalization.

"I'd want to avoid a vehicle that crashes," I defended the examples that Jayns used. Maybe the soldiers were right. I walked to his sink.

"How do you know *which* vehicle will crash? There are a lot of cars out there. These assholes are avoiding riding in *any* military vehicle, in *any* military airplane, and on *any* ship. They avoid men, stop signs, turkey dinners. Nut cases!"

"Okay," I said. I walked over to Jayns's medicine cabinet and opened it. I wanted to use his mouthwash to gargle my sore throat, but he warned me not to drink his. When I asked why he said that it was too strong. Shrugging, I sauntered over to his roommate's medicine cabinet, but Jayns said that his roommate's was stronger. Cadets often disguised vodka with food coloring to hide liquor in their rooms and Jayns privately to me had pointed a finger at his roommate as being alcoholic. He told me to go ahead and use his, but not to swallow, just swish. I complied, noting that he had an off-brand bottle that tasted worse than usual.

"Jayns, not liking something and avoiding it seems sane to me," I argued after gargling and sitting back down on his bed.

"Third," he announced, ignoring my comments, "Soldiers with PTSD generalize their poor thinking to the point of changing the way they think about themselves and others, even the world."

"What does that mean?"

"It means their asses are crazy," he laughed. "Instead of reasoning, they rotate their emotions and behavior against themselves. They think that all of us are somehow dangerous. They are the ones that are jacked up in the head. I'm not watching their silly videos in my head, and they shouldn't be either. They cannot help themselves."

Jayns was a senior. He still remembered these concepts perfectly after two years. "Did you like this class?" I asked.

"Loved it," he laughed. "God, yes, I loved it. It's one of the best classes here. When you graduate, you are going to have keyed-up PTSD soldiers, who can't sleep or concentrate. They may get irritable and angry, unable to keep a lid on themselves. They are off-center. You can almost tell by their walk, their talk."

"People can be like that for little reason at all sometimes," I pointed out.

"There is always a reason why people are the way they are," he nodded, "and I appreciate getting to know the list of characters from psychology that are most vulnerable. Every chapter of the class details another sorry temperament, easy to move off his center. The army asks us to work with these shitheads. I need to be able to identify the weakest players on the board. It's always good to know this information. I'm playing to win." Jayns brandished that wisdom as a commissioned officer upon graduating in 1990.

I earned a B in psychology, but I never fully got it.

Colonel Blue, 1990

After Jayns and Twig graduated, I leaned on others for support during my junior year. Colonel Blue was a favorite professor of all of the minority cadets and, for many of us, his was the friendliest, most unconditional smile we received on post. He saw the lighter, more positive side of everything and always offered salient advice. He helped run the Social Sciences Department and he had a deep understanding of both politics and human nature. I lacked expertise in both, and I felt like I learned something every time I breathed the same air as him.

Some of us visited his house on the weekend expressly for the home-cooked meals and relaxation time these visits offered. The tension during my second year prevented me from relaxing in the barracks. I confided little about my treatment during this period, since I didn't know whether my experiences were normal or not, but I often sat at his house and wondered if others received equal time with him. The best part of going to Colonel Blue's house was getting an idea of what to expect once I put on a real army uniform. Everyone flocked to him–everyone except Jayns. Colonel Blue knew little of Jayns–another red flag, but my eye refused to distinguish what color red flags were.

Convenience, 1990

I began my junior year with a conundrum: the classes required for my major were mind-numbingly boring. I declared my concentrations in systems and civil engineering, the same courses of study Jayns and Twig had pursued, but I feared that my lack of interest would murder my GPA. There was no way I could pursue these subjects and be myself.

Jayns was on the phone constantly, telling me to settle down. He felt the same way, he told me, and the curricula worked for him and Twig, but I knew I was nothing like them. I entered a panic mode. How could I get out of this decision I had made? The army can be unforgiving with bad decisions, so I sat in my classes each day, afraid of the electives I had chosen.

One day in social science class, the teacher called my name. She had caught me sleeping, not listening at all in her class. I had clearly irritated her. "Read until I tell you to stop," she ordered. A neighbor whispered the page number to get me started. I fumbled through the text waiting for permission to stop.

"Enough," was all I needed to hear.

To another cadet she ordered, "Pick up from there."

I tried to regroup. The temperature in the room rose, and I found myself physically sweating while trying to remain awake. Exhaustion was starting to creep into my cadet life more and more.

When class finally came to an end, the instructor called me to the front of the room. "Report to my office sometime tomorrow, Cadet Brame. I have class in the morning," she ordered.

"Yes, ma'am."

I panicked. Can you get kicked out of the United States Military Academy for sleeping in class? Since you have to do one activity every semester, I had tried all kinds of extracurricular activities at West Point. I ran well. I ranked nationally in power lifting. Furthermore, I was the star of the Speech and Debate Team, which was run by the Social Sciences department. Nothing was easier for me than Speech and Debate. I would go on to be the president of the team, to win the coveted Whitfield Award, and to win more individual speech awards than anyone had before me in cadet history. If I had control over my tiredness, I would have chosen a different class to sleep in perhaps an engineering class, for example.

The next day I reported to the instructor's office. She was a major and her husband was a reservist who had been called up to West Point on assignment. She had come with him.

After opening up conversationally about her hometown, she confided, "I know about you."

That could mean several things, so I waited for an explanation. Even the fact that Speech and Debate was in the Social Sciences Department did nothing to clarify her meaning. In what way did she "know about" me?

"We have a lot in common," she told me, before going on to talk about her husband and her marriage. She used the term "marriage of convenience," which meant nothing to me at the time. What I didn't know then was that, in the army back then, a marriage of convenience meant that one or both partners were gay, and that they were married to hide this fact from the military.

Like "lesbian" when I first came to West Point, "gay" was not part of my vocabulary, save as an insult among cadets. All I understood was that the major's marriage of convenience had somehow brought her to being a teacher at West Point.

She went on to tell me that she liked me a lot and that I was making a mistake by majoring in engineering. Finally, the first logical thing she had said to me! I had no idea what was convenient about her marriage, but did know that I abhorred engineering.

Still, I tried not to get too excited because I did not fully understand why I was there or if I were in trouble. She interpreted my apprehension as not being interested in discussing my major further.

"Maybe it would be better if someone else told you. I think I've scared you." She left the room, reemerging with an appointment slip. "You have a pass to Major Hill two days from now. She is brilliant, and we will see how that goes."

Dismissed, I nearly ran through the halls to find Colonel Blue's office. He was the assistant chairman of the department. I might be changing majors.

Major Hill, 1990

Major Hill allowed me to come into her office and sit down. She was a small, appealing, superbly learned woman. No one else in the department had a doctoral degree, but she wasn't fussy about which title we used. She frowned just a little when she talked, not to display anger but to remind you to listen.

She opened by stating, "Let me say first that I don't usually get involved with other people's life decisions." In the twenty minutes she took to get involved with mine, I realized that I had no business studying engineering any further than what the academy forced me to take for my mandatory engineering minor. I knew then that I belonged in international relations.

As I left she called after me, "Sleeping in class eh?"

I was instantly ashamed, and told her I did not know why I was so tired. PTSD people are tired a lot, but a more readily reason why I fell asleep in class was simply because I was a cadet and sometimes the rigors of the Academy left us tired.

She sensed my humiliation. "Your grades with us are stellar in this department. Sleep in your dorm, Brame."

We laughed.

International relations was the right fit for me. I never looked back.

Junior, 1990

Jayns's insistence that I would regret my major change upon seeking employment meant nothing to me. He ramped up phone calls and sent flowers weekly, sometimes daily. He invited me out to Monterey, where he was in language training for the field artillery, for a long weekend. I was proud of him for doing something so social as learning another language. I thought it was an honor, and wished that the army would train me in a language as well.

I flew out to Monterey and we wound up in a bar playing pool almost immediately after I arrived. Jayns drank Heinekens, and I tried to analyze why he seemed rather aloof. At one point he brought me a "fruity drink" that did not smell fruity. To his chagrin, I refused to drink it.

"You're going to wish you had kept that alcohol," he muttered darkly, foreseeing something in my future that I could not. Time would prove that that drink had been a failed she-was-drinking-at-the-time defense. His were premeditated plans to rape me.

He returned to the bartender to exchange the drink for a Diet Coke, but his actions drew my ire. I scolded him. We left the bar after his third beer because I was scared that he was going to get drunk, and I could not drive a stick shift.

Undeterred

He drove erratically. I suddenly realized that I was in a strange town with no money, being driven by someone metabolizing a few beers. If I exited the car, I had no place to go. Jayns seemed to know exactly where he was going, so I tried to relax.

After weaving in and out between the other cars and zooming through traffic lights, the car came to an abrupt halt outside a hotel. I did not ask why we had come to a hotel, rather than his apartment; I was just relieved that I could walk away from the ride alive.

"Leave your bags," he ordered harshly. I never saw the front desk, which means that no one else ever saw me either. Neither of us spoke. When the hotel room door opened, a short wall led up to the queen-sized bed.

I never had a chance. He was on me immediately.

"I am not in the mood" I told him, struggling.

He continued.

"Stop!"

He threw me on the bed.

"You are drunk." He may or may not have been. "Jayns, you are raping me!"

He knew.

The bite saved my life. He ensured that I could not perform any of the rape-prevention moves that West Point had taught me. His defense was well-studied, thanks to me. Still, I raked my teeth across his scalp with one productive chomp of my jaw. I probably caught all manner of dead and living cells in my mouth, and along with it, DNA, the details of which were on file with the Department of Defense for every soldier. He would later demand that I brush my teeth twice to dispel his DNA.

I could not stop his attack, and when the pain of his brutally raping me became too much, I passed out. My body simply said, "Enough terror."

My changing majors was only a minor reason for Jayns to rape me. He would later express a lot of additional reasons, the most important of which was that he sensed that I was homosexual and that I had admitted that I might go into politics. He dated me to hurt me for those very reasons, giving meaning to Mrs. Angel's theory of people hunting people.

My brain suffered from the memory loss of these traumatic events, which meant, as long as I could not remember the rape due to my PTSD, Jayns could continue to hunt me until I recognized him as a predator.

Monterey Airport, 1990

I arrived in Monterey on a Friday during the first semester of my junior year. I was excited to go anywhere since my family could rarely afford to bring me home for anything other than Christmas or Thanksgiving. We saw the sea lions the next day, Saturday, while I was deeply in shock and still in pain. I slept the entire day on Sunday until my flight back to New York.

I was a bit more awake in the airport, though I still did not realize that Jayns had raped me. PTSD blocked the memory from my consciousness. We stood against the gate's wall, and I tried to rest my head against his shoulder while we waited for boarding to begin. In those days, everyone could pile around the gates to say goodbye to their loved ones. We did not yet fear terrorists from beyond. We certainly identified few terrorists from within.

I was exhausted; one of the side effects of shock from the rape. Though tired, I spoke normally and I was as logical as ever. My brain simply could not access memories of his horrific crime.

"Do you think that you are going to keep that engagement ring?" he asked me in a low, direct tone.

Not fully understanding, I asked gingerly, "Do you want it back?"

He stared at me with taut lips. I waited. "It will come back to me. You will not be permitted to keep it."

The half-carat diamond ring was a promise to marry him, but after this weekend, we both might chose to forego matrimony. To be honest, I did not care if I married him or not. Despite having accepted the ring, I did not love him as much as I thought I did, or even at all. Jayns's best characteristic was my grandparents' approval.

Undeterred

He had asked my grandfather for my hand in marriage on a trip back home during my sophomore year. My grandparents thought he was a fine fellow, which helped him a great deal in my book. Had they not liked him, I would not have been in Monterey at that moment.

"If you want the ring back, here, take it." I worked it off my finger and offered it to him.

He stood, focusing first on the ring and then on my face behind it. I let him weigh his options. Finally, impatient with his hesitation, I urged him again: "Take it." My tone was tenser this time.

Traffic at my gate began moving. "Things might change once you get back," he told me cautiously. "A lot has happened. I cannot tell if you can't remember that or if you are trying to pretend."

"The ring is not pretend," I informed him, annoyed. "Now take the ring, or stop whining." He had complained a lot that weekend, from my shower, to my walk, to the way I slept.

"I'll let you keep it," he said.

"Gee. What a favor. Now neither of us wants your ring." I continued to suspend it before his eyes.

"I'm sorry. I'm just nervous. Maybe next time we can play chess. I know you like that. You slept so much this weekend. Please keep the ring."

Jayns hated to play me at chess. I beat him every time. Book smarter than I, he misconstrued the pieces' movements and moved without any forward-thought. We played all the time, but one time he overturned the board in anger, throwing pieces for having made simple errors. Years would pass before I realized that, in raping me that weekend, he had bludgeoned my queen.

Cadet Clinic, 1990

Monterey, Sunday Flight

The flight attendant had to shake me mightily to wake me once we landed in New York. When I finally did awaken, she hurried me to deplane the by-then empty aircraft. I wearily flagged down a taxi outside of LaGuardia Airport and slept all the way to West Point.

I was returning from a three-day weekend in Monterey, California, with my fiancé, a rapist then unknown to my consciousness. Jayns's purpose in inviting me to Monterey was to rape me, not to introduce me to the sea lions. The savage act soothed that violent part of him that lay just beneath his surface.

I got back to West Point in time for Sunday evening formation. Military formations give the army a chance to account for who is present and who is not. Cadets need permission to miss formation, as accountability is vital to maintaining safety and strength in the military. Sunday evening formation accounts for everyone who returned after the weekend. After formation, I went to my room and slept deeply until my new roommate, who had transferred to our company, shoved me to move again.

"You are going to be late for *breakfast* formation," she warned. I must have looked confused because she added, "It's Monday morning. Let's go."

The night was gone.

"Hurry Tracey!" She ran out the door.

I took stock of my surroundings. I knew where I was and why. I simply did not care. I was too exhausted to care. PTSD victims are routinely enervated after a trauma, sometimes for days or weeks. The prospect of lying back down seemed delicious, but I managed to fumble into my uniform and find the stairs since I made it a point to never miss formation.

By the time I got outside, I felt like I was going to pass out. I considered my options: I could proceed to the right, to morning formation, feeling light-headed, or I could walk straight into the cadet clinic directly in front of me. I looked up at the sun and felt the heat getting the best of me. I moved toward the clinic.

West Point cadets all go to the same clinic near our dormitories. The hospital required a drive and was for the very sickest. In shock, I did not think to go to the hospital. After all, the clinic was perfectly fine for most of us. By the time I arrived at the clinic, I was crawling on my hands and knees, too dizzy and weak to stand.

"Attention over here! Someone help me with her," a voice called.

I eyed the bench seat closest to me. It was a few crawls away. I almost made it, but didn't. Several people assisted me off the floor.

Prepped

"What's your name?"

I looked around before focusing on Major Walker beside me. He alone served the Corps of Cadets in the clinic. His office was neat and sterile, with US Army posters on the walls to motivate us. A handsome, caramel-colored man, he never missed a chance to thoroughly explain something to his patient. He kept an upbeat outlook and encouraged cadets to do the same.

"Tracey Brame," I answered wearily.

"Good," he said. At the very least, I knew who I was. "And where are you right now?" He washed his hands vigorously while watching my every move, including my inability to remain upright. He ordered me to lie back down.

"The clinic," I identified my location. He told his assistant to lower the table further to the ground, to reduce the chances of a dangerous fall. I lay back, fatigued.

"How did you get here today, Tracey?"

"I came over."

"What day is it?"

"I don't know." He asked if it were Monday or Friday to test my awareness of time. I had no idea what day it was. I could not remember, and I was so very tired. The Corps of Cadets had just returned from long weekend. I should have known it was Monday.

"What did you do this weekend?"

"I went to Monterey to visit my fiancé."

"It's beautiful out there. What did you guys do?"

"Nothing." PTSD allowed me to remember little.

"What does that mean–nothing?"

"I don't know." Major Walker did. Through his gentle inquiries, he was casually stepping backward in time to see where my memory failed me. PTSD victims who lose their memory can remember events up to a point, and then they miss a block of time surrounding the trauma. The lost time in my memory is called a blackout. Something relating to the weekend escaped me. Major Walker was going to dig harder to bring it out. He crossed his arms and stood in front of me.

"You did nothing?" he clarified.

"We saw sea lions and cops."

"Explain that."

"Cops were gathered by the sea lions." I fell quiet. That was the extent of my memory, and I was too tired to try to remember more.

"What day was that?"

"I don't know."

He kept pushing though to see if that had been Friday, Saturday, or Sunday. I fumbled with the possibilities and just guessed, "Friday."

Undeterred

"That's a long flight from New York to California, Tracey. You landed on Friday and went straight to the sea lions that night?"

He had me. I did not know what day I was missing in my memory bank. I did know that I was dead-tired, and his inquisition prevented me from napping.

"Are you two sexually active?"

"Yes."

"Do you mind if I do a quick pelvic exam to look around? I'll be brief."

I did not care. I just wanted to sleep the rest of my junior year away. If he could do it without disturbing my slumber, I didn't care if he removed my head surgically, let alone performed a pap smear.

"Prepare her," he ordered the assistant and left the room.

Rape Exam

In the cadet clinic, Major Walker reentered the exam room and washed his hands again to perform my rape examination. Drying off, he walked around to the left side of the table where I lay on my side, trying uncomfortably to get more sleep. He watched me and smiled, reassuring me that the exam would not take long.

"You're going to need to be on your back, Cadet Brame." Being curled into a ball waiting for slumber to befall me despite my discomfort was not going to help the exam process.

The prospect of moving again proved excruciatingly difficult. Major Walker had already observed that I was too lethargic to fully undress myself and therefore needed help. His assistant helped me move, and then blurted that I had a light feminine pad on as well.

"Are you on your period?"

"No."

"Are you spotting?"

"Yes."

I wanted to beg him to stop asking questions, but that would have required energy I simply did not have. Instead, I lay on the table, praying that he would just go away. He needed me to scoot down and spread my legs wider. He needed me to relax. He needed a lot, it seemed, and I just needed to sleep.

The cold medical utensils did not soothe the deep cuts around the opening of my vagina. Where skin was missing, there were random gouges leading inside my vagina.

"Cadet Brame?" He was not looking for an answer, so he continued. "Do you and your fiancé use toys when you have sex?"

"No."

"What kind of foreign objects do you use?" I did not understand the question.

"Knives?"

"No."

"Combs?"

"No."

"Do you play with anything at all?"

"No."

"Well, a human penis cannot leave these markings, and I have not even entered your vagina yet. Is there something that you are not telling me?"

"No." I could not remember.

"Hmm, I have to use my speculums. They are cold. You are going to feel some real discomfort." He sighed deeply.

Addressing his assistant the instructed, "Please go to her side and hold her hand."

To me again: "We are going to hold your hand, Cadet Brame, to see if that makes it better. Please be patient. I will try to go as fast as I can."

It was excruciatingly painful as he worked that steel clamp into me and then stretched those open wounds further. I did not want it to last, and he did not want to see what he found inside of me.

He repeated "oh my God," "Lord," and "please help me" several times.

He stopped touching me.

Every inch of my internal vaginal walls was missing skin or showed tattooing from what looked like a fine-toothed comb. Major Walker asked me over and over again if I owned a tiny comb. How did it get in my vagina? How could anyone make these perfectly even comb marks throughout my vagina? Gouges left red welts where no lining existed, as if a fork had ripped off sections and left others streaked. Tissue that had not fallen out dangled. During my rape, no surface on the inside of me had been safe. He had attacked every part of my vaginal cavity.

"Cadet Brame!" He stood. "I am going to need to move the speculum to see the extent of the damage. I have to rotate it. It's not going to be comfortable for you. But I have to see how much damage is here." He instructed his assistant to move closer and hold my hand tighter.

I shouted for help as the steel clamps rotated inside me to reveal all the affected areas. It felt like he made a complete 360-degree rotation. My back arched as though I was undergoing an exorcism. I could barely take it. Screaming did not help, but I could not stop myself. When he finished, I fell back to the table, breathless, practically lifeless.

He paused, so I thought I had made it.

"Hold her hand!" He pinched some raw tissue off of my sore vaginal walls to remove it for further inspection. It felt like torture. I rose and wailed for help yet again. Perhaps that was when his eyes watered. I fell back to the table when he finally released me.

Major Walker stood and removed his gloves to make notes, dismissing his assistant. He pulled his lips taut to his teeth and held them there as he thought. In the silence that followed, I closed my eyes.

When I opened them again, he had rolled his chair to the side of my bed. His eyes were wet, and he assured me that he was there to help me, but that he needed honest answers from me as to what had happened.

I did not know.

"Tell me about where you had sex."

I did not know.

"Do you drink?"

"No."

"Do you smoke cigarettes?"

"No."

"Smoke anything else?"

"No."

"Tell me about the drugs that you take. Are there any?"

"No."

"Please!" He begged me to help him help me. I lay there, exhausted.

He put his head down and whispered, "Please, tell me how he did this to you."

My silence won me a transfer to the hospital, where I was granted the right to sleep for as long as I wanted.

Military hospitals have rows of soldiers sleeping off trauma. The brain needs to re-stitch itself after being traumatically torn in two. I was a step ahead of most patients, in that I willed myself to stay on my feet. When you do not know what happened to you, you do not think you need to take a knee.

Hospital

I heard everything they said.

The two men talking close to the door of my hospital room had familiar voices. One was Major Walker and the other was my company captain. Their voices were low, but they were discussing my progress, each elated that I had finally opened my eyes.

There I was, the star of the show–little old me, in an open-backed gown, after catching some Zs. I said I felt great. They asked if I really meant that, and I assured them that I did. Both smiled.

"Well, you have slept here only two days," said Major Walker. "Every patient is different." Some PTSD patients sleep for months.

I eyed the saline drip that I had watched him start when I arrived. I had never had a saline drip before. Upon arriving, my body had been burning up with fever, heat and exhaustion, and when he started that intravenous line in my left arm, I had felt a remarkable chill spread over my arm and shoulder that was like nothing I had ever experienced before. Given my exhaustion, I welcomed it. I needed the hydration because I had hardly had anything to eat or drink over the weekend.

"You look great. How's your discomfort?" asked Major Walker.

Undeterred

All you can do in a situation when folks are gawking over you in bed is smile, so that's what I did. The major moved around the captain to start with his questions. Major Walker asked me repeatedly if I had been raped and I repeatedly answered, "No."

Maybe they liked my answer or maybe he hated it. He would certainly prefer that I had said, "Yes, but I don't want to press charges." Those were magic words for him, because they would let him off the hook.

Mine was an unusual case. If I could not remember the rape, and I had obviously been raped, then I was in shock. The army spits out shock victims, which would mean no graduation and no commission.

Major Walker bowed his head and sighed in frustration. Medically, he had an obligation to report my case to the military police. The Department of Defense wants severe PTSD patients out of uniform, but the Army doctors falsely pass many PTSD soldiers at the patient provider level, keeping men and women in uniform beyond their due time out of sympathy or ineptitude of the doctor. I had done nothing wrong, but through no misdeed of my own, a decision had to be made that could end my cadet career. I had no say in the matter.

The rape examination had been horrific, both to experience it and in the results it yielded, but I did not recognize myself as having been raped. I went into shock about the examination too. My brain associated it with the terror of the rape itself, and tucked the experience away to be forgotten as well.

When doctors mention a rape, a patient with dissociative amnesia may not even hear the word rape. It may sound like audible scratches, like on an old record. The doctor's face may be blurry, as will the perpetrator's face upon recall. For patients with PTSD, sight and sound can become distorted during the trauma or during references to the trauma even long after the crime.

I wasn't sure why the doctor's examination had been painful, or why I still felt discomfort in my groin days later. To me, nothing was related to a rape since *I* surely <u>had not</u> been raped.

The doctor made his decision. The hospital released me the next day and allowed me to return to West Point and continue pecking away at my studies. If I could handle the rigors that remained before me, I was set to graduate from the United States Military Academy, despite being in complete shock from an unimaginable and horrific rape.

PTSD Reactions

Different people respond to trauma in different ways.[1] Physical and emotional responses can vary, whether we are stricken with PTSD or not. PTSD responses are usually standard, typical. It's the trauma involved that is nonstandard, atypical to most people.

Individuals with PTSD can experience a range of emotions in response to their trauma, including sadness, hopelessness, denial, confusion, fear, withdrawal, anxiety, numbness, guilt, self-blame, and shock. Physical symptoms can include pains, aches, a racing heartbeat, insomnia, fatigue, agitation, difficulty concentrating, and tension.

These symptoms are most acute immediately after the event, and then fade with time, as the victim processes the trauma. This can take hours, days, months, or even years. Even when they feel better, PTSD sufferers may recall the event or the emotions it caused when triggered by any person, place, or thing that reminds them of the event.

Over time, we learn what kind of responses we have with PTSD as we survive with the disease. As for me, I am emotionally prone to feelings of shock, guilt, denial, sadness, and numbness when first triggered by terror. Physically, I am most likely to feel fatigue and muscle tension at first, both of which subside with time. The memory loss, however, lingers.

Europe, 1991

Despite walking around in a state of unknowing shock, I still managed to achieve my goals. The Social Science Department chose me to represent the United States at a junior NATO conference in Denmark and to work at Supreme Headquarters Allied Powers Europe in Mons, Belgium, the summer before my senior year. These are the highest privileges that the department could bestow on a student. I had never been overseas before, and I was excited to have the opportunity. Only one cadet per class earned these honors in each class.

Jayns's attitude to these successes was caustic and bitter at best. He warned me that if I went, we were done. I gladly went and was equally glad to be done with him. I simply did not understand why he was so angry that I was enthralled by a world different than his. I heard his disapproval over the phone, but what I failed to hear was that he was taping our conversations. After the rape, he taped every phone call we had, not because he wanted to hear my voice, but in order to convince anyone that listened not to hear my voice.

Upon arriving abroad, I quickly learned that Europeans are a lot more open about sexuality than we are in the United States. I saw women in Denmark openly holding hands in the street in 1991. No one cared. So much of what the United States condemned, Europe generally disregarded. At one point, a tall, blond Danish woman took an interest in me, but I ran from her metamorphically. I tried to evade her, but she insisted that I take her number. I never called.

After Denmark, I moved on to my second station in Belgium. From that vantage, I was able to travel most of Europe, taking in many countries.

The food stumped me. I lacked the maturity of palate to enjoy most of the foreign dishes that I tried, from Danish pickled fish to German schnitzel. I resorted to bread and butter for weeks and put myself on a diet when I returned to the United States.

The Homeless, 1991

Both on the way to and from Europe that summer, I spent time talking to the homeless people milling around LaGuardia Airport. Both LaGuardia and Newark allowed the homeless to sit inside the first floor to warm up. In my full dress West Point uniform, I would sit in a chair or on the floor, talking to a homeless person over coffee or soda. If they were willing to talk, I listened to their story. If they did not wish to speak,

I did not speak either. I worried for them, though they would argue that they were better off there than outside. I wondered what has to go wrong in a person's life to ground his or her progress to the airport without a fare.

They seemed normal, if a little sooty, but when I looked into their eyes, I saw regular people. When I listened to them, I heard regular stories at best. I was trying to understand where their flights in life had veered off track. Sometimes they just talked about the times when they'd sailed through life without problems. Tears flowed if they reminisced back through their own crashes. I could see myself, or anyone, in them. In all probability, my brain was trying to reconcile my own turbulence. I had not seen many homeless people in Indianapolis. My grandmother had always warned me to move along and not miss my transportation.

I deemed understanding them an important part of my education. As the incoming president of West Point's Speech and Debate Team, the least that I could do was learn to listen. Stories hail from all walks of life.

Jayns, 1991

The story of my own shock was still taking shape. I did not know to avoid Jayns, though I was certainly annoyed with him. Most people with PTSD try to avoid the triggers of their terror. I did not know that Jayns had raped me. This lack of awareness, coupled with dissociative amnesia, is the most dangerous part of PTSD, since those of us with it do not even recognize that we are still in danger. A victim who looses their memory, as I did in Monterey, can unknowingly walk away from a rape examination, visit sea lions with her rapist, or rekindle a relationship with a violent criminal.

When I returned to West Point from Europe, Jayns blew up my phone line, begging me to get back together with him. In my mind, he wasn't my rapist. I had not been raped. He was just an obnoxious guy I had not definitively broken up with yet. His controlling behavior irritated me. I am sure that the only reason that I got back together with him was to please my grandparents and to go to Greece. I was in my senior year, and I was unsure of my next direction, but his new assignment to Greece appealed to me.

Having talked to my mentors in the Social Science Department about visiting Greece, I agreed to visit Jayns after graduation in the spring. Major Hill thought there nothing wrong with Greece, but there was something wrong with my host. Jayns had called her at the end of the previous school year and had words with her for sending me to Europe. Being a lowly lieutenant, his protests gained him nothing.

Graduation, 1992

My family journeyed to New York for my graduation. My mother came, a beautiful woman with an easy-but-shy smile. She and I had our own complicated history, since I had wanted to live with Mama, rather than her, as a kid. Like Papa, Mommy never tried to dissuade me from going to West Point. She supported me in spite of Mama's discouragement. I was happy to see her, my grandparents, and my aunt and uncle. I did not know it then, but I would increasingly look to my mom for help over the rest of my life.

Walking across the graduation stage, I felt a staggering fatigue. Some may have believed that a girl with convulsions and possible shock as a child couldn't handle the rigors of West Point. I had entered with ease, but found new trauma, while still maintaining grades that kept me at the academic forefront of my peers. Graduation offered me a chance to silence my internal anxieties, but my personality was such that I would continue to pick up more.

Still in complete shock from my rape, I wearily crossed the stage and accepted my diploma from Colin Powell. Neither he nor I knew of the battles raging within me, nor of the ones that had yet to commence. I had no idea what, if anything, the honor that he conferred on me that day would mean to my life. I waded into the army with a disease that caused other soldiers to exit in droves. I was being all I could be.

GREECE, 1992

Thessaloniki

When I arrived in Thessaloniki Greece, I learned that a military post is rarely in the heart of a big metropolis. Indeed, the service invests in less congested areas, most likely to keep costs down.

The country was beautiful and there wasn't a bad stretch of weather while I was there. There were few tall buildings where we were, but I was a little disappointed to see that roadside Greece was a lot like the US. Green or yellow weeds and plants filled the open spaces between towns and opposing highways. I kept asking myself, how do you know it's different here? Of course, I only had to wait for the locals to open their mouths to speak. At that point, I conceded that I was lost.

When Jayns picked me up, I hugged him and thanked him for the trip. It was the first time I had seen him since the rape, which my brain still did not recall. At this point, my dissociative amnesia was so firmly established that I would have denied my doctor's suggestion that I had been raped, and would even have argued with him profusely. Accordingly, I was excited to see Jayns, but he seemed standoffish, assuring me that there were a lot of things that we had to discuss.

Like he had done in Monterey the year before, he almost immediately told me that another guy on post shared his exact name. In Monterey,

Undeterred

he had told me that this person had been using drugs, getting in egregious trouble, and wreaking havoc on the post. In Greece, this different someone with his name had just left post without warning one day. He was quite insistent that if I heard something, I should be aware that it was not his doing, but rather his nemesis's.

Odd, I thought, before dismissing it.

He next insisted that I go sailing with him. He had convinced his mother to pay for sailing lessons, and bragged that he was a certified sailboat captain. It sounded interesting, so I gave it some thought.

When we got to post, though, the explanations began. He told me that he had trashed the soldiers' recreation room one night after drinking. He had destroyed everything in sight, even shredding the furniture. I did not understand, and he tried to explain: "I was so stressed out about our relationship, I leveled this place. Everything you see in this recreation area is new."

I looked around and realized that it was indeed all new. I studied him closely and asked, "What were you thinking?"

He admitted that he was in trouble. Money from his two official intelligence officer vaults had disappeared after someone cut the locks. He and his sergeant had each separately lost $40,000 of the army's money from their respective vaults. They had both been found not criminally culpable for their respective funds in a major investigation, which was a relief to me, but Jayns alluded to another investigation about financial liability for the debt.

"Did they catch the thief?" I asked.

"No," he responded. Greek nationals were conducting the investigation.

"I just lost it that night. I'm so glad that you have stayed by me. I am alone here."

I had been lonely in Europe the previous summer, so I understood his feelings. It's always good to have someone like family around. I said this to a man who admittedly hated his family; he seemed unmoved by the sentiment.

Jayns also seemed to be overly acquainted with the females on the post, many of whom waved or winked at him while we were out and about. I wondered if he had paid them to behave that way to make me jealous, since no one in the States had ever held such admiration for him.

His promotion ceremony loomed. In spite of the stolen money from the vaults, Jayns had made captain. Excited, he asked me to film the ceremony using the video camera he had bought me as a graduation present. Soldiers usually have their loved ones pin on a new rank, but Jayns insisted that I film him instead. In fact, I suspected that his promotion ceremony had been the motivation for his choosing my gift.

After the ceremony, I stood at the rear of the room, as people came forward to shake his hand. Suddenly, a Greek national in uniform whispered something in Jayns's ear, causing him to involuntarily glance at me. I looked behind me to verify that their gazes were indeed directed my way. I saw that two other uniformed Greeks stood behind me. Jayns and the third approached me.

The conversation that followed was entirely in Greek, and it resulted in my being handcuffed. A senior officer on the US side stopped everything when I was loaded onto the back of a Greek military truck. Could Jayns actually speak Greek? How could real communication lead to my being handcuffed?

Video cameras, as it turned out, were outlawed on post. One might think that the Greek-trained linguist and intelligence officer would know not to give his girlfriend a video camera to film his promotion.

The higher-ranking US officer curtly explained the situation to the locals, who turned to the truck and motioned for me to be released. I stepped down from the military cargo vehicle with the senior officer's help, as he explained the nature of the "misunderstanding" to me.

Jayns stared sullenly at the ground. He was brilliant with books, but he often disconnected from people for some reason, focusing anywhere but on the other person's eyes when talking. This habit had long troubled me, and seeing it now made me nervous.

I spent the rest of the summer with him. I waded through the problems he amassed and, more than anything, I tried to reassure him about his strengths. Still, if he could arrange for a video camera and arrest, could he purposely loose $40,000? I wanted to believe him, but such counter-logic preoccupied me. The reputation he was earning for trashing or loosing government property was bound to stick if not reversed, and soon. When does the army decide that someone is refusing to be all that he can be?

Rock

If you arrive at West Point with little-to-no swimming skills, you are labeled "a rock." A lot of poor black and Hispanic entrants fall into this category, as these groups are the least likely to have had access to swimming pools while growing up.

Failing swimming is grounds for dismal, and it weeds out a lot of minority West Pointers. You get one second chance, but failing twice guarantees erasure from the Long Grey Line. I only narrowly escaped that fate.

"*Get in the water,*" my instructor ordered. *He was a tall, handsome, dark-haired man wearing army-issue black pants and a grey shirt. I sat by the side of the pool and quietly, politely refused. I was too scared.* "*Get in the water,*" *he repeated, more directly.*

"*No.*" *I spoke softly at first, but with his subsequent order I was firm. I did not know how to swim and was terrified.*

Only I defied him. He eyed me. He set everyone else in motion, then returned to me a few minutes later and extended a hand, as if inviting me into the water.

My instructor could tell I was going to require extra work as soon as I hit the cold water. I failed to catch my breath. The smell of chlorine nauseated me and just standing in the water changed my breathing patterns. I hyperventilated as fear and the water's temperature constricted my breathing, but I stood there as wet as everyone else, quivering.

The rest of the class was sent to the six-foot end of the pool right away. They all put their heads under water, blowing bubbles while holding onto the side of the pool and coming up for air.

The instructor kept me in the shallow section. I was remedial.

I failed that first day of swimming. Everything he asked of me defied logic. When he dismissed the class, he ordered me to stay behind.

"Before today, what has been your experience with swimming?" he asked, kindly.

"I nearly drowned in three feet of water when I was eight years old. My brother saved me by telling me to stand up."

He didn't laugh like my cousins had. He simply tried to understand. "You are a West Pointer now. We swim. You can get through this class." He spoke to the top of my head because he was tall, and I sat slumped in a sitting position with my chin shamefully buried in my chest.

"Look at me," he ordered with a low tone. I met his eyes. "You can get through this class. It is entirely possible, but if you ever in your life fail to take a direct order from me or any ranking officer, you will take off your uniform forever."

I realized the depth of my trouble. Grades and fitness were not enough. I was going to have to learn to swim as well.

He demanded to know whether I understood him.

"Yes, sir," I answered, miserably.

I went to gather my clothes, only to find that the only person who had seen me take off my high school class ring and hide it in my shoes had probably stolen it. Mama had saved up to buy that ring from a department store, where it had cost less than what my high school's vendor charged. The day could not get worse. But ultimately, that same kid did not make it at West Point, so I suppose fate took care of things.

Back in the barracks, Twig had heard about my performance. She and Jayns, still buddies at that point, paid me visit to rally me. "No one can graduate without swimming, Brame," she reminded me. "We cannot coach you or practice with you. That is not what you need. What you need is to focus and refuse to fail."

With nearly straight A's and B's my freshman year, I hated the idea that swimming could be the class that would remove me from West Point. Fear settled in me as I sat there at my desk. Can you castle on purpose, or is it an involuntary act? *I wondered. I needed to trick my mind to put away my fear of the water. In the end, I managed to convince myself that dying would be okay–going back home would not.*

Undeterred

At our next swimming class, I immediately complied with the order to get in the water. An assistant showed up to work with me, since I was clearly going to need extra help. To deal with the frigidity of the water, I concentrated on my breathing. After all, breathing underscores any sport. Once I was able to control my breathing, I passed the breathing exercises, like my other classmates had the day before.

I still sank when I tried to tread water or float, and it took me longer than everyone else in the class to master the required skills or concepts. I struggled with everything, but I attempted it all. The instructor gave me more attention than anyone else in the class. Mastering my own breathing assured him I was worth the added time he had to spend on me.

During the final two-mile exam, I could not see him, but I felt him there. He walked the perimeter of the pool, and I sensed his presence. There was little thought involved in swimming the distance, and I focused on my breathing. When I touched the concrete for the last time, I looked up, and he was there. He did not smile; he simply nodded.

I passed the swimming course and the two-mile test with a heroically low grade that hurt my GPA that semester but saved my career as a West Pointer.

Cadet Twig celebrated with me by sneaking me off post to buy a leather jacket that I still have. Jayns gave me a nod in the hallway.

Swimming

Having passed the West Point swimming test, I did not flinch when Jayns wanted to go swimming in Greece. He had found a tiny, deserted beach that he seemed excited to show me.

We walked into the murky water together, holding hands at first. The water's depth and cloudiness made me nervous, but I rationalized that I disliked chlorine too. I knew I couldn't spend my life disliking water. Besides, the beach's sand was so white and untouched. It was pretty. Still, I did not like the sand's slimy feeling beneath my feet. I grew uncomfortable as the water reached my chest. It was not cold so much as it was dirty, and I did not want it in my mouth.

Jayns, only three inches taller than me, moved further out into the water and then turned to face me. It was hard to tell if he was smiling or sneering. "Come to where I am," he beckoned. I failed to see that he was no longer standing and had started treading water.

I thought that it would be easy enough, so I walked further out into the waves. Just before I reached him, I felt my feet drop down into nothingness. The sand that I had been walking on was not there anymore. I flailed past Jayns and noticed that he went back towards the shore, standing again. I coughed and thrashed, asking him to help me. I could not reach him and he made no effort to reach for me. His face held a broad smile. I continued to search for something to ground me. I imagined myself flailing, drowning.

I found what I was looking for suspended on the left bank of the shore. In West Point's black shorts and gray gym instructor shirt stood a vision of my swimming teacher. "*Cadet Brame, listen to my voice.*" Despite Jayns's presence, my instructor's was the only voice I heard. "*Find and face your direction. Look where you're going. Let that arm lead you. Open your eyes, and most importantly, Cadet Brame, breathe.*"

Opening my eyes, I saw a car parked on the beach. Young people piled out, preparing to sunbathe on the white sand. No one dies in the water when young people are driving up to lie in the sand. I stroked.

"*Great job,*" said my instructor, disappearing. Jayns said nothing, did nothing.

I stroked. I looked. I breathed. I swam until I felt rocks and sand with my hands. Only then did I stand to catch my breath. Jayns walked out of the water past me and continued towards the car.

"Why didn't you help me?"

Raising an eyebrow, he casually summed up his conclusion, "You seemed to have it."

I did not believe him. When he asked me to go sailing with him a few days later, I refused. One shot at killing me in Greece was enough. I broke up with him, but he cried real tears, as though I had hurt him.

Undeterred

Maybe I had been too harsh on him; after all, I had managed to swim back on my own. But we were leaving Greece in a couple of days: Congress had voted to close his base, and I needed to get home to my family. I saw no future with him.

About halfway through my stay in Greece, I noticed that Jayns was slipping out of the room for a few hours each night. Whether he was meeting with or speaking to someone escaped me. I just started losing track of all the senseless things that he did.

I did not know it at the time, but Jayns was the soldier named Jhomes who was doing drugs on post. Several people on base had asked me if I could get him help, but I did not know what he needed help with. My assessment left me believing that he needed mental help. Little did I know that psychological help and help with addiction are found within the same discipline.

Back to the US

The flight from Greece to JFK International was a long, crowded one. I do not recall a layover, but I do remember our in-flight movie.

Everyone liked Denzel Washington, including me. When I saw that one of his movies would be screened in-flight, I was elated. It meant that much less time where I might have to converse with Jayns. Every time I asked him a question of late, he paused and thought about what might sound truthful. He never seemed to have a genuinely honest, spontaneous answer. His words were increasingly losing value to me.

It was the summer of 1992, and the movie on our flight was called *Ricochet*. Washington played a Los Angeles attorney terrorized by a criminal he had helped put in jail when he had been a cop on the LAPD. John Lithgow played the criminal and he played the part so perfectly that I stopped watching movies starring him after that flight. Perhaps avoidance is the best compliment I can give to an actor who so perfected the role of an absolute scoundrel.

In the movie, Lithgow escapes from prison to avenge himself on Washington's character. He uses drugs, women, and sordid conjured sex tapes to incriminate and persecute the drugged cop-turned-lawyer before the final scenes, in which Washington escapes, kills Lithgow, and regains his life. The movie's twists contained shockingly hateful turns.

"I hated that," I whispered to Jayns when it was finally over.

"I loved it," he returned, as though a thirst had been quenched.

"What was there to love about that?" I asked, startled.

He met my eyes. "Everything."

I thought it was a sick response and we barely spoke again until the plane landed. I planned to deliver him back to his parents in Virginia and then travel on to Indiana to visit my family before heading to Officer Basic Course Training. Except for his directions, our conversation entirely ceased between New York and Virginia.

I did not want to see Jayns's family. They had not done anything to me, but he had never reported anything favorable about them. His mother was a constant source of ire for him. He frequently repeated that he hated her, but offered no reason beyond the fact that both of his parents insisted that he attend a free academy to forego paying the Ivy League tuition at Brown University, his first choice. I didn't know it at the time, but his father, tired of funding Jayns's habits, had cut him off financially while he was at West Point, which left Jayns to pay for our dates with credit cards that he had no way of paying off.

When his family visited West Point, he always walked ahead of them or did not speak. I could not imagine treating my grandparents or my mother in such a fashion. When we arrived in Virginia, I dropped him off at their house without a word. I stayed overnight so I could pick up my grandmother's wire transfer the next morning. After that, I would be gone.

Jayns's Mother

In the morning, his mother counseled me. His parents had a large, beautiful home thanks to his father's engineering job. She sat on the couch in

Undeterred

front of the TV, the only place I had ever seen her in her own home. By the time I had arrived at her house the day before, I had concluded that her son was a brand of evil that would allow his fiancé to get arrested or drown in Greece. I said nothing to her.

In her mind, her son was hard to understand and, while he had a good heart, it was difficult to discern. "He is my most intelligent child," she said, "but his sister will do better in life because of the way he treats people and what he is doing now."

I considered his mother's words at length, and I asked her what she meant by "what he is doing now." Were other people drowning?

She reminded me that her husband drank. This was true; one time when the four of us went out to dinner, he drank two bottles of wine and sang sloppily all the way from his seat at the table to his seat in the car. Had Jayns not supported his father under one arm, the old man may have crawled. I had never seen a drunken person up close before, nor did I register him as one at the time. I just assumed that he was not feeling well.

"Well, Jayns is doing things," his mother declared, "worse than his father. He thinks that I don't know it, but the neighbors saw him outside smoking the few times he has come home. They tell me everything."

"I have never seen him smoke. We don't like cigarettes," I assured her.

She studied me. She spoke not of cigarettes. As I sat there, she gathered that I was clueless, and I certainly was. The opportunity to educate me mattered little to her, though. With partial disclosure, she watched my reaction to her next words: "Neighbors have seen him smoke something."

She returned her attention to the television, figuring it was not her place to tell me more. All she learned from that conversation was that her son was not confiding in anyone. All I learned from that conversation was that Jayns's neighbors had a vision problem. I was truly naïve.

I said goodbye and left his ring. I left him.

My grandmother had wired money overnight. I withdrew it that morning to gas up my Mazda Protégé. Fourteen hours later, I had made my way home without the aid of a AAA map.

Firsts, 1992

First Time Stranded

Mama and Papa bickered about the smallest things of late. He would ask for a piece of bread, or complain that no spoon accompanied his coffee. He could get it himself, she responded, but she did not allow him in the kitchen. Their exchanges were petty, but Mama started and finished every one. Everyone in the family laughed about it. Papa never touched her or so much as raised his voice, often quietly waiting for her to finish hounding him. Mama always won the argument–always, even when she lost. I gather that's the secret for sixty-plus years of wedlock.

Glad to see them, I regretted having gone to Greece instead of coming home, but I imparted stories, along with the trinkets I had purchased for them. I wanted them to live through my experiences.

Mama called the residents of other countries "them foreigners" all the time. According to her, I needed to be careful with "them foreigners." Still, she labeled a host of people right here in the US as equal threats. I needed to be careful with them too. Nothing and no one seemed safe to Mama.

My giving Jayns's ring back disappointed them. They liked him and saw him as a great potential provider. But they had spent so little time

Undeterred

with him that they did not see what I saw when I studied his eyes, words, and actions. I thought him unpredictable. They felt that, with time, we might work things out.

At one point, I started to notice fluttering movements in my belly that I'd never felt before. I announced that I needed to go to the grocery store, and set out in my car on my own. I did not tell my grandmother that I was buying a pregnancy test.

The closest store in Cloverdale, Indiana, was also its only store. It stood by the town's only stop sign–not a traffic light, a stop sign. I pulled up to the weathered, wooden house that housed the store and spoke to the clerk. They did not carry pregnancy tests. She suggested only one alternative drugstore, in Martinsville.

These were the days before GPS, so I kept an atlas in my backseat. I drew up a route and headed to Martinsville, a town most black people in the area knew not to be caught in at night, as it was the headquarters of the Ku Klux Klan. Some daylight still shone. I thought I could make it.

Back roads in Indiana are sometimes confusing to the unfamiliar. I found the Martinsville drugstore and bought my test, but got turned around on the way back. I thought I could make the adjustments in my head to get back on track, but I ended up having to turn around several times. Stopping to read the map again consumed time. The sun disappeared below the horizon, leaving me with just the light on my keychain with which to see. I identified my location and headed out anew.

As I headed out of Martinsville, I hit something, causing my back driver's side tire to deflate completely. So there I sat, stranded in the dark somewhere in Martinsville, Indiana, home of the Ku Klux Klan, exactly where my grandmother had always told me that I should *never* be caught after dark. No street lights shone in front of or behind me. I called my grandparents on my cell.

Mama went into hysterics when she heard where I was. "My God! Thomas, she is in Martinsville! Nothing at the drugstore is this important! Thomas, go find her!"

Papa did not own a cell phone and he did not know where I was, given that I lacked street names. He told me to call the insurance company and then call back immediately.

I had never had a flat before, but Papa had taught me how to change a tire. While I waited for the insurance company to call me back, he walked me through it again over the phone. Unfortunately, the lug nuts refused to turn.

The insurance lady called back to narrow down my location based on the store I'd left and a few landmarks. She patched through a man's voice, and he was able to zero in on where to find me. He ordered me to hang tight and said he would be there soon.

My grandfather told me not to be scared, which was unnecessary, since I wasn't. Mama's reaction alerted me to my peril, but from childhood I knew the danger of my location. Making matters worse, my phone battery dwindled. Still, I felt calm. I started assuring my grandparents that I was fine and that they should not worry. They were both on house phones, but within seconds all went silent: my cell phone had died.

I listened to my heartbeat. In the silence, I finally started to feel fear. No one was around. I sized up the wooded area ahead of me beside a deserted building. There was no safe place to my rear, but there was the hope of traffic. A stretch of weeds parted me from opposing drivers who would never see me from that distance in the dark. What good could they do anyway? I thought hiding in the woods might be best, but having never called an insurance company, I wondered if anyone would change tires for a deserted car. I stayed put. Facing my fear ruled out over camping all night in the brush.

First Flat

Each of the forty-five minutes crept by at a snail's pace. Cars passed, but I hailed none of them. Finally, a set of lights approached from behind, slowing down until I could hear chains and clanking noises on a

Undeterred

strangely shaped truck. It came to a rest close to my rear driver's side. Soon after, a large hand knocked on my window. I lowered it.

"Hey," the man said by way of greeting. His eyes were brown, and he had short brown hair peeking out from under a skullcap and a full beard and mustache like Jack Nicholson. Dirt and scuff all over his overalls and shirt detailed a day's work that I could not have performed. "You can get out."

Was he my first brush with the KKK? I did not know. I just exited the car. His eyes left mine and took in every inch of my body. He didn't even hurry about it. Once he'd reached my toes, his eyes met mine again before he raised his head. I froze.

"You ever changed a tire before?" His cadence dragged as slow as his gaze.

"No."

"How old are you?" Cars passing on the opposite side of the road were so far away you could barely hear them.

"Twenty-three."

"Hell, you look all of twelve to me." He didn't even laugh at his own joke, assuming it was a joke. "You ain't from around here?" He barely made it a question.

"No."

"What are you doing here?"

"I am visiting a friend in Cloverdale."

"What's the last name?"

I lied and gave him my grandmother's maiden name, Lyman. I didn't want him to be able to identify my family or me. He searched his mental bank of residents and could not find a 'Lyman' in the lot.

"You scared?" Cars coming toward us highlighted me as I faced him, returning us to darkness once they had passed.

"No," I lied again. I teetered in and out of fear just standing there.

He sighed. "You sounded white on the phone. What are you–educated?"

"Yes."

"Hmm." We stood there. "Well . . . I guess I can teach ya how to do this. Pop your trunk. You got the muscles to do this."

When I finally arrived at my grandparents' front door, you would have thought I had arrived home from war. Mama shouted "Thank you, Jehovah! In Jesus's name!" long after I'd settled in. She started speaking in tongues while Papa and I simply embraced. I told Papa a new trick that I could use as a woman to get the lug nuts off–my feet. We let Mama continue to bless the Lord for all of us. Papa swore he knew I'd return all right. That may have been the only white lie he ever told me.

First Child

I felt rattled. Still, I took my pregnancy test into our compact bathroom, and reading the instructions provided, impatiently performed everything commanded. When I was done, I put the contraption in the trash, balled up in the paper sack. I was not pregnant.

Mama was whispering to Papa in the family room when I awoke the next morning. Our small family room seemed overly full with furniture. In one corner was Mama's puzzle table, a pastime we enjoyed together during my youth. Pictures of their daughters, grandchildren, and great-grandchildren, the last of which I barely knew, covered the wall. All morning long, every time I left the room, Mama's whispers with Papa started again, and stopped when I reentered. I ignored it.

Papa and I moved to the dining room table while Mama maneuvered in the kitchen. They wanted me to recount the previous evening's events, so I did in detail.

"God delivered you," Mama promised me.

Papa and I worked in the garden all day while the dogs danced through the yard. Papa never badgered me about Jayns and the possibility of reconciling. Knowing that he would refrain on this front won him my help for the day, rather than doing housework with Mama, whom I knew would start the subject.

Undeterred

Papa was getting older, and gardening was getting harder for him. He stopped frequently to wipe his brow, sighing and searching the sky for a way to stop the rays from sapping his strength. The most tiring work I have ever done was with my grandfather. As long as he kept at it, so would I. Together we could do just about anything.

"Sandwiches are ready!" Mama announced. We had been gardening for hours.

"Nice!" I exclaimed. I checked Papa's face to gauge his hunger. A telling smile told me that he was ready for a break. We halted our work.

Mama used to say, when all of the grandchildren were gathered, "Let the food shut your mouth." We often heard this when we took vacation drives, because she thought unruly, loud, children in public were nuisances. Often, when we took trips as a group, strangers complimented how well-mannered and quiet the five grandchildren were.

Today, Papa and I sat at that table for lunch and played her most well-behaved and silent guzzlers. I thought I would never be able to drink enough lemonade. Papa kept sighing after large gulps. Mama asked me how I felt, and I told her I was fine. She asked if I were sick. I responded with a casual "nope." She came back with another question: with all that work in the garden, wasn't I nauseated? I shook my head.

"Well, when are you going to tell us you're pregnant? I saw the test in the bathroom," she finally demanded.

I froze. Skilled at maneuvering Mama's pounces, Papa, the patriarch, wisely said nothing. He kept eating as though he had not heard Mama's question or tone. I, however, had to respond to her inquiry.

"I'm not pregnant. I took a test, and it was negative."

"I read the test this morning. Right now it's positive," she assured me.

What a medically sound way to find out that you are with child! Mama took me into the bathroom and showed me the blue marks that must have evolved after I'd thrown the test away the night before. How one can ace organic chemistry, yet not be able to read a second blue mark on a pee stick is beyond me. Mine was a true case of not seeing what I didn't want to see. Suddenly, I felt nauseated.

"You have to tell him. He has a right to know," was Mama's immediate verdict. Papa did not weigh in.

I waited until I could stomach the act and then called Jayns. His mother answered and found him in the basement. He sounded groggy, scary, growling like the literary monster, Grendel. I asked repeatedly what was wrong with him, and he claimed to not be feeling well. I had never heard him when he was drunk and did not make the connection. After telling him my news, we disconnected.

"He is coming here," I told my grandparents.

Papa advised me to hear him out and state my feelings honestly. "He may actually want to do the right thing for this child," he said. At that time, Papa did not know Jayns as well as he would come to know him. But then again, neither did I.

When Mama left the room, I whispered to my grandfather, "Papa, he is not fit to be a dad."

Jayns arrived on his best behavior. Everything he said indicated his readiness to share a parental role. My grandparents listened intently. For the moment, pressured by my encouraging grandparents and their religion, I would go ahead with the canceled wedding only for the sake of the child. I stored grave doubts and foresaw myself as a future divorcee.

First Crush

Captain Denise Redd introduced herself as my instructor for the Officer Basic Training Course (OBC). OBC is the school that teaches fresh West Point graduates how to do their jobs after graduation. Her oath in life included taking me from student to capable personnel lieutenant, and she required only three months to accomplish the mission.

Redd was a handsome woman and she was the first woman who was not on TV that I thought of that way. Her hair was a brownish red I'd never seen before. Little about her could be classified as feminine. She walked like a little dude. She talked tough. She wore cologne that kept me wondering, "What is that?"

Undeterred

I couldn't stop looking at her, or following her, or listening to her. I went to the mall and smelled cologne after cologne, trying to identify the one that she wore. She was the first woman I found attractive, but I could not name what drew me to her. I felt that if she were a lesbian, I needed to further investigate the very word that had almost ended my cadet career. I studied Redd.

I relocated to Fort Benjamin Harrison, which was just northeast of Indianapolis. The location had everything to do with my branch choice, because I could have gone into aviation instead of personnel. But, this being 1992, the army would not let women fly combat missions, so I decided not to incur the extra time commitment. I think I was the only aviation-qualified West Point cadet that did not choose to fly, but I may have also been the only entering freshman in the class of '92 whose varsity letter requirement was satisfied by Speech and Debate. I'm okay with being different, and Redd seemed okay with me.

Jayns hated her. He trained with us a few times in the morning, and neither of them told me until later that he was always staring her down.

I exercised. He prepared for war.

Redd talked to me a lot. She recognized me for what I was, probably even more so than I did at that point. When I told her about my upcoming marriage to Jayns because I carried his child, though, she assumed a not-so-fast stance. She did not know me well, but given my upbringing, she did not want me to be lassoed to a loser. No woman deserved that.

She assured me that she had connections. She could change my assignment, so I could stay in Indianapolis with her, which was very appealing. I was flattered that she liked me enough to want to keep me around the school.

I considered not having my child. I was torn. I fully support a woman having a choice in her life, but I wavered about my own choice. Redd researched places that I could go, and I drove by one. I even walked in. They abruptly scolded me regarding my grave intentions that, in their opinion, summarized a big religious mistake. They did not believe that I was merely researching. They strongly raged against abortion. Perplexed as to why they were listed as an abortion clinic, I deemed their sermon unhelpful, yet planned, trickery.

One woman left the office ahead of me. When I got outside, she put an arm around me and confided that the office I needed was next door. I thanked her and followed her directions.

Abortion clinics were busy. They set an appointment for me even though I was not sure I wanted to have one. They assured me that if I did not have an appointment, I would not be able to get one in time. I took their card and thanked them. I asked questions, and they obliged me with direct answers.

"Lieutenant Brame, I will personally take you myself," Redd urged. The problem was that I did not want to go. During that trying time I had learned that I support a woman's right to decide, and I had decided to carry my child and raise him. Unlike many women, I had the means to raise him, even if I eventually might have to do it alone.

I married Jayns in Indianapolis after OBC in the fall of 1992. At the altar, only one of us was conscious of the fact that he was my rapist. Had my family known, I would have woken up single the next day. When asked if anyone objected, no one knew to stand up; not even me.

Fort Bragg, 1992-1993

New Station

Papa took me to AAA to get me my own North Carolina map. I was officially on my way to Fort Bragg, North Carolina, where Jayns and I were both stationed. The long drive left me with time to reflect on my feelings. Those living with PTSD have a range of emotions, such as anger, shame, fear, and hopelessness. Fortunately, I felt none of these emotions, and I could confidently speak, approach people, and fully participate in life. Other emotions though, such as worry, denial, and guilt, all latched onto me and held on as tightly as the original shock.

I worried about my child and my career prospects. I wasn't sure how I could have a child in the army and make it as a single parent, which was the fate I projected for myself, despite being newly married. I felt sad and guilty for letting my grandparents down with a probable, eventual divorce, despite the ring on my finger. I worried to the point of denial or numbness. So much was unsettled in my mind.

Wanting to avoid the fate of being a single mother divorcee, I hoped that Jayns and I could make things work once life would settle down and we could just live. Despite my unremembered trauma, I reasoned that it was Jayns who needed treatment for his ever-growing incidents of poor judgment. I thought he was just acting out.

When I arrived at Jayns's apartment, I did not mind all of the army furniture that he had saved from his time in Greece. Our living room looked a little like an army waiting room: a boxed couch with wooden sides and woven fabric sometimes made it feel like I had not left work at all each night. The nicest thing he owned was his sound system, which is great if you want to sit on your speakers, but we needed chairs. I said nothing, because I figured that, as a guy, furnishings were not the first priority.

Though unaware of the rape, I still felt uneasy about living with Jayns for some reason. There were other issues, of course, like his controlling behavior, but I had always ended up deciding and acting against him anyway: I had changed my major and gone to Europe, after all. I wish I had kept track of every time I dumped him and then took him back. That statistic alone might have raised my eyebrows. I knew Jayns needed help, but I could not put my finger on why. I lacked references from my family to compare him to.

I was assigned as a staff officer to my first unit, a transportation battalion. I did not have as much to do as I would have liked, so I created various tasks to feel accomplished. The colonel did not seem to mind, but my major said that my energy made him nervous. He walked around the office with bare feet a lot, though, so it was hard to take him seriously.

There was no war for Jayns to fight or field training for me to go on while I was pregnant, but it seemed like Jayns's unit was never home. He was with the 82nd Airborne Division and they trained harder than anyone else. I worked in Support Command, which was a more relaxed unit. I put in long workdays and returned home at night like most everyone else in America. Since Jayns came home late, or never, we slept separately, a personal and sexual relief to me. I secretly prayed that the 82nd would live in the field for the foreseeable future. I could spend the rest of my life in a marriage like that.

Undeterred

First Rumor

Far from our apartment, across post, a drug dealer disturbed the peace. Fort Bragg soldiers filed in and out of a club designed to give young, junior-ranked enlisted soldiers a place to defuse. They wore civilian clothes and flirted with each other, dancing, smoking, drinking, commiserating, and celebrating the end of another week. While officers and sergeants gave orders all day, these soldiers were the young Americans who had enlisted, destined to follow orders.

Most rank-and-file soldiers hailed from inner cities, suburbs, and country farms. The lower and middle classes often could not afford to plant their seeds in college after high school. Army recruiters promised to nourish and educate these sons and daughters while visiting parents in one living room after another. Those without resources often pinned their hopes for a stable future on the military.

To the side of the Fort Bragg club, away from the lights, sat a black Mitsubishi Eclipse sports car with Virginia plates. In that vintage vehicle sat a black man, an army captain who, after smoking crack and coming off his high, was ready to sell his favorite pastime to America's soldiers: drugs, all types. He had a reputation for being fearless, and had established customers in uniform both on and off post.

The captain's first high came from consuming a cut of his inventory of drugs. He got his second high from hooking anyone that he could get his hands on; another established customer.

Finances

"Here, you pay my car bill," Jayns ordered.

I almost did not understand the statement. Why should I pay Jayns's car bill when we were both officers and he outranked me as a captain? He made more than I did because he had a two-year head start.

"You're not paying the bills," he pointed out. "You have been living here for weeks. I keep asking you to deposit your paycheck with mine so I can manage the bills. Since you won't do that, pay my car bill."

I laughed and an argument ensued. Every week, he demanded I hand over my paycheck. His logic tired me. What I wanted instead was to go over the bills together and understand our joint finances. It made no sense to intermingle our money without having a view of the iceberg looming just beneath the water.

His accountability for the $40,000 from Greece still was undecided. While the army had cleared him criminally, I was unsure, given his dealings with the Greek nationals and his willingness to watch me drown. The army did deem him financially liable for not properly securing the money, though, and they had garnered his pay for the amount of the stolen funds. And yet, with this history, Jayns maintained that he had a superior ability to manage funds.

Rather than finish the argument, he left for work. It was Saturday, and even on weekends he disappeared for extended periods of time, resurfacing later with a story of having had to report to work.

In his absence every night, I toyed with a spreadsheet to automate the monthly staffing report. It was simple math and an Excel spreadsheet like we'd used at West Point, but I could not print or align my results properly on army forms. That was probably by the army's design, claimed my boss.

Second Rumor

Another black captain, a coworker of Jayns, pulled his pants down to his ankles and lay back in his chair. He cashed in on Jayns's gift to him: a thin, nearly emaciated hooker who "belonged" to her pimp, Captain Jayns C. Jhomes.

All three of them were in her apartment, a lower-class flat with sufficient appliances, but little furniture. Jayns sat at the hooker's card table, which doubled as a dining area, his back to his fellow officer. Jayns counted and tallied stacks of money and crack rocks spread on the table, some of which he had to turn in to his own dealer.

The hooker called Jayns her "Old Man" because when he asked his wife to show him the same respect of title, she refused. The prostitute had one more deed to do before getting her cut of the group's earnings:

Undeterred

her Old Man's friend. She obliged. To refuse would have left her beaten like their other scraps.

Both captains covered for each other both at work and on the street. African Americans face a lot of pressure to be as good as if not better than their counterparts in corporate America. That pressure exists no differently in the army. There are pockets of people in the United States that would rather not work with blacks or other races. They certainly don't commingle with them outside of work.

In this room as one co-worker sat finding his orgasm, another frantically counted to see if he had left enough money and dope for his "other boss." Had he smoked too much crack? Did he take only his cut? Street drugs are another accounting system that West Point does not intend to teach its graduates.

Only Jayns hailed from West Point, but both men were in the same field artillery unit. Jayns knew better than to don a US Army uniform and walk in and out of as many crimes as he did, but he did it anyway. He collected felonies with sheer arrogance.

When the hooker finished, both men reported to their superior.

Mommy on Jayns

At this point, I talked to Mommy as much as I did to Mama. Her experience was more relevant to my situation, and she had supported my going to West Point. She assured me that the army would not make a lesbian out of me; if I were gay, it had been solidified by birth and upbringing, and no armed force, military or religious, could exercise it out of me.

"You're not demonic," she assured me, thinking of her own mother's words. "You are just a person with feelings. You can control a lot with your head, but sexuality is a wiring system that won't be clipped or cabled by the army or the church."

She sounded like someone I should be talking to on a regular basis. I started calling her every other week or so.

"What's his problem?" she asked one day after I had been complaining about Jayns.

"I can't tell. I think that he is becoming mentally ill, and I am worried that the army is going to throw him away. I hear the doctors in the services don't treat mental illness well."

"Describe his behavior."

"It's erratic." Memories of the swimming trip and sailing requests in Greece flooded over me. They were soft examples, but I would not trust him with my life like that again. I told her about how he looked at the curling iron when I showered, as if it gave him ideas. Once a clean, tidy man at West Point, he had become filthy away from the academy. We no longer touched, but that was no complaint for me.

"Is he drinking?"

"He loves Heineken, but the same two bottles sit in the refrigerator untouched all the time. And listen to this," I continued, "neither of us smoke, but the other day he came in from the field with brown teeth and tried to kiss me. It was gross!"

"What was it?"

"He's chewing tobacco and smoking, I guess. I hope his teeth are not rotted. I haven't kissed him in so long I can't remember. I think I should go to his unit and talk to his commander. I think that he is losing his mind."

"Tracey, has he hit you?" Mommy asked.

"No, but he accidentally bounced on my ankle when I was lying on the floor. And he accidentally smashed me behind the bedroom door. He races around the apartment like there is a fire all the time. He seems to have big business going on in his head. I'm really worried about his mental health."

"And he doesn't reek of alcohol?"

"No."

"Not a vodka drinker?"

"No, but his roommate at West Point hid vodka in their mouthwash."

"Is that what he told you?" Mommy asked, wiser in the ways of the world than I. "He also told you that the other guy with his name in California had gained a reputation for breaking laws. And that guy stationed in Greece with him. *They always, always, always point the finger somewhere else, Tracey.* He may even be on drugs. Can you see if his pupils are dilated?"

"No. I refuse to get that close. He is too smart to be on drugs, though. He would know better."

"Brilliant people do know better, but brilliant people still make the choice."

"It would make no sense for him." I paused, thinking, then continued, "Mommy, he is purposely not letting me sleep."

"What does that mean?"

"He is up until all hours of the night. He keeps the lights on and slams things on purpose. The other day while I was curled up under a blanket on the couch, he stared me down while rotating the floor lamp through the bright, dim, and off positions. I'm starting to hallucinate when I drive because I can't get any sleep. I worry . . . Here he comes. I gotta go; he argues about our phone bills. Kiss, Mama." Click.

The door opened. He said nothing to me. He carried the mail, but there was none for me, of course. I suppose that's what you get when you don't have a key to the mailbox and the only holder of the key screens your mail. My high school boyfriend was at the Air Force Academy, and wrote to me all the time, but I never saw his letters. Jayns claimed that the office would not issue two keys to the mailbox if I did not sign the lease. I refused, aware that commingling our credit, especially given his problems from Greece, promised disaster for me. I maintained a keyless, mail-less penitence.

Fire Drill

A fire drill at work left my unit scattered across the lawn one afternoon, lounging about while waiting for the signal granting our reentrance to the building. I sat with two black lieutenants, luxuriating in the sun. Upon learning my name, they interrogated me about my husband and my married life. I did not know them, but they seemed to know Jayns. The conversation interested me little, and after a while the female switched to the third person, inviting me to ignore the rest of their conversation.

"She is clueless," she said

"I don't know," thought the male.

"He is wreaking havoc everywhere, and she sits at home probably watching TV."

"It's hard to believe."

"Do you watch a lot of TV at night, Lieutenant Brame?" the female lieutenant asked.

"No. I just busy myself," I responded, not paying much attention. The talk about TV made me think they were discussing a favorite show.

"She is clueless," the woman confirmed to her companion.

"I don't know."

Every junior officer at Fort Bragg knew something, save me. I was in denial, in my PTSD cozy spot. After all, you don't have to worry about something that is not happening.

Pregnant and denying their chattering truths, I lay back and ran my fingers over the lawn. Fort Bragg scorches in the midday sun, and the penetrating rays, a stifling fire-retardant uniform, and a child borrowing my nutrients combined to make me dizzy and tired. I distinguished the blades of grass beneath my hand, but did not realize that my life was wrapped tightly around the most famous and menacing human weed on post.

Break-In

Driving to and from post grew perilous. The lack of sleep while Jayns acted in a grand one-man show each night, at a time when I needed even more sleep than usual, took its toll on me. I worried that I would fall asleep at the wheel and wreck my car. Never having been through an insurance claim, I worried that if that happened, I would not have a car to drive. I would loose my commission and wind up unemployed.

My doctor calmed my fears with stories of cars she had totaled and replaced, so many that she had stopped naming them. She said that if

Undeterred

my inability to sleep continued, she would secretly provide medication for me. I was so miserably tired, I could barely answer her questions. She ran through every probable cause for my sleeplessness, only to find that my cure necessitated Jayns's unit be deployed to another galaxy for the remainder of my pregnancy. Alas, no such orders came.

When I arrived at work after my doctor's appointment, everyone was engaged in his or her afternoon routines. My desk was a mess most of the day, as I tend to work on piles of things at a time. I spread everything out to take care of it simultaneously. I know I'm done when all the piles are tidy and ready to be removed. I have been that way all my life. My grandmother could barely stand to see my bedroom floor until bedtime. She assured me that I was messy, but it always looked fine in the morning.

I remember going into my office, but I do not remember falling asleep. When my eyes opened at eight or nine p.m., the sight of my own desk startled me. I did not recognize my whereabouts until I looked around and realized I was still at work. My desk was covered in disheveled papers and regulations. I noticed that everything was shadowy. Through my door I saw the supply officer's area, which faced the street. Light flooded in from the outside door. I felt hesitant and peeked in rather than entering.

My other door led to the soldiers' office area. Desks reflected our commander's clean-desk policy, and nothing was out of place. I opened the door to the hallway. Doors were shut all along the corridor, with flags, hallowed pictures, and crests giving a spooky ambiance. Away from the street-facing side of the building, the offices were pitch black. I was alone.

Fear crept through every synapse in my body, which was unlike me. A building that, when lit, housed productive soldiers took on shadows and forms designed to assault my imagination at night. I approached the lit-up exterior door and could see my car in the darkness, undisturbed. Old-fashioned common sense told me not to open the door and run for it.

I tip-toed back through the offices to my own little closet-like space. From what I could tell, I was locked in alone, but fear made me look in the direction of every noise as the building settled. I sat down at the supply officer's desk in the light of the door window and listened.

My belly felt okay, but I wondered if my son was scared too. I had not eaten since breakfast and I did not know how I would make it through the night without feeding my little monster. I did not bring food to work because I did not cook at home. Something about a testosterone-driven man vocally expecting me to cook after working the same hours he did encouraged me to eat out. We sat there, just my son and me.

I heard something slam outside suddenly, and dove under the supply officer's desk. I felt cramped, holding my legs tightly so as not to be seen from the window. Someone banged on the front door. I remained still, but my breathing speed up. I alternated between holding my legs and my belly. How could I put my child in this position? Despite checking the doors, I feared that someone still could hear my breath. The banging stopped.

I listened to see if the car drove away, but it remained. Suddenly, someone attacked the office door, pounding the frame and window loudly. I imagined it would kick open and expose us. I constricted every part of me to contain my unborn son and myself in that tiny space. The pounding abruptly stopped.

A flashlight danced along the chair beside me. For the first time, I heard talking, some of it sounding like faint squawks. I thought of my grandparents. The army forbids calls home on military lines, but I wanted them to know we were okay. Assuming we were okay, that is. I could not be certain, so I maintained my hiding spot. I was scared for my son, guilty that I had put us in harm's way. What damage had this fear done to my child?

Two cars eventually pulled away. In time, I crawled back to my office and picked up a stack of work. Not wanting to use my light, I took stack after stack back into the supply office and finished what had put me to sleep in the first place. It wasn't the way I preferred to do things, but it worked for the moment. I caught myself up, and then worked a full day ahead. At least I would not feel guilty for falling behind.

Undeterred

The morning took its time arriving, but daylight eventually broke. When my major arrived to work, my feelings of guilt prompted me to tell him everything I could remember: that I had fallen asleep at work and when I had woken up in the middle of the night, tried to make up for it by working ahead.

In response, he jokingly he asked, "Did you steal anything?" I must have looked shocked, because he laughed, calling me a "lieutenant true to her word," and sent me home to get some rest. I drove home alert.

"Where have you been?" Jayns demanded hypocritically when I got home. He never felt the need to tell me where he was when he was out all night.

"I was at the office," I explained.

"All night? You are lying. Where were you?"

"I fell asleep at the office, Jayns."

"You did not hear us calling you? A cop and I were trying to get in."

I was tired of arguing. The truth was that the terror of the potential break-in incited my PTSD. I did not remember anyone banging on the door. I did not remember hiding under the desk. All I remembered was waking up in the office and getting more work done. As I had many time in the past, my memory blocked the trauma and anything associated with it.

Cops

In chess, you have to plan a castling move in advance. A horse and bishop sit between the castle and the king. You cannot castle for safety until you move those two pieces out of the way. Stranding himself without the horse and expelling the bishop's religion create space for the king to duck behind the lesser forces and hide.

In real life, PTSD sufferers don't plan their castling. We just move through life. Events happen. Ironically, even someone attacking an office door created a chance for me to drift off into shock. I suppose that is a case of the game playing a move on the player.

One Thursday, I sat in our apartment, thinking about how I had a lot of chores to do. Whenever the army relocates you, your home goods trail behind for some time, but you know the day they'll arrive. My home goods were coming on Tuesday, and I wanted to be ready.

I asked Jayns if we could schedule a time to be at home together to rearrange the apartment so that we could share the space better. I was still living out of my grandmother's luggage and I thought we should work together to make our home a little more "ours."

Jayns asked what day my belongings were arriving. When I told him Tuesday, he coughed out an excuse about having to work part of the weekend though Wednesday without hesitation.

In my book, the 82nd Airborne stayed out in the field entirely too much. I suspected that units like his were to blame when soldiers blew a gasket from having too little balance in their lives. My husband was never home at night or on the weekends, and I felt for the families who missed their spouse or parent. In my case, the benefits of not having him home certainly outweighed the detriments. I did not know that he fabricated his need to be gone. I just relished his absence and the resultant peace.

After work on Friday, I went to a local furniture store and hunted for a chair that I could rock my child in. I knew the chair might impact the future of every other room, so I perused everything, knick-knacks included. The salesman waited until I gave my order, and he lamented that my singular, black leather rocking chair could not be delivered until Tuesday.

"Perfect," I laughed. Relieved, he cashed me out. We needed furniture. I worried a little about Jayns not liking the chair, but I reasoned that it only sat one and he did not have to sit in it.

I felt unsure as to how to create the teamwork that Mama and Papa had without giving myself up in the process. I possessed no interest in cooking Jayns's dinner as ordered and his interests rendered me nothing more than a potential paycheck cushion. I tried to like him, given that I did not love him, but I found even that difficult, given his increasingly erratic behavior.

Undeterred

I knew that he failed to resemble, in any shape or form, the person I had wanted to marry some day. I felt uneasy about that, because my feelings were not his fault. Maybe what he wanted was a storybook female. Why hadn't he listened to me when I told him that I wasn't one? Why hadn't I listened to him when his behavior spoke volumes of how he wasn't a story-book male himself? I didn't know what his excuse was. I did, however, think that my goals identified that I had no interest in being his housewife.

On Saturday, Jayns and I sat in our living room watching TV. At one point, he picked up on some imaginary cue that I wanted to have sex with him and he tried to kiss me. Since I had not sent any such signal, I pulled away. He pressed and pulled, I said "no" repeatedly, but still he continued to try to kiss me. I soon realized that we were both using more strength than should have been necessary.

I hollered, "No!" and stood to loose myself from him. "What are you going to do, rape me?" I demanded rhetorically.

He said nothing. I never dreamed that the answer to that question could be "yes."

He stood facing me, his nose flaring rhythmically, furious. I did not realize it, but Jayns knew that someone was now on high alert outside of the apartment, ready to jump into action, hanging on our next words. I did not know that we were constantly watched in our own home, but Jayns did. He was the most-wanted drug and prostitution lord on Fort Bragg and the apartment housed federal bugs and wiring devices.

He stormed out.

Later that day, I went to get something from my car and noticed two men, one black and one Hispanic, sitting in a sports car next to my Mazda Protégé. As I walked past them to open the car door, the black guy rolled down his window and asked, "Hey, is he hitting you?"

"What?" I asked. I had surely misheard him.

"We can't tell if he is hitting you."

"Who?"

"Your husband. If he touches you, scream. Don't be scared. Just scream."

To me, Jayns seemed mentally ill rather than dangerous. Still, the black guy in the sports car had spooked me. *Why would my husband hit me?* I wondered. After some thought, I assumed he had me confused with someone else. In reality, Jayns was hitting women, just not the one living in his home.

In fact, federal tap wires had called the apartment home before I did. The Feds, curious about Jayns's doings long before I showed up on the scene, knew my location at all times. Technically, our apartment was never the scene of the crimes that they were investigating. The real crimes happened outside our apartment, in the city or on the post, where drugs and women were bought and sold, and where men looking for both drained their potential in the streets.

Cleaning

On Sunday I cleared all of the horizontal services in the apartment, wiping them clean. I reorganized shelves and drawers into a newer, tidier state. I vacuumed in front of, behind, and around everything. Though pregnant, I pushed and scooted furniture into new positions. The living room and dining room both looked and smelled better.

In the kitchen, while emptying the trash under the sink, I found another trashcan just as tall hiding in the back corner of the cupboard. You'd miss it if you stopped reaching when you got to the dishwashing liquid, which I always did. I struggled to pull it out of its awkward cubbyhole. It hid hundreds of perfectly compacted Budweiser cans.

When had there been a party? Jayns did not drink Budweiser. I always assumed that he drank tap water from a cup every night, because I heard him run the water a lot. I was wrong, of course, but the cans did not convince me I was wrong. Nothing registered. Denial ruled.

I opened the refrigerator to find the two lone Heinekens that had been there since I'd arrived. *When was the party?* I wondered repeatedly. I prepared the ruins of the Budweiser cans for the garbage.

Undeterred

I moved on to the pantry, which I thought would be quick. After all, there is not a lot you can do with dried goods when neither of you cook. What we did have though included two coolers that, when I tugged on them, seemed full. Like the Budweiser trash can, they were wedged into a tight corner. I used both hands and all my squatting muscles to yank them out from under the last two shelves.

I opened the first cooler to find icy water and Bud after Bud. The second was the same. Without giving it a second thought, I lined up all the cans in the refrigerator and gave Jayns a shelf to keep his beer. The ice and water drained down the sink, and I stored the first cooler inside of the second, placing them back out of sight. I did not suspect anything.

I dreaded the bedroom. I had avoided it entirely for a month, and it reeked with the stench of old greens and garbage. The window screen lay against the wall, and the window, left open a crack, let in the welcome outside air. When I stepped toward the window, I saw that filthy underclothes lined the floor. I heaved three pairs toward the middle of the room, intending to turn to the laundry later. I shivered in the chilly winter air. I re-fit the screen and closed the window, consuming time and making it difficult for me to feel my hands.

It took some effort to be able to pronounce the floor and bed visible again. I took a break and wondered if it had been longer than one month since I had entered the bedroom. Had I been given the choice of the living room or the bedroom, I would have chosen the bedroom. Jayns hadn't given me that choice though, probably because the cover of the bush outside the bedroom window gave him somewhere to hide when he lit up.

The smell differential between the bedroom and the living room invited me to catch my breath on the couch. You don't ask how someone lives that way. You ask, "Can I really tolerate living with someone who lives that way much longer?"

I'm not a big TV watcher, but anything on the screen could potentially have dissuaded me from finishing what I'd started. That is exactly why I turned it off, held my breath, and muscled my way back into Jayns's little cove.

The closet took a while. The strangest thing I found at first was a laundry basket filled with hundreds of mini tapes labeled with my name or a subject referencing my family or West Point. Who collects beer cans and telephone conversations? I didn't need or want either. He had both. I would have taken the tapes if I had seen value in them; it made no sense to even have them though, so I left them alone.

I also found a strange beaker-like container filled with water and pieces of paper trash floating on the surface. I did not find it extraordinary because I did not know what it was. I put it in the kitchen to be washed with the rest of the dishes not knowing that it was crack paraphernalia. I kept cleaning, denying to myself that anything was wrong.

The sand particles and bags of rocks everywhere made little sense either.

His top left sock drawer had some socks up front, but it was filled with what I assumed to be sand particles behind them. Jayns was an airborne jumper, I rationalized. He hurled himself out of airplanes and landed on the ground in a sandpit because the army said so. I'd never seen sand particles as large as the ones I saw in his drawer, but what else could these rock-like structures be? Perhaps they'd fallen off his socks. I did not question why these "dirty" socks were folded in the drawer, though. Unaware of what Jayns was up to when he was away from home, and being in shock still, I made sense of everything I saw as best as I knew how.

I opened a package of the rocks and sniffed them. I couldn't count them and they were of all sizes. I was glad that I had found the drawer's contents before our child was born, because if he found them, he could easily choke on them.

I was tired of cleaning, and since I devalued these souvenirs as not being from a beach I knew, I pulled at the drawer full of rocks, hanging it loose from its hinges. I rotated the drawer to its left, front corner, careful not to spill a crystal, and I congratulated myself on a job well done

Undeterred

for the day by discharging all of the sandy contents and residue into a drawstring garbage bag with all the other trash.

I dragged the bag to the bathroom. I expected no conundrums there, as I used the bathroom myself and I quickly cleaned all the parts that I used routinely. I did not use the cabinet below the sink though, and when I opened it, I found dozens of prescription medication bottles.

I was cheered at first, thinking that maybe Jayns was finally getting medical help. But when I looked at the labels, I saw that they were not in his name.

That is odd, I thought. *The people whose names were on these prescriptions should not have left their medication under the sink for us to discover once we moved in. The apartment's management should have cleaned that out.* It didn't occur to me to realize that Jayns had lived in that apartment for some time before I arrived; after all, his hoarding other peoples' medicine did not make sense. I threw them all away as well.

I had a bag or two more of trash than I expected, but I managed to carry them to the door and out to the parking lot. I set the bags down to catch my breath and calculate which trash bin was more likely to accept them–the one to the left or the one to the right. Making up my mind, I noticed my good friends, the black guy and the Hispanic guy, in a different car. I did not recognize them, but in their eyes, we were friends. When they waved, I offered an official nod just to be nice. I took a right, ditched my findings in the dumpster, and closed down my mission for the day.

My personal belongings arrived on Tuesday, as I'd been promised. I unpacked and put everything away in drawers and compartments, as though I lived in Jayns's little apartment too, which smelled much better than it had. Until then I had felt like a stowaway; now, with my things and a little space of my own, I felt more like a cohabitant. *Things might work out with some organization and shared goals*, I thought. *It might also help if we actually saw each other occasionally.*

What would really have helped, of course, was if I had seen the danger I was in. People with PTSD make sense of their surroundings while lacking all of the relevant information. We all do to some extent, naturally, but a person with PTSD may not sense fear. Even when there is no trauma, we are less aware of danger than other people. My life would have changed had I recognized the items that I found in Jayns's room and so casually threw away. Unfortunately, it would take time for me to put all of the pieces together.

Jayns's Reaction

The door opened around dinnertime. It was winter, and darkness had already fallen. Jayns said nothing, just looked around at the rearranged living room that accommodated my sleek new La-Z-Boy rocking chair in his favorite color, black.

"What all did you clean?" he demanded. He looked like he wanted to charge at me.

"The kitchen, everywhere." I was proud of myself.

He sauntered to the kitchen. The pantry door swung open, the refrigerator swung open, the sink cabinet swung open. All slammed shut in their turn. I heard his fist crash down on the counter.

He inspected the bedroom and bathroom next. I heard drawers hit the floor and the bathroom cabinet sounded like it had been ripped off its hinges. "Where is my crap? Where is my beaker?" he demanded. I informed him that it was drying in the dishwasher, cleaner than ever.

"What is wrong with you?!" he screamed.

Answering seemed useless. He went from room to room, pulling things out of their new homes, shouting, "Where is my stuff?" again and again.

I found a moment to tell him that I had thrown away nothing of value. He looked like he was going to batter me, but he stopped an inch away from my face.

"*Where is the stuff* that was in that top drawer?" His tone resounded lower and more calculated than it had when he had first panicked. I noticed that recessed, dark circles surrounded his eyes. I was not often this close to him anymore. He appeared to be having a mental breakdown.

Undeterred

I did not know what he meant by "stuff," but when he described the sand particles, and I offered the truth: "Jayns, I put those sand crystals in the trash."

"*Where is the trash?*"

"In the dumpster."

He sank. I heard and saw him swallow. He collected his coat and tried to walk to the door as if nothing were wrong. When I looked out the window, he was running at a full sprint toward the trash bins.

The dumpster had filled up since I had cleaned on Sunday. One white garbage bag resembled another; even the drawstrings matched. He seemed to be bargaining with something invisible near the collection area. Finally, he wiped his eyes, readjusted his clothes, and even cried for a moment, alone. I felt bad for him, but if the crystals were from a beach or something, why wouldn't they be on display instead of in a sock drawer? He made less and less sense every day.

I jumped into my chair when I saw that he was returning. He came in mumbling things like, "What am I going to do?" "How am I going to explain this?" and "How did this happen?" Over and over again, he turned to address me venomously, "You threw my *crap* away!" He wailed and whimpered as if he needed help.

I tried to assist him at first, but if I neared him, he started screaming so loudly that I ultimately resolved to stay in my new chair to keep some distance between us. I brought my feet up to my chest when he attempted to rip my dangling legs from the edges. That must have set something off inside him.

"You *retarded* bitch!" He started screaming about how I had cost him money and rendered him broke. He blamed me for his parents' suspicion. I'd ruined his family, his life, and his career. He cursed me for hours and hours.

Most of what he said was not worth responding to. I did tell him that he would have a better life if he did not hate his family, namely his mother, so much.

"Your mother–" I stopped when his hand cocked to punch me.

"Say anything about my mother and I'll kill you!"

"Stop saying that you hate her and maybe you will live life better. We need our mothers."

"You will get the hell out of the apartment," he advised. "I hope you find a place in the gutter. Find someplace else to stay. I want you and your unwanted child gone tomorrow."

That was our standoff. He walked away and came back verbally swinging again. I curled up in the chair. It never occurred to me that I had another option in that moment; all I had to do was scream, and those federal agents in the car outside would bust through the door.

Those cops would miss me. I always stayed home, so they had a quiet, easy job, unlike whoever tailed Jayns. Looking back, I wish that I had taken them a glass of soda or cocoa. It was steaming hot out there in the summer, freezing cold in the winter, but I did not recognize them as probable friends, the good guys. Perhaps I did not know what real good guys looked like at this point. Those days weren't the only time that I could not distinguish a good egg from a bad one. My inability to register one over the other would cost me more and more with time.

Jayns angrily picked up my medical records, which I had not yet turned in after arriving to post. He rummaged to a specific date relevant only to him and ripped out two pages that I had not nor would ever read. "You were not raped at West Point, were you?"

"No." My surprise at the question assured my truth. At that point, you could not have convinced me that I had been raped.

"Let your records reflect that, dumb ass." The medical records of my rape had become a souvenir for my rapist.

I said nothing. I thought nothing. Numb, I felt nothing. In my mind, I had not been raped so my records should not have reflected that I was. I read nothing into Jayns's tone because he was in the middle of screaming at me about nonsensical things anyway. I ignored him as he committed a grave crime: tampering with my medical records.

The doorbell rang. A black man in a trench coat, buttoned and with the belt pulled taut, walked in. He did not greet me, but he did not lose eye contact with me either. I stayed in my chair, the only furniture that I owned in the apartment. I do not know what they discussed or did in the bedroom. I could not call my mother, so I slept. With two criminals a stone's throw from me, I slept.

The Apartment

The next day I must not have been in shock from the previous night, because I set out that morning to get a paper on my way to work. I was on the hunt for a new apartment. Had I been in shock, I would not have remembered to look. I flipped through every page of the paper, but I did not know what to look for, so nothing stood out.

I casually asked the other officers I worked with, but no one knew of anything open. They all lived in houses with their wives. The enlisted soldiers lived on post, but I did not want to alert them to changes in my life any more than I wanted to forewarn my major, so I moved around that day saying nothing. I got so busy with work that when I looked up at the end of the day, I found that I had no place to go.

I cautiously entered the apartment. Jayns appeared to be wearing the same mumbling, pacing paths in the carpet. He stopped and faced me.

"Why are you here?"

"I could not find an apartment."

"Thousands upon thousands of apartments in the area, pages upon pages in the classified ads, and your stupid butt could not find an apartment?"

His spew wound up, but all I heard was *classified ads*. That's where they are! I could not have known that; Papa and I did not read that section. While Jayns berated me, I checked my bag. Of course I'd left the paper on my desk.

That night was a long one, offering little slumber. Jayns rummaged in the same places he had when I'd experienced his wrath the night before, cursing, damning, pacing, and spewing. A hotel did not occur to me as an option.

Early the next morning I secured my newspaper from my desk. By noon I had signed a lease. I could move in on Saturday. Freedom had begun.

When Jayns found out that I was indeed moving, he apologized profusely. Then he asked for his ring back. I said no. Jayns threw a tantrum. I packed up all my things, curled up in my chair, and waited.

If someone had foreshadowed when I was growing up that my husband would kick me out of my house while I was pregnant, I would have wondered why I had to have a husband. "Is that mandatory?" I might have asked.

Freedom was not fully at hand and I was hardly cured of my PTSD. Leaving Jayns did not indicate that I knew of the rape or his status as the most-wanted drug lord on Fort Bragg. But it would keep me further away from him. Going forward, the federal government would no longer know my every word at home. They would now know Jayns better than I. In fact, they already knew him better than I ever would.

My mother advised me to wait to divorce him until after our child's birth to ensure that I did not experience any more stress during my pregnancy. I didn't feel stress, though; people with PTSD feel numb in the face of tumultuous fear. Feelings that are too painful to face are submerged. What I did feel at that point was guilt for going along with the marriage in the first place.

Jayns eventually visited me at my little box of an apartment. I had only one bedroom, but it gave me a chance to use the notes I'd taken at the furniture store. I invested in a great bed, living room furniture, and a backyard table I could use as a dining unit. When Jayns came in, he looked irritated but conceded that I'd tried to create a home, and perked up about my taste in decorating. Over a few visits, he seemed to embrace my new freedom.

But I saw him everywhere. I'd see him buying groceries, at the gas station, at the department stores. It's understandable that he would need bed sheets too, but on the same day as I did? Everywhere I shopped, he seemed to accidentally show up.

Undeterred

The last time he came to visit, I asked him why he was on my side of town so much. He admitted that he tried to catch me in places. He was searching for a way to rekindle our relationship.

I wasn't. When he dropped to his knees and proposed to me again with the ring that I still had not taken off my finger, my answer was no. He begged. No. He was going to get help. No.

The prospect of his getting help piqued my interest, since I had been hoping for that for some time, but I thought it wise not to open a can of worms so close to a pregnant woman's ice cream time, so I maintained my disinterested *no*. I'd bought a special blender for ice cream time. He needed to leave, and I told him so.

When he put his hands on his hips, I saw a nine-millimeter on his right hip. I asked if he had stolen it from the military. He claimed that he had bought it for personal and professional use. I asked why he needed a gun while out of uniform, and he asked me to sit down.

I sat, freezing in place when he took the gun from its holster. He didn't point it at me, but he handled it cockily. Pulling a chair in front of my belly, he started asking me question after question. They were seemingly random, yet highly specific, and entirely unforgiving: "Count from 1992 to 2010. Say the months of the years. Say the numbers one through thirty. Say them again. What do you think of this? What do you remember of that? Have I ever raped you? Repeat this as if in first person." The answers he expected weren't all full ideas, and were sometimes just words. I had to repeat my answers until he was satisfied. "There is a statement Bobby Knight gave about women being raped. There was something that Malcolm X said about this . . ."

He was taping me. I was so in shock from and focused on the gun that I did not care or even notice that his right hand held a mini tape recorder.

At some point, I fell asleep and awoke alone, not remembering anything of the exchange. The front door sat wide open, though the screen door was closed. I felt afraid at having been so exposed, so I locked the doors and finished my evening routine.

Fort Bragg, 1994-1995

Followed

Animals hunt for food. These days, people hunt for sport. Either way, there is a chase and kill pattern. Jayns was stalking me.

Everyone visits the post variety store, and a few days later I saw Jayns there. He was still following me around. Even when I didn't see him while I was out running errands, his black male friends often followed me with talk of my needing a man in my life. The combination of these men constantly following me around was starting to take a toll on me. Jayns assured me that it was a coincidence, but not everyone exchanges his car at the dealership so that he can comfortably follow his estranged wife around all weekend without her noticing.

I suspected that this might be happening, so one day in front of a side street near my house, I halted. I knew no one who drove a red Nissan Pathfinder, and I waited for the driver to pass me. When he didn't, but instead halted behind me, I dialed 911. Jayns got out of the vehicle and approached my window.

He claimed that he had borrowed the Pathfinder to impress me with my favorite car, and he asked if I wanted to buy one. He asked questions, probing to see whether I remembered the night with the gun and the tape recorder. I did not. I didn't even recall him owning a gun.

Undeterred

When the cops came to my house, I told them about Jayns and his friends following me around. I showed them rocks that someone had thrown against my windows at night to keep me awake. I felt terrorized. They deduced that it was Jayns, already a well-known figure to them, and that his partners were helping him. They paid him a visit, but my worries mounted.

Jayns's Unit, 1993

The next day I reported to his unit of my own volition to discuss the behavior of Captain Jayns C. Jhomes with his superiors. My presence rattled many and several black male captains tried to use their rank to influence me, a mere lieutenant, to retreat.

"Listen to my voice," said the most handsome black captain. "My voice is going to destroy you on those tapes. You'll see."

The threat meant absolutely nothing to me. Any doctoring he and Jayns had done to our taped conversations was known to the feds, not me.

A major offered to speak with me, but I insisted that if the colonel had an open-door policy, then I wanted to talk to him specifically. In unison, several officers informed me that the open-door policy was not for me, but rather for them. I decided to test it anyway, so I waited.

The colonel was skeptical. I explained to him that I thought Jayns was losing his good judgment, not to mention his mind, and that the army should seriously consider helping him to save his career. He seemed surprised by my angle. Throughout the conversation, he asked strange questions, gleaning that I did not abhor Jayns's mother. No, I never said that women should enjoy rape; that was Bobby Knight. Yes, I did indeed imitate a better live orgasm imitation than Meg Ryan in *When Harry Met Sally*. No, I had never tried drugs or alcohol, and, no, I had not had sex with a dog or with a person outside of my marriage.

These answers perplexed him, and he demanded to know why I would say these things. I wondered why he would think I had said them when I had just negated each statement. I do a lot of things, but lying is unusual for me, I assured him. I reserve lying for well-mannered moments when someone's home cooking isn't as good as Mama's.

I expressed to the colonel that the constant public run-ins with Jayns and his associates spooked me, especially when it came to his friends telling me that I owed a debt on his behalf. I likened this latter accusation to tying me to his Greek debt, for which I had not been present.

The civilian cops were now watching out for Jayns in my neighborhood, but what could his commander do? I did not know. Jayns and I both lived off-post and the colonel lacked jurisdiction. His advise to me was to not talk to Jayns over the phone again. "Just stop talking to him, period," said a man who now realized that his criminally minded officer had taped, cut, and pasted sordid statements from me and circulated them on post.

Not realizing what Jayns was doing, I had expected a different response. I was trying to win psychological help for Jayns as he spiraled out of control and I had failed.

I failed again that night when I called Mrs. Jhomes. I thought she might be able to reach out to him. She laughed at me instead, telling me that I was worse than him. She would not entertain the thought that her son needed mental help. Perhaps I could undergo it for both of us, she joked. Confused as to what I needed help with, I felt her denial in that moment understandable. She hung up on me with a dismissive chuckle.

Going to the army again for help would not work. My own colonels had even less authority over Jayns than his commander. I had no one else to call. Jayns had created a cocoon around himself to keep from sinking. My only victory was that I had parted from him without going down with his ship. I just did not know whether to celebrate my position or fear what he planned to do next.

Dissolving

Living alone, I feared going into labor on my own. When I lay down each night, I had to convince myself that if I went to sleep, I would not go into labor and then have to rush around in the night, trying to save my child. When my eyes finally closed, I was calm and felt safe, but as soon as my eyes opened again, these fears returned, pursuing me.

Months later, Mama arrived for her great-grandson's birth, a milestone that she coveted and I feared. She arrived early, and planned to spend time with me both before and after the delivery. She drove me to the hospital when I went into labor, but I did not know that she had invited Jayns to the hospital as well. He tried suiting up for the delivery, and nurse after nurse heard my wrath. He was ejected from the room and Mama cut my son's umbilical cord.

I had cut Jayns out of my life, but Mama did not understand. She learned the hard way, after inviting him back into my apartment to see his son.

He assured us that he wanted to visit the baby, but he never even looked at him. He just wanted to fondle me in the bedroom. Unable to move quickly, given my fresh stitches, I resorted to blood-curdling screams until Mama came in and asked him to come back into the kitchen with her.

In the kitchen, Jayns assured my grandmother that he had documented proof that I had taken drugs while pregnant. Mama knew that I had never taken drugs to get high, and he sounded completely insane to her.

Jayns next tried to convince Mama that I had cheated on him, grabbing a picture of a West Point classmate, which I did not even know I had, out of my Bible. Alone with Jayns in the kitchen, Mama grew increasingly apprehensive as his sanity appeared to dissolve. She lacked familiarity with him, but he did not sound rational. She asked him to leave, but found that an elderly woman could not remove a muscular man in the prime of life who did not want to be removed from a space. She called Papa, who threatened to call the cops.

At the mere mention of the police, Jayns scattered, like most criminals. As soon as he was gone, Mama transferred the phone to me so I could hear Papa tell me that I was right: I had to divorce Jayns. I hadn't heard the entire meltdown in the kitchen, but Mama regretted every detail that she recounted. Divorcing Jayns was already on my schedule.

Serving Corps, 1993–1995

My career took off within months of leaving Jayns. I moved to a bigger unit and was selected to work in the headquarters of the 18th Personnel Group as the personnel strength-management officer for the entire 18th Airborne Corps, which spanned seven posts. My role was essentially a glorified recruiting position combined with software analysis. I later found out that the personnel executive team considered every lieutenant on post and chose me because I was known to be smart and articulate. I handled tens of thousands of soldiers' needs and was honored to work at such a high level. Colonels routinely called me and requested that I do important tasks for them. They exuded faith in me, so I borrowed that faith and started to look forward to each day again, willing myself to keep going, in spite of my secret, on-going exhaustion, a lasting relic of my PTSD.

It only took me two weeks after the birth of my son to build up the strength to ace the army physical fitness examination. During morning formations, I often sang cadence and ran around the soldiers like a mad woman, trying to motivate troops to be what the army deemed "Hoorah." I could set an excellent example for others, but in private I suffered, dragging like a ship in water. I moved at a good clip, but the friction of my stress constantly pulled at me. I could not put my finger on what was wrong.

My colonels knew Jayns's reputation, even if I did not. They repeatedly checked in on me, but I thought they were just being nice to the only lieutenant in the unit.

Unbeknownst to me, meetings were being convened on post on how to bring a West Point graduate drug dealer to his knees. A federal task force had been formed, and the military police and the feds were working with personnel to get all of the I's dotted and T's crossed before they made their move. Jayns struck no one as a good match for the army. He was certainly not being all he could be.

"Tracey!" A voice called me from behind as I walked down the hall to go downstairs. It was 1995, the year Jayns's officer commission ended.

I turned at Lieutenant Colonel Maron's summons. He was my direct supervisor. "Walk into that conference room," he directed me, "and show them your smiling face." He indicated the door next to me.

I opened the door, and about ten men in suits and green army dress uniforms stopped conferring and looked up. They composed the federal task force working to bring down Jayns and his associates. They knew me. I knew nothing of them, nor their mission. I stood in the doorway, unsure what to say. Colonel Smart, the commander of the Corps' personnel group, smiled at me. "Good afternoon, sir," I greeted him.

"Lieutenant Brame," he nodded.

"Sir, Lieutenant Colonel Maron asked me to walk in here," I told him, hiding my uncertainty. Several people chuckled.

"Well, I'm glad you did," he smiled. I looked around to see black suits and army greens mixed together for a single purpose.

"Where are you from, Lieutenant?" Everyone in that room already knew where I was from. They had scoured my past, and had ruled me out as Jayns's accomplice.

"I'm from the great state of Indiana, sir."

"Good deal! Thanks for stepping in." Everyone chuckled. "Good coincidence too." More laughter. I was slightly confused by the whole scene, but hid it well.

I returned to Lieutenant Colonel Maron's office, and learned that everyone in that room had my best interest in mind. He explained that the task force was working to bring down a captain on post who was ruthless in his treatment of other soldiers and women in general.

"Sounds good to me. Whoever he is, I wanted him caught!" I exclaimed.

Lieutenant Colonel Maron recognized and understood the source of my fatigue. He had seen combat action in many countries and everyone on the task force knew that I had unknowingly been living with a monster. As a result, he deduced that I was probably in shock. He had seen it many times before. He did not push the issue, and simply asked on occasion how tired I felt. I always denied it, though. After all, my work had not suffered.

One day, he told me to stop working alone in the office on nights and weekends. "For your own safety, you need to stop being here without anyone around you. Certainly stop bringing your son to the office."

When I asked if the building would be closed, he said no. "This is just my personal order to you." My office lay off the beaten path, so he did not want my son and I alone up on the fourth floor without witnesses until the drug lord was caught. I was frustrated at first, but I obeyed.

Jayns had made official threats that he planned to kill my son and me. I had to call my son's daycare on more than one occasion and tell them not to let him play outside. In the following weeks, there were several times when an MP or an 82nd soldier waltzed into my office to see if I was okay. They asked when I had last seen Jayns. I was still deeply in denial and suspected nothing.

The fact that I second-guessed none of this was a telling sign of the seriousness of my PTSD. I carried on with the daily routine that I had known before, not worrying. I just moved through the days. Others feared for me.

Though little fazed me, I was increasingly stricken with exhaustion. I did everything I could to simply focus on doing what life required of me from day to day, moving from one mission to another. I assumed that others had found out about Jayns's mental illness and that he was getting help. I did not know that I needed help.

Lash

I drove to another personnel unit one day to talk to a fellow lieutenant in the lower headquarters. Lieutenant Lash ran the personnel records section. She maintained every record of every soldier on every post of the entire 18th Airborne Corps.

Undeterred

"Hey, girl," she greeted me.

"How's it working down here?" I asked.

"Crazy. We are working on a big case with a black West Pointer. Get this: DC is on post hunting this fool. Federal task force, hear me?" Lash knew the man they were trying to bring down was my estranged husband, but leadership in the personnel units instructed everyone not to let me know, for fear of startling me. The higher-ranking officers suspected that I was in shock. Everyone was protecting the queen.

She continued on about the perpetrator without naming him. "This man has sold drugs to soldiers, and they've gathered accusations that he beat and sold women on the street. All this is going on right here in Fort Bragg and in the city of Fayetteville. It's crazy!

"No one has put him away yet. He may sing and take a dishonorable discharge. We are researching ways to not let him on another post for life. This is one of America's finest and best. West Point, girl. You hear me now? West Point!"

Of course, the West Point emphasis was aimed directly at me as a fellow West Pointer. "And hear this," she continued, "he has a marriage of convenience."

"I've heard of that before," I said, thinking back to West Point.

"I bet you have." She nodded with eyebrows raised.

"What does it mean?" I asked, curious.

"What do you think it means?" she wondered.

"I don't know, really. I think they live together, have kids, and then stay together because they are too chicken to get divorced," I reasoned, thinking I had nailed it.

"Not exactly," she corrected me. "One or both of them is gay, and the marriage is just a cover so the government can't knock their heads off and snatch them out of uniform."

I thought back to the female professor at West Point who had singled me out in class, suddenly understanding. I started thinking about possibilities, but Lash continued.

"I know the wife is gay."

"You know her?!" I exclaimed. This was getting juicy.

She nodded. "You want to see his file?" she offered.

"I think not." I hadn't worked in her department and felt uneasy about the offer.

"Well, come by if you want to. Everybody thinks the wife is Little Miss Perfect. But how can she not know that her husband has a completely different life, breaking every law on post with multiple other women?"

"How do you know the wife is gay?" I was curious.

"She comes to visit me all the time. I don't swing that way."

"Right. But maybe she's visiting you for the same reasons I do."

"Why is that?"

"Because you are my friend and a most pleasant joy to be around." I smiled while she had a laugh too. She was far from pleasant, and she knew it.

My own job dealt with binary numbers and analysis. Sometimes I would spend all day data-mining problems and solutions like an analyst. In binary, everything is either a one or a zero, there or not there. In my realm, soldiers either existed or didn't. They were airborne or not. I either did or did not have permission to reassign them to one of our seven posts to boost our personnel strength. Once they got to post, their personalities and work ethics either rendered them desirable to the army or not. It was Lash's department that documented their behavior and standing.

The worst of us could earn our way back into the civilian world or even end up in jail. The vast majority of soldiers serve perfectly. The few that wrote a path to Lash's attention most often constituted problem children with the thickest, most horrific files.

Lash had applied for my position and had undergone an elaborate interview process, but my colonels had passed her over for me. I enjoyed talking to her, but I also approached her with caution. She harbored the rawest of information and opinions. I had no interest in the small handful of psychopathic loony-toons terrorizing post. What about all the other Americans that constitute the droves good citizens? There were so many other soldiers doing the right thing. Lash protected our files too. I bid her farewell.

Bosses

Lieutenant Colonel Maron and our boss, Colonel Smart, routinely checked on my well-being when I briefed them. I was a hard-charging lieutenant, and I think it pained them that I lingered in harm's way.

"Tell me he doesn't hit you. I am not a fan of that at all," one would say. The other would agree. At one point, I thought that they were saying this because Jayns was black and they were stereotyping him. I failed to realize that I was probably one of the most at-risk women on Fort Bragg. They were simply looking out for me.

After I had left Jayns, they were relieved. "Never open the door for him again," Colonel Smart advised.

No one looked out for the women he beat up, though. I wondered if he hit them harder because of my absence. I wondered if he hit them harder because of Twig's absence. She was the person he had tried to impress at West Point by taking the drugs that leveled his twenties. Was her rejection the true source of his self-destruction? Was it his parents, who refused to pay for regular college? A lot could explain Jayns's anger. He wanted something to make him feel whole, but he had no clue when enough was enough. He tested the limits of the army and the law, but the source of his malevolence lay beyond me.

Deployed, 1995

My phone rang, and it was Lieutenant Colonel Maron on the other end of the line. "Tracey, we're live. Get in here."

I had already taken my son, Jordan, home to Indianapolis to stay with my mother. President Bill Clinton had declared that US troops would attack Haiti for its leader's war crimes if his regime did not lay down their arms. The 82d Airborne Division, the premiere unit of our

Corps, was prepared to jump in, including select members of my unit. I was one of them.

Lieutenant Colonel Maron had selected my team in advance. As soon as we jumped into Haiti, we would regroup and I would take charge of the casualties. There were rumors that the Haitian government had anti-aircraft missiles, so our military mission was to defeat the then-president's forces once on ground. Though many in our unit were afraid, I felt calm; it was an instance where a pinch of denial did me good.

Many US presidents would have ignored a Haitian president murdering his own people, but President Clinton said what the US had to say to stop bloodshed: "Enough is enough."

No one would tell us what route we were taking from Fort Bragg down to Haiti, but we loaded up and landed on another, unknown airstrip several hours later. Another soldier and I joked that we were actually in Miami and just not permitted to visit the beach. We were attached to the first-string unit, but in that moment, everyone was only familiar with his or her immediate team. My team was peppered with diversity, though I was the only female. Some seemed scared, but we were all ready.

Lieutenant Colonel Maron found a room with a TV at our new, unknown facility. CNN showed an empty podium with a backdrop of what appeared to be the Haitian president's mansion. Former US President Jimmy Carter was inside that mansion, trying to negotiate some sense into the Haitian president. Lieutenant Colonel Maron assured me that it was the Haitian president's last chance. Our orders were to take off and jump into Haiti with guns ready as soon as President Carter left the ground.

I appreciated that Colonel Maron trusted me enough to handpick me for the mission. I was a qualified airborne jumper, and fortunately, hurling myself out of planes never once brought on shock for me.

President Carter finished negotiating. Cameras and shutters clicked and snapped as he walked toward the podium after leaving the Haitian mansion to announce the results of his efforts. He had succeeded: the Haitian president agreed to stop killing his people, and our wartime

Undeterred

mission had now changed into a peacekeeping mission. Our unit would now occupy the airport to maintain order there. Some of us felt deflated; others, relieved; and yet others, indifferent. I followed Lieutenant Colonel Maron. Nothing fazed him, so nothing fazed me.

"Back on the planes, guys and gals," he announced. We left what was probably Miami for what was then our Haitian peacekeeping mission.

We landed at the Haitian airport. Murmured or screamed expressions of confusion surrounded us wherever we went. I followed Lieutenant Colonel Maron everywhere. The Haitians gathered along the airport's perimeter fence, gawking at us, their bony fingers curled to grip the wire fence that was our cage, as though we were the most interesting animals in the zoo. As time went on, I concluded we were just that: green creatures stomping around in an enclosure with an unknown purpose.

We occasionally ventured into the towns. Despite having grown up poor, I had never seen poverty like that in my life. Back roads hid shanty after shanty, crammed along both sides of a narrow street. Cloth rags hung here or there to dry, to provide shade or simply to announce that the garment or sheet was being used for some purpose far from its original intention. It saddened me that we were forbidden to give away our food for fear of ravished infighting among the hungry locals. Some of the children had open sores that were blood- or pus-filled. I worked far away from home in a place I had never studied.

A naval ship rested in the water off shore. One day, Lieutenant Colonel Maron ordered me to take my best soldier and tour the ship. When I asked him why, he laughed and said, "Because."

The official reason was because the naval vessel supported the Mobile Army Surgical Hospital on land, to which we were attached. It provided our huge hospital on the Atlantic, the MASH's back office, so to speak. Once aboard, you almost immediately forget that you are suspended in the ocean. It felt like a land hospital. We received tours and briefings from the navy and were treated better than by the air force, whose only role in the operation was in kicking us out of planes.

We toured the entire vessel. I learned a lot, but I could have gone without learning the word "malingerer."

We entered a psychiatric ward, and the rows and rows of crew cut heads peeking out from underneath sheets and blankets astounded me. We gathered in the center of the ward, where the orderly talked to us without whispering. He signaled that the people around us were either not listening or were unable to concentrate on what he said. "Consider them asleep," he instructed us.

"What's wrong with them?" asked a member of our party.

"They have PTSD. That's post-traumatic stress disorder. Something traumatic they experienced induced them to repress the memory or in some other way caused them troubles that land them here."

Each patient was silent, as were we. I walked down the center aisle and could see rows and rows of shaved heads in one direction, and rows and rows of blanketed feet in the other. Superficially, they all appeared well-rested, even if they were wracked with turmoil on the inside. When the orderly paused in his explanation, no sound filled the room except a tapping toward the back row.

I asked what the noise was and the orderly assured me that I would soon see. A mop of African American hair peaked around the edge of a bunk. Seeing me, its owner stood up and started walking around, randomly tapping a book so that I would see her. I stared at her, not only because she clearly wanted me to, but because I wondered if she were safe. In a bay full of guys, albeit sleeping, I saw no other woman. She mumbled and pointed.

We looked at the orderly for an explanation. He promised that her stay would be short. I questioned why. Without losing his military bearing, he explained to the group that the unit had one and only one malingerer. I alone did not understand the term.

"She's faking," he explained. We all understood that.

"How do you know? Is she in pain?" My questions started.

"Nope. If she were suffering, she would lie down and deal with it like everyone else. Our patients sleep, coming out of shock. They repress the event so they can cope. They have no energy to hang on to a bible and pray. There is no religion involved."

I thought of the chessboard, of the bishop having to desert the area before a king can castle. There is no religion involved.

Someone else asked where the patient was going, and the orderly assured him that she was headed anywhere but home. There's no reward for faking to get your piece off the chessboard. Play the game.

Going Home, 1995

When I returned from the ship in Haiti, Lieutenant Colonel Maron asked me if I wanted to take a road trip. I asked where to, and he said, "Back to Indianapolis to pick up your son." I leapt in excitement: he was sending me home. I left Haiti within a week and returned to Fort Bragg.

He soon returned, too. Colonels were bargaining over the lieutenants again. It's strange to have people haggling over you, but I chose to take it as a compliment.

Everyone in my unit knew that Jayns had conjured faked tapes of me saying damaging things to cause me harm. They were distributed on post, so many of my colleagues had heard them. I just kept living and doing my job, oblivious to it all.

Guarded, 1989

One Sunday I had guard duty in my company. Every West Point sophomore graduated from a hellacious plebe year to simply dreading being the cadet-in-charge of his or her company dormitory. Sophomores rotated to the job each day, one per company, to thanklessly deliver phone messages and packages, check and recheck doors and lights, and field every question from freshmen who could not find anyone else to pester.

This particular day started off easily. We were allowed to go to classes when on duty, but the deliveries and floor checks heated up after the cadets started filing in from classes in the afternoon, getting ready for sports and other activities. Our commander had left to watch a sporting event for the evening, so only I held company duty.

I heard Cadet Quill as soon as he entered the building. He was a handsome cadet, tall, blonde, blue-eyed. Unconcerned about academics, he was someone who didn't let grades hold back his lifestyle. Everything about his personality dictated that he preferred fun to school. He created mayhem naturally with his boisterous laughter and behavior, so his being loud surprised no one. Something crazy had apparently happened during the day, and he horse-played with others as a means of expressing himself. I noticed that his voice seemed strained, almost desperately loud.

When freshmen walked by him on the stairwells, he greeted them loudly, his voice travelling through all levels of the building. He could be obnoxious, but in our age group people liked that–a wild and crazy young person.

After half an hour, I grabbed my inspection chart and began my rounds by checking the phones and storerooms in the basement. We had to check the phone booths for trash and debris; upperclassmen sometimes left bottles of dip spit behind in cups after calls. I mustered a few unfortunate freshmen to attend to that. Past the phones were the storerooms. I had to check that no couples were hunkered in there doing weed, or each other.

I cruised through the first floor, but as I entered the stairwell, I could hear Quill howling up on the third floor. It got louder as I ascended and checked the second-floor. When I finally opened the door to the third floor, I heard, rather than saw, Quill being shoved into a room where another person slammed the door abruptly. I continued my checks.

That same door flew open again and Quill came flying out, dashing into a freshmen girls' room, followed by startled shrieks. No one egged him on, though enabling cadets followed in his wake to save him from himself.

I met him trying to leave the girls' room. He pushed by me, raising his eyebrows and laughing. "Woo!" he cheered as he continued down the hall, before his followers dragged him into another room.

In that valuable fraction of a second, I smelled no alcohol and I chose to rule out vodka. His pupils were wider than his mouth, though. I quickly left the floor, deciding to save the final checks for later.

In the company guardroom I called the active duty officer in charge. Captains on post rotated into that position everyday. The officer who picked up did not take me seriously at first. I detailed Quill's behavior and dilated pupils, so he thought it would be wise to come over and check things out.

He let himself in and followed the sound of Quill's ruckus while I finished checking the upper floor. My shift soon ended, but when we all woke up the next morning, Quill's belongings were permanently gone. West Point had a zero-tolerance policy for drugs.

I got backlash from Quill's supporters, in addition to the other upperclassman waiting to pounce, but Jayns encouraged me. "Don't sweat it. He got sloppy."

I would later learn that Jayns had sold Quill those drugs. Quill, a rich kid, had paid better than Jayns' other customers.

Phone Call
Surviving the ordeal with Jayns at Fort Bragg was so stressful that I could not raise the rape to consciousness; other terrors still held it down. I trusted Jayns with my address and phone number in case he needed someone close by who could help him, but he abused that privilege more than he appreciated it.

Not long before our divorce trial, he called my apartment twenty-five times one day until I answered. He told me that he had left a piece of paper outside my door and asked me to read what was written on it to him. I refused. He asked me a couple of general questions, and I answered those. They were not important to me.

"I cannot believe how dumb you are. I hate the sound of your voice," he said.

Nice, I thought. "Jayns, are you going to get help?"

"I've helped myself to you. I resolved to do anything to keep you from going into politics. That is why I raped you. I called to tell you that I raped the hell out of you to destroy you. That is why we rape you. It's not for the sex. We rape to destroy you. It's just to ruin you. The shock that you're in, I planted it as a seed in your brain, so that when you least expect it, it will set off the ticking time bomb that counts down to your last days upon recall.

"I violated you, and then I rammed a Heineken bottle through you fifty times. As I did, I resolved to kill you. I have no idea how you lived. I just jammed that bottle in you with the force of a truck, and every time the metal cap raked out torn skin from you in globs. I had to clean the walls after slinging the bottle in the air to get you off my beer. Your guts were everywhere. It cut holes in you. You played with your own skin, you dumb bitch.

"You'll never come back from where I dumped your future. I got excited all over again and just kept ripping and ripping, ramming and ramming.

"You bitches are messy, I tell you." He laughed, repeating himself, reliving his pleasure. "I flicked that crap. Parts of your sorry ass were flying through the air. You passed out because you're weak. I kept pounding you like hell. It was fucking funny.

"You played with your skin in the shower," he laughed. "I should have made you eat it. You are the dumbest bitch I have ever met. You're why we don't need women in the army. All we have to do is rape your sorry asses and you won't remember where the barracks are.

"A black woman should suck a black dick, not gallivant around giving speeches. When you shut up, we can get our blowjob. That's all we want with dinner. But you bitches want to be men with us and take our flipping jobs.

"You're a dyke, Tracey. I *hate* dykes. You have the sexual development of a thirteen-year-old thanks to your dumb grandparents. That's another reason that I raped you. I'm going to kill them just to hurt you more.

"I avenged Quill. Loved that guy, you damn narc. And I am going to go through all the tapes I have and see how much damage I can do to

Undeterred

you. Every time you hit me for child support, you are going to lose your job. It's a *man's* world, bitch. I cannot believe they let you graduate from West Point.

"And by the way, despite being smarter than you, *I am on crack.* I *love* it; I *love it* so much, I hook others too. Every ho' I sell on the street is hooked because I say so. So forget you!"

The phone disconnected. My rape, even my marriage, had been hate-infused.

Jayns had made that call from his wire-tapped apartment. What the federal government no doubt caught on tape had me curled against the wall, desperately trying to forget. I could not make out some of what he said because my ears were physically hurting.

People with PTSD can experience auditory and visual distortion in traumatic situations. The senses attempt to protect us through blurriness and scratchiness.

I managed to call his commander's wife, who assured me that her husband was making calls as we spoke. He had actually already fired Jayns from his executive officer's position, and he was now talking to Jayns's new commander in the piddly position he held while the service built their case against him.

She confirmed that Jayns was a drug addict and was wanted on various charges: battery, possession, trafficking, and prostitution. She was a drug and alcohol counselor and had identified his substance abuse problems the day she met him. Reading people like Jayns was her specialty.

It was more information than I could handle. My main concern now was that Mama and Papa were in jeopardy. I worried for them, living alone on a country road in Cloverdale, Indiana, far from neighbors. Though his former commander's wife assured me that I would be fine and that she'd always doubted my involvement, she stayed with me on the phone until my breathing calmed. According to her, Jayns would hurt himself even more if he showed up in Indiana. She was confident that my grandparents were fine.

During my rape examination years earlier, Major Walker had commented that he saw comb-like markings inside me. Those markings would be consistent to the ribbed edges of a bottle cap. Jayns had raped me with an unopened beer. Fifty blows would certainly leave me as butchered as Major Walker found me.

I called Papa and warned him that they might be in danger, and then I fell asleep. We were getting close to our divorce trial and Jayns was increasingly spiraling out of control. When I awoke, it was as though the entire conversation had never happened. PTSD refuses to permit recall of the worst events.

Trial, 1995

The night before our court proceedings, a black man with darkened eyes and an unkempt appearance came to my door. It was already dark out and he did not look like someone that I wanted to get to know. He offered me the privilege of a complimentary carpet cleaning, because new carpet sheds. I was living in a brand new house that I had just had built. Everyone in the neighborhood had shedding carpet.

He held up a dirty cup holder with a "Don't worry, be happy" smiley face–my free prize should he gain entrance to my home. Though I wondered where that dirty item had been, I could not help looking past him to the van that he had come in, and I could see movement in the back.

One would be proud to know that I got it. Though I have PTSD, I completely understood the danger that I was in at that moment. The trial beckoned the next day; this was clearly a last-ditch effort to hurt me tonight.

"No, thank you," I answered calmly.

"Help a brother out." His gold teeth caught the light on my lit porch. He was ridiculous.

"No, thank you."

He grew agitated, and I sensed even more that he had a drug habit. I informed him that I would get my gun if he touched the door latch he was studying.

Undeterred

Squarely, he said, "You don't have a gun. You don't believe in them, remember?"

"If you are standing there when I look again, you won't live to know whether you were wrong." I disappeared to call 911 because his taunt rang true: I did not own a gun. The man vanished.

Jayns said nothing in domestic court the next day. I received custody of our son. He fought for visitation rights, but never came to visit. His lawyer asked if we could be lenient because the army had already found him financially liable for the $40,000 in Greece. He offered me the option of receiving less to help Jayns pay off his massive debt to the army. I declined. I did this not out of spite; I did it because I was not involved with his debts from Greece.

I did not recall the conversation where he bragged of my rape two days earlier. Castling, my mind blocked the call, his crimes, everything. I just could not handle it at that time.

Jayns was arrested in 1995 in a drug sting, along with several other people. He was allowed to out-process and join the civilian world, but he did not receive an honorable discharge. Someone from his unit assured me that the army forbade him from ever setting foot on a military post or government property ever again. This only happens when the worst criminals in uniform escort themselves back to the civilian ranks. Those are the people that, for the rest of their lives, cannot associate with the spirit of the corps.

Exit

In October 1995, I exited the service with the blessings of my superior officers. Even with a disease as disabling as PTSD, I had served three units superbly, including a stint in the most coveted position on post for a personnel officer lieutenant: Corps Readiness Officer.

At the same time, I suffered from crippling fatigue. I fought feelings of guilt, sadness, worry, and denial daily. I still did not know what I wanted to be in life, but I was starved for rest. My armor had collected so many invisible chinks, I worried that I was not able to be all that I could be, and I did not want to stay in the army without the energy that had helped me rise to the level of my position.

Jayns and the trauma at Fort Bragg accentuated the depths of my struggle with PTSD to that point. I still had no recollection of my rape. Because my brain blocked the vital details, I was unable to avoid further harm. Instead, I had married my rapist, lingering in harm's way. I ended my career in response to the constant fatigue. Mine was a textbook case of PTSD.

Fort Bragg did not treat me for the mental and medical landmines I tripped over. Upon exiting the service, I returned to Indiana as part of Pfizer Pharmaceuticals, which was so packed with veterans that many called it the Pfizer Army. Pfizer assigned me to Bloomington, Indiana, the new headquarters for the Indiana Ku Klux Klan. The Klan would take an immediate interest in me and my struggle with PTSD.

Part Three: KKK

Bloomington's First Vote

My grandparents were still living in Cloverdale, Indiana. When Pfizer offered me a job in Bloomington, Indiana, billing it as a great college town, I took it largely because my grandparents lived nearby.

I did no research on Bloomington before relocating. The US was the US to me, and Indiana was Indiana. My territory included a square of area between and around Bloomington, Columbus, Bedford, and Seymour. My job was to encourage the doctors in my territory to write more prescriptions for Pfizer's medications.

I went through rigorous training, which included rote memorization and scientific journal studies. I learned my articles so well that I could pull one from my bag, hand it to the doctor, have him or her make note of it, and see the memorized proof without actually losing eye contact.

When a drug rep walks into an office, he or she knows exactly what prescriptions the doctor wrote the month or quarter before. With that information, the drug rep knows what direction to take for a sales call. When a doctor says, "I never use that drug," the rep knows if the statement is true or false. Reps talk amongst themselves with a special emphasis as to which doctors are or are not "important" to them.

Tracey Brame

I worried a little about my new role. The job came down to several short speeches or deliberations a day with whichever doctors I met. I had a quota of presentations to give each day.

The territory around Bloomington had languished without a representative for some time, and Pfizer was losing revenue and market share. I started out ranked last in the state and my superiors did not expect me to earn commission for a long time. It seemed that some companies find it hard to keep representatives in Bloomington.

Zoloft, my biggest drug, was a newer antidepressant and it primarily competed with the hometown favorite, Eli Lilly and Company's Prozac. Zithromax, a five-day antibiotic, novel for treatment of many respiratory infections and used off-label for skin problems, ranked second. Nurses hunted me down for Diflucan if they had a yeast infection, which infectious disease specialists and surgeons used daily for the worst systemic fungal infections. I also had a good add-on for treatment of hypertension and a strong antibiotic used in hospitals.

Getting around proved to be the real challenge, given the five-hundred-plus doctors in my territory. I could take it slow and grow sales in a limited fashion, or I could really work my patch and see results. Coming out of my inexplicable lethargy in the army, I was excited for the opportunity to be back in my home state. I wanted to hit the ground running. The first night back, I laid on the floor with maps and numbers, formulating a plan.

I invested in business pantsuits and scarves. The military had always chosen what I wore, but checking out fashion is a common new task for recently departed soldiers. Brooks Brothers and Talbots sold me my entire wardrobe of six shirts, half with cuff links and half without. I looked around for a while but, running out of time, I just bought a handful of the same shirts in different colors, and so I was dressed for business.

The first negative thing that resonated was, "Why does she dress like a man? We don't need that here." Apparently, southern Indiana in 1995 preferred its female sales representative in skirts and dresses, not pantsuits. I ignored this because, as a newly returning veteran, I had sunk all

Undeterred

the money I had in clothes. And besides, who judges someone by a cufflink or a pantsuit? For starters, southern Indiana.

Packing

When I walked into a doctor's office, I had a game plan. I primarily focused on the larger family practitioner offices and psychiatric offices because I needed Zoloft sales. I also kept a list of ten key players for each of the other specialties and frequented them more.

The pharmaceutical companies fed doctors every day through us. It offered a time for the doctor and staff to sit down and learn about the drugs.

However, if a doctor had been prescribing a certain drug for several years, he or she knew the drug; they didn't know me. Every community passes judgment on a drug sales representative, but in Bloomington, it was a common practice for doctors to actively accept or reject representatives, to embrace or destroy their employment chances. Bloomington was unusual in that the doctors there felt at liberty to make it clear that a given representative was not welcome.

Companies found it hard to keep a representative in southern Indiana during the 1990s for that very reason. Doctors in the area judged the drugs less than the person marketing them. Not knowing this, I would test the lengths to which Bloomington would go to cleanse itself of an unwanted drug representative, by running them out of town through coercion.

Historically, such is Ku Klux Klan behavior. We have all seen the pictures of the hooded men standing around a burning cross. They were old, angry men in history textbooks, with seemingly little relevance. We've all seen images of black churches burning to the ground on television. By 1995, the Indiana KKK did not want that much attention. Rather than burn down a building or cross, they instead attacked individuals, which is far less visual. If they could find a way to make a person leave town without talking to the press or writing a book, they would.

As it turned out, one of the most powerful members of the Indiana KKK was a doctor in Bloomington. Most of the rest of the doctors in town either followed his lead into the Klan, or lived in fear of them. As a result, the KKK, and because of them, the doctors in town, voted on every new drug sales rep in the area, threatening the rep's success and livelihood. Voting yes or no was their way of deciding if the representative stayed.

I was nervous to begin with, because the town seemed cliquish, which only compounded the pharmaceutical companies' struggle to keep representatives in the area. As I began making my rounds, several stone-faced family practice doctors, the older, settled ones, would often ask, "Have you been to Dr. Blank's office?" where Dr. Blank was another older physician, with the long tenure to potentially be a big prescriber.

If yes, then my response was, "Yes, sir."

The follow-up question might be, "And what did he think of you?" Not the drug–me. It was something I had to think about, because Dr. Blank usually just listened and walked away without saying anything.

I always responded that he, and it was almost always a he, loved me. The truth was that I did not know, but why wouldn't he love me?

"Hmm," they would respond in thought.

If, on the other hand, I had not met Dr. Blank yet, the other doctor would say, "Well, go over to his office today, because he may like these drugs. Be sure to tell him that *I* sent you."

This always sent me packing to that office because I thought some good might come of it. Dr. Blank would not be expecting me, but when I dropped the other doctor's name, he would come to the window and either sign for my samples or refuse them. I had great products, but I felt like I had something short of a referral.

What I didn't realize at the time was that the oldest doctors were passing judgment on me. Each was voting as to whether I could keep my position in town, or if they should coerce me to leave. If the majority of them voted that I should leave town, they would put together a plan to coerce me to leave.

I carried on. Some would sing or taunt that "the vote was still out." While I basked in the oblivion of my candidacy, yeas and nays, and they were mostly nays, quickly piled up.

Dr. Kalen

Crucial to my least-important drug was Dr. Kalen. A six-foot tall woman with blonde hair down to her waist, she wrote over half of my cardio scripts. It was not a drug that made a lot of money, so I could not focus heavily on cardio or I would starve. Therefore, I appreciated Dr. Kalen's numbers as a rare "extra." I made it to her office within my first month and gained permission to bring lunch the following month.

Most of the office staff caters to the doctor; after all, that is their job. Dr. Kalen's staff was no different. Her older sister, Degan, served as the nurse and Degan's husband, Don, was the office manager. While Dr. Kalen ate lightly to maintain her thin frame, her sister and brother-in-law preferred excess. In conversation as well, Degan and Don needed the attention that Dr. Kalen forewent, often asking rude or nosey questions in an effort to pry. The receptionist, Haley, a friend of the family that never stopped smiling, stood out as my personal favorite in the office.

Degan studied my mannerisms early on, and quickly made a point of telling me that Dr. Kalen was not like me, not any more. In addition to her towering height and blonde hair, Dr. Kalen had a somewhat deeper voice, but was feminine, always wearing mini-skirts and dresses. Given our differences, I could never imagine when she had "been like" me.

Degan was the opposite of her sister, too. While Dr. Kalen was quiet, her sister was obtrusively talkative. Dr. Kalen was thin; her sister was wide. Dr. Kalen was nice, while her sister fed on other people's misery.

One day Degan voluntarily told me that in high school, Dr. Kalen had been admonished for either a relationship or some kind of encounter with another female. The community descended on the future doctor and "cured her" of the orientation. I felt empathy for Dr. Kalen having been harmed, but I could not tell what had prompted Degan to air such laundry to a person she barely knew. Degan nodded, as if she had put my intentions to rest. I had no intentions with Dr. Kalen. Most sales reps knew of her love of tennis, not her love from high school. Though repressed, I preferred someone like Redd, not a fair, long-legged alternate. To me, Dr. Kalen was nice and nothing else.

In other offices, staff often asked me how I fared as I waited for my appointment to begin. Degan pried more into my personal life. Early on I suspected genuine interest, but in time I learned that she didn't care for me and lacked the desire to hide it.

"Where do you live in town?" she asked one day.

"I live in Cloverdale with my grandparents. I will be moving soon."

"Where are you moving?"

"To Morgantown, just under Martinsville. I may buy a house there. It's directly between my two biggest towns, Bloomington and Columbus. I think it will be better for driving."

"I know where Morgantown is," she said flatly, with no trace of a smile. Obviously, a local would know where Morgantown was, but you would also think that she would be happy for me.

"Why are you buying a house?"

I was confused. "So that I can live there." It seemed the obvious answer.

"You don't even know if you will work out."

I never looked at it that way. The statement stumped me. "Well, I'm pouring myself into making it working out," I smiled.

With no smile to return, she said, "Seems presumptive to me." She started to turn away, but met my eyes to assure me, "No decisions on you have been made yet."

She asked to take a picture of me. I obliged. She showed it to Don, her husband, and asked if it would help. He hunched his shoulders and declared that nothing would help. I asked what I was helping with. She assured me that nothing about me would save me. She asked what I thought were my best attributes. I thought myself smart and articulate. She assured me that a lot of people in town hated that about me. With that, she walked away.

Undeterred

I bought a house in the country–five acres and two ponds for less than $100,000–a true steal. Its central location meant quick jaunts to my two largest towns. It would save me hours off the week traveling so far from my grandparents. When they came to visit, a great place to fish immediately satisfied Papa. A stream connected both ponds, and Papa could see just what he wanted lurking below the surface. He and I would have a great time, he assured me.

Home

When Mama came to my one-story, three-bedroom house with two ponds and a detached garage, she started cleaning, not because I was messy, but because she liked to reorganize. I hated that, because she put all my stuff in places that I had not intended. We set up a great little room for Jordan, my son, but he stayed with Mama until I was more acclimated and travelled less.

Out of the seven territories in the state of Indiana, I was still coming in dead last. My boss encouraged me not to beat myself up about it. Once I raised my numbers a little, the scripts would flow and Jordan could come home, I assured myself. I felt it would not take long.

My grandparents were excited for me. Mama kept saying, "You are so far out in the country, but at least you're not in Martinsville. That is where *they* are. Stay in at night." Papa did not want to rattle me, so he took a less flustered approach and reminded me that I had what it took to do a good job. Hard work and smarts were a good recipe for success.

I ran down my country road one day. I felt like Rocky, making it in a rustic environment. There were four teenaged boys lollygagging around a John Deere. They stopped laughing when I got closer. Their silence lasted until I passed and one said, "An N-word should be found at the bottom of a pond!" Since I was approaching my house, I kept pace until I got to my mailbox. The cool-down walk to the front door helped me assess those to be my good neighbors to the west.

Prepped

The other two towns in my territory had a handful of doctors, but if I started early I could cover Columbus or Seymour and Bedford in one day. Every bit of logic told me that I needed Bloomington to survive. I slowed down when I got to Bloomington and called on everyone there.

One memorable new doctor, Dr. Reenie, a petite brunette with wavy hair, practiced as a specialist in the office of a high-prescriber named Dr. MacTech. Dr. Reenie may have written a handful of scripts, while Dr. MacTech wrote hundreds. I saw Dr. Reenie more often than I saw Dr. MacTech, who was always busy and whose competition did not stay in town long. I was told that if a doctor did not like their competition, they could put them up for vote to be run out of town, the same as with sales reps. Once kicked out of town, they weren't competition any longer.

Dr. MacTech and her partner seemed to have more staff than some other offices. They were all young women cooped up in the office, so I brought them treats more often than some offices.

While taking orders for the ladies' milk shakes one day, Dr. Reenie pulled me into a patient exam room and admitted that she worried for me. Having talked to other non-KKK doctors, she felt I was in danger. "What are you going to do?" she asked referring to my fate.

I did not understand the question.

"Are you going to move?"

"I just got here." The thought made no sense.

"Talk to your company."

"They just moved me here. I have to stay two years before I will be eligible for another move."

She gazed past me. From what she was hearing, she did not think I would make it two years. "Talk to your company." She was trying to prepare me for what was to come. Confused, I offered to get her a milkshake too, but she shook her head.

With a casual office and a young staff, it seemed easy to cater to Dr. MacTech at first. She prescribed my anti-fungal med off-label for nail infections. She spent time with me, but firmly commented with a smile, "The decision is still out on you." Again, not on my products. Me.

I learned to ignore comments like that. I did not have a choice but to continue to do my job. My numbers remained flat initially, but my goal remained to be nice and informative to everyone.

Brian was my hiring boss, and he'd bet the farm on me when we met. He liked soldiers because we worked hard. Many drug reps became lazy over time. If it rained, they stayed home and counted inventory. If the sun were shining, they may not have willed themselves to work at all. Soldiers do not care about the weather. We tough it out.

I toughed it out until Jayns's tapes arrived. Unbeknownst to me, he sent them to many of my doctors, Pfizer's clients. In the tapes from Fort Bragg, he had asked me sordid questions while in shock and cut and pasted my answers to defame me. According to his work, I was his accomplice, a drug addict, a woman of ill repute, etc. He laid his life and problems on me. Pfizer had the tapes too, thanks to him.

"How could you do that to a dog?" an office receptionist asked me one day after the tapes had arrived in town.

"How could I do what?" I was curious.

She proclaimed to God that I made her sick to her stomach and walked away. No one helped me in that office, or many others that day. Later that day, a doctor asked me if I felt all right. Of course, I did. He leaned in to me, studied my eyes, and made a comment that I could feel better, and I probably wanted to. I did not catch the reference to drugs because, no matter what the tapes said, I had never done drugs.

I travelled to another office and experienced a similar chill. Some even refused to speak to me. I drove home wondering how I could do my job without communication.

This treatment continued. One office that had scheduled a luncheon with me allowed me to set it up and wait, but no one came back to eat or talk until sometime after I had deserted the building. At office after office I was treated the same. To top it off, Pfizer called me out of the field for drug screenings twice in two weeks. Jayns's tapes were affecting my work. I drove to Indianapolis to take the drug tests, and they put me off my schedule for a full day.

The voting process in Bloomington escalated with Jayns's tapes. To a trained medical professional, the tapes hinted at some form of marital abuse, from which I suffered post-traumatic stress disorder. No one said anything to me. Bloomington ended up convicting me based on the fabricated tapes, but they were coming to the same conclusion before the tapes arrived.

Get Out of Town!

Indiana does not follow daylight savings time, and it was dark on the morning of January 22nd, 1996, save for the streetlights. It had rained every day for a week in Bloomington, a cold rain that made working outside miserable. The entire month had been wet. It was the Monday before the Super Bowl, and I listened to my windshield wipers interrupt Sting's *Summoner's Tale* album. When I pulled into Bloomington, I took the southbound vein through town to the obscure numbered streets by the hospital where many of Pfizer's clients spent their workdays.

I pulled into the parking lot of a long building sectioned off into small doctor's offices. I called on the last three, but had ruled out the others as clients for my products. Sting belted about "heavy clouds, no rain," which reminded me that he was nowhere near the pouring storms I hoped would subside soon. I looked up at the yellowish parking light to see thousands of dew points drifting from an obscure sky to the frosty earth. I had plenty of clouds in Bloomington and an equally damp rain and snow mix.

I waited in my car for half hour or more; doctors and their staff never rose as early as my military training encouraged me to. The rain stopped. I checked my watch.

Bundling my coat around me, the coat I bought specifically for Indiana because I did not own a heavy one while living in North

Undeterred

Carolina, I ventured from my car, listening to my feet shuffle across the gravel. Tree branches encapsulate in thick frost and ice crunched under my shoes. I had giveaways like pens, notepads, and clipboards. I felt light on my feet despite the frost, knowing that other drug reps would sleep in and give me an advantage that morning as one of the few people working. I might even get a few extra offices in. I was the early bird.

I opened the first office door to find no one behind the desk. A stale sweetness told of the age and ventilation of the tiny space. Several stackable office chairs and coffee table and side tables welcomed patients to sit and peruse magazines with the doctor's name and number scribbled off. The carpet was worn in several places and may have been the source of the room's scent, but I cared as little as the staff did. If they were comfortable with their work environment, then so was I.

I was a guest. I rarely sat unless offered a seat. I stood a lot from nervous energy and fear that someone would order me to move because I was not a patient. I waited at the receptionist's desk. Someone heavily stomped across the back hallway to see who had come in, but she disappeared quickly upon seeing me.

I waited longer. After awhile, two heavyset and heavy-footed women approached the receptionist area from the back hallway. The first to show her face started screaming, "Get out!"

"I'm your Pfizer rep," I assured her.

"Not any more. Get out!" She entered the room scowling.

I wanted to tell her that I was not a burglar, but the second woman rounded the threshold behind her and screamed, "Get out of town!"

Both in unison hollered louder like corpulent raptors, screaming, "Get out of Town!" repeatedly. They looked to each other when I stood stunned and confused, and raised their voices, as though the problem was in my hearing, not my understanding. At the height of their volume, they screamed, "Get out of town!"

With all the shouting, I did not hear the doctor make his way to the entryway. He was a thinner man of medium height, who, looking at me and hearing his staff, made eye contact and pointed his thumb to the door. "You gotta go," he said. He was matter-of-fact at first, but his face quickly tore up like theirs. "Let's go!" he raised his volume as well.

All three looked deranged to me. They were all white, and their faces, strained red with anger, made me feel empathy for their highly emotional outbursts. What could be wrong this early in the morning? Was there no coffee? I tried to tell them that I was still their representative just like the weeks before, but they assured me that I was not their representative any more. "Get out of town!"

I felt like they were addressing someone else. Of course, I thought, they must have confused me with someone else. But whom had they mixed me up with? There was only one other black pharmaceutical sales rep in Bloomington and he was male.

Pfizer trained us to take advantage of every second with a doctor, so I tried to do my job despite their anger. I addressed the doctor, "Sir, how are you today?"

The first woman, hearing me attempt to speak with him, screamed, "Get out of town!" She and the other woman put their wide, heavy bodies between the doctor and I.

The second woman yelled, "You were voted out. Out! Out! Out!" She shooed me like an animal.

Voted on me. I wasn't a politician. I couldn't be voted out of anything. I did not understand. Who votes for regular people? What do they vote on? The term was confusing.

"Miss," said the doctor, "get out of my office." I looked at the door. Why did they not want me to do my job?

"Get out of town!" yelled both women again, crowding me in the tiny reception area, backing me toward the door. The first shoved me by the shoulders. I did not even think about shoving her back, for she was corpulent, and I was still a sleek soldier. Was she Aletha from fourth grade, embodied in a white face? I had hurt Aletha, knocked her and her cousin to the ground when both pitted themselves against me. Was this 'fight' another grapple that I had to go through?

Undeterred

I felt sorry for the first lady. She was clearly ready to fight someone much stronger than she. The arms extending from her extra-large blouse were laced more with bubbled, shaking fat than with lean, useful muscle. What mental illness was theirs? Had they been on the streets of Indianapolis, someone would have cut or stomped both of them. However, Pfizer would fire me if I punched an office person, even if they deserved it. Mine was not fear, but shear self-interest in what could possibly be wrong. They clearly lacked the self-control of a decent human being.

The first woman pushed me again. "Move it!" Could she not hear my thoughts? The second waved a fist. I tripped over a chair leg but remained on my feet with a hop and wobble. I worried that I would slip on a patch of tile by the door because my shoes, issued by West Point long before, were wearing on the soles.

"Get out of town!"

I stopped hearing "town" and focused on "get out." How could I get out if I was scheduled to work the entire week in Bloomington? I could not understand what I did to these people or what they thought that I did to them to earn this kind of reaction. If they would let me get a word in, I could ask the doctor what was going on. Why was I not able to get my own words in? I was silent. They crescendoed.

"Go!"

"Get out of town!"

"Miss," the doctor maintained his tone, "please leave."

I looked back at the doctor. We were taught that the doctor was always in charge in an office. Staffers had no power, yet he stepped up right behind them, concurring with their screams and pushes, ensuring that the only space I had was what was needed to open the door and leave.

When I stepped outside, the staff of both of my other offices in the building were outside, wrapped in jackets and coats. They stood in their doorways or on the sidewalk and steps, screaming, "Get out of town!"

Those were the offices next on my list. I walked toward them, and the calls for my departure grew louder. "Get in your car!"

"I have to speak to the doctor," I said calmly, looking at the physician in the second doorway with a smile. He shook his head, and as I approached, he turned and left, leaving more door-blockers to rescind my welcome.

"No one will speak to you!" screamed his nurse. "Get out of town!" The lady from the third office joined in, and soon I had two new faces snapping at me.

What my denying brain heard was: the office is closed, not just for you, Tracey, for everyone. That was the only thing that made sense, so I returned to my car to the jeers of all four women. *When you do not get the notice that they are closed, Bloomington offices become temperamental and unwelcoming,* I thought to myself. My delusion would catch up with me soon enough.

I made it to my car, careful not to slip in my old shoes, not knowing that the votes had been tallied and the KKK had declared me unacceptable. Seeing my frosty breath in the air, I tried to imagine whom the offices had mixed me up with. In my state of denial, I concluded that these offices were doing only administrative work that day and could not hold meetings. I decided to rework my week's schedule, and circle back around later in the week when they could see me.

Leaving town never dawned on me. Why would I leave before I had finished my work? That did not make sense to me. I would feel guilty if Pfizer lost business due to my laziness or ineptitude. Alone in the car, I muttered to myself that I must get to the next office.

I felt numb, a common feeling for people with PTSD, which drowns out other feelings that are too painful to face. Beneath my numbness, I felt an overwhelming sadness and guilt. I knew these were offices with which I could not grow business. My chest felt tight and like it was pressing inward. I covered my heart with one hand and my neck with my other, as a form of self-comfort. All I wanted to do was my job.

There was a lot to do that Monday, I reasoned. I would simply try back later when they were less hostile. *Not everyone is a morning person*, I reminded myself, putting the key in the ignition and inviting Sting to again fill the car.

Undeterred

He sang of having "seven days, a kind of ultimatum note," from a woman. I had been given seven seconds, and nothing in writing, but my delusional thoughts focused on the next five days I had scheduled to wrangle scripts from the town. I had plenty of time to have a good week. As I pulled away, heading to another office, my tires churned against the gravel on the pavement. I filed their wretchedness away as unintended. I had a lot to do that day, and kept a positive outlook.

First Rampage

Bloomington's rejection hit me suddenly and pervasively. With animation, close proximity, and physical pushing, people screamed, "Get out of town!"

On occasions like these, the KKK repeats itself with an official slogan like, "Get our of town!" With little variation, people screamed the same thing at me all week. Women and men in doctors' offices yelled at me to get out of town immediately, or else it would be too late. People got in my face, walked me to the door, and sometimes closed and locked it behind me. I thought they were all just in a bad mood. I smiled and tried to be helpful and friendly, but they would not let me finish a sentence. My PTSD, protecting me from such hostile emotions, failed to let me put it all together.

"Get out of town!"

"We hate you!"

"Get the hell out of town!"

"We voted you out."

"Out! Before it's too late."

"Get out of town!"

I silently studied them as they moved quickly around receptionist counters, emptied out back rooms, or held the door open to the cold air outside, demanding, "Get out of town!" It was the same in every office I visited. An office's rich decor did not render better behavior. They all repeated the same statement: "Get out of town!" This became an hourly, daily, weekly onslaught.

Tracey Brame

They were not getting through to me, not because I was being defiant, but because of sheer mental illness. Neither they nor I knew what had happened that was causing me to respond with a smile and empathy in the face of their cruelty. Thanks to Jayns, they suspected that I was sick, but as I was not their patient, they did not have to help me, lend credit to my positive attributes, or tolerate my differences, and so they didn't.

I feared for Pfizer's current and future business in the territory. Guilt straddled me with the realization that my numbers might sink even lower than they had been. I worried so much that I worked harder, including Saturdays. Where I was seeing eight offices in a given day before, I started seeing ten. I had to find people who weren't angry, so I reached into my database and pulled out folks that no one else was calling on. Meanwhile, the mob waited for me to respond to my dismissal.

In shock from my treatment, I wondered why everyone in Bloomington was suddenly so angry. What had happened to them each day to make them so evil? Through the fog of PTSD, I tried to make things better. I empathized with them. I gave out more pens, paper, candy containers, etc. I actually thought that those around me would cheer up soon. After all, people like free things. My calm demeanor and congenial insistence on doing my job with a smile in the face of such open anger and hatred revealed the depths of my mental illness. Any other person would have run.

In hindsight, I realize that my PTSD failed to let me assimilate the events around me or correctly interpret my environment. I lived through events and conversations, but I could not put these incidents together to draw sound conclusions regarding the danger surrounding me.

My inability to comprehend their hate clearly registered me as damaged. Their words, phrases, shoves should have bothered me, but instead I exhibited numbness and a bit of complacency, not arguing back as an unaffected person naturally would. I tried to make sense of each situation as though it was unique, not a pattern, with no success. Bloomington was senseless to me.

Undeterred

A person whose PTSD was demonstrated through anger or mood swings would have fought this brand of violence with a brand of their own. Though numb, I still did my job, which seemed repetitive and carved into my muscle memory like a guitar pluck. I prepared articles to present and carried in lunches that were cancelled after I set them up.

I was soon able to dismiss their hateful aggressions, just like I had with the rape. Some people with PTSD avoid aggressors. In Bloomington, my aggressors looked like people, all types of livid white people with beastly expressions. I did not try to avoid them like lethal animals in the zoo. I just made eye contact with them calmly and tiptoed past their cages with the belief that they could not bite me. My response kept me walking into malevolently rude receptions in an effort to do my job.

Only one opinion stuck and made sense to me: Bloomington had fallen on hard times. I had seen it at Duke; when the team lost, the campus mourned. Sometimes I'd sit next to Christien Latener, a famous Duke basketball player, in political science class. I'd watch him unfold and refold his long legs in an effort to get comfortable in our cramped seating. He never winced and, though it might have been painful to squeeze himself in among us shorter folks, he did not seem as though he wanted girls crying over his performances.

"Did you guys lose the football game?" I asked the receptionist at one of my Bloomington offices one day. "It seems everyone is in such an agitated state when I'm here. Is the team doing poorly?"

"It's *basketball* season! We have asked you several times to stop coming here! Why are you here? Get out of town!" With her volume, others came out of the back office, alerted to my presence.

As she came around the desk, I headed for the only place she directed me, the door. So much for empathy. Bloomington apparently did not appreciate empathy. They just appreciated a chance to holler and scream or push and pull at another human being. They pursued me vehemently, getting in my face, fussing all the way to my car, grabbing at my arm. If they walked to the sidewalk, they sometimes even spit in my direction, repeating, "Get out of town!"

Going into the details of every encounter seems impossible. If I made it into an office, they ordered me out. If I managed to ask to check to see if they needed more samples, they screamed that they would not use my product until I left or died. When I tried to leave a gift, they attacked me for littering their office. I would remind them that the pens or whatever I left were free gifts. They reminded me that they or I could just as well take my eyes out with them, it did not matter which. I tried to leave a candy dispenser to fill on each visit, and it came back aerially, aimed straight for my head. As I ducked, I heard a crash against the wall. I was not welcome even with goodies.

My boss maintained that Bloomington suffered from bigotry. True, it was a college town, which were usually liberal, but that meant nothing away from campus. Brian did not know that the KKK had moved from Martinsville to Bloomington, but it wouldn't have fazed him. Prejudiced people make room for more prejudiced people. Brian said that southern Indiana housed small minds. I concluded that they enjoyed less spacious hearts.

The hazing lasted several months. I did not try to hang on or hold on. I never understood what exactly made them so bent on crudeness. Confused by their reactions, I visited and revisited doctors' offices, the vast majority, probably 85 percent, of which were KKK. I judged this by the fact that, of the eight-to-ten offices I visited each day, seven or more kicked me out.

The non-KKK offices were strangely silent compared to the noisy receptions I received elsewhere. They existed to serve those people the KKK refused to serve. These offices were so calm and peaceful, I wondered if they were actually open. When I walked in, I stared at people who simply stared back. When they did not charge at me or scream at me, I asked if they were okay. They assured me that they were, and that I was okay too.

One non-KKK office allowed me to sit down and catch my breath once. I studied the office staff, trying to determine when they would erupt into tyranny. They didn't. The receptionist pointed toward the back office where their doctor sat, and said, "He's not like them." The volume with which she spoke was so normal, I felt I should speak back at a whisper. When I left the office and visited their neighbor across the hall, the howling began anew. Bloomington made absolutely no sense to me.

The KKK did not need Jayns's tapes to hate me, but the tapes did not help my chances either. I continued walking into the line of fire each day, over and over again, because my self-made schedule called for it: eight offices this day, ten offices that day. My PTSD did not allow me process why, who, what. I moved from day to day, not understanding that my race, my intelligence, and my articulation were culprits as much as Jayns was.

Lull

And then it stopped. The screaming, pushing, hurling, spitting ceased. Folks muttered cautiously, resentfully pleasant. The crowd, pensive, watched me as if gauging my response for a change. Another decision regarding my fate had been made with no input from me. The KKK suspended its effort to kick me out of town because they realized that I was too mentally ill to budge.

During that lull of hatred, the team physician for Indiana University basketball, Dr. Bando and his partner, Dr. Alterwood, held an after-dinner meeting to announce a new medical building construction project. Their office was grander than the other doctors' in town, thus their selection as the event hosts. Theirs was a stand-alone building with rich wood decor and separate windows and office spaces for each. Other offices were typically brighter, with almost flimsy furniture and decorations by comparison. I was invited only because Pfizer was underwriting the occasion.

As I waited for the event to begin, a doctor cornered me to explain why I had been "saved," despite my race. Unaware that I had been "saved" from anything, I struggled to understand the meaning of this conversation, which was clearly not Christian-related. It was rather based on a socioeconomic or even a scientific view of me as a part of some class of unwanted people that could be "useful" if "retrained." It was an almost-religious conclusion on his part, and it was so distinct from the way I had been raised that I found it uncomfortable to linger in conversation with him. I excused myself. He followed me to warn me to proceed with caution in Bloomington.

The crowd of attendees grew. "We have the power to revoke your stay at any time," the man kept saying. The words were like an insult laced with a lukewarm smile that should have heightened my sense of danger. His voice sounded scratchy, a sign that my brain sensed my danger and was distorting his language to protect me. I felt unwelcomed and searched for the host, Dr. Bando, explaining that the other doctor was harassing me.

"If you are going to be allowed to stay here, you have to get used to how we think and talk," said Dr. Bando in response. I did not know it yet, but Dr. Bando was KKK royalty. His best friend, Dr. Francis Hrisamolaz, was the reigning grand dragon. Their sons, Bando, Jr. and Dr. Tohmios Hrisamolaz, grew up in the Klan together and were life-long buddies.

I left noting that Dr. Bando was the one person lately who had said that I "might" stay. The town had reversed its decision to expel me. I still did not know I had been expelled in the first place.

Family Sense

At this stage in my life, I talked to my mother as much as I talked to my grandmother, both of whom suspected something was wrong. Communicating the specifics of my day to them exhausted me. A psychiatrist would note that by evening, I had already forgotten my day. If asked how I was, I defaulted to "fine." Still, both Mommy and Mama noted my struggle each night, in spite of what I did not say. I failed to quench their inquisitions with details.

My grandmother's father sported the palest blonde hair and near-transparent blue eyes. As kids, we would take turns sitting on his lap and

Undeterred

staring into his eyes, which made him giggle. He stood over six feet tall, and two or three of us could sit on his lap at a time. After I'd had my turn, I would run and bury my face in Mama's neck, because I found Grand Pop to be a bit scary. His hair favored corn silk and his eyes were too pale. I thought everything about him was faded from work in the sun. Mama laughed and deemed me "silly."

Grand Pop had nothing but kind words and smiles for us. His family graciously welcomed his twelve kids and dozens of grand- and great-grandchildren. However, in Indianapolis, they had to live in the black areas of town because whites would run them out of a neighborhood.

Grand Pop never showed prejudice to his full Native American wife or any of the "yellow neggras" he brought into this world. Whites and blacks alike used that term in the 1920s and 1930s. But my grandmother never forgot how she had been treated in Indianapolis, and I think she always quickly jumped to a racial conclusion, given that history.

In Mama's mind, Bloomington treated me differently because of my race. She could tell both by what I said and what I could not say during her nightly inquisitions. She knew herself to be right, but I didn't know. I just tried to get to bed each night before utter exhaustion overtook me. It seemed that when I lay down, the weight of my day came crashing down, but when I got up each morning, I could not recall a single slur, put-down, or disgrace. My disease was both protecting me and leaving me in harm's way.

"It's your race," Mama kept assuring me. She insisted that southern Indiana had a history of hating and hurting black women. Her intense and motherly cautions did not penetrate my PTSD-fogged brain, though. The issue of my having served in the military eluded her as a potential cause. For the Klan, the KKK was the ultimate authority. Serving any other was anathema.

My treatment was indeed changing, but my race may not have been my only offense. The KKK knew that I was mentally ill, but the lure of hurting a non-heterosexual West Pointer was delicious.

Dr. Kalen's Questions

Every sales rep got a one-on-one appointment with Dr. Kalen. Most people would assume that a one-on-one with a doctor dictates that you discuss your product, touch on current events, and then leave. At my one-on-one though, Dr. Kalen had a number of other questions for me. She was the inquisitor and I answered.

We talked in her tiny, horrifically cluttered office the first week of April 1996. Her office building was a small, drab converted house with rooms that begged for more space and light. We always hear that cluttered spaces indicate a bright mind and, ready to give credit for anything, I assumed Dr. Kalen must be brilliant.

We discussed my having gone to West Point and my confusion about what I would do in the future. I had attended West Point to start a military or political career, but I lacked an agenda. Dr. Kalen tried to burrow into what my agenda might be, and I told her that I did not have an overall plan, but that I thought that my public speaking abilities and desire to help people would translate well into politics.

"Are you conservative now that you graduated from West Point?" she asked me. Her tone hinted that she wanted to hear a response of "Yes."

"I've always been conservative," I assured her.

"Really?" She seemed surprised.

"It's my upbringing."

"Your grandparents are conservative?"

"My grandparents are Pentecostal, old-school style. I do not know if they vote conservative, but we are conservative."

"You mean socially conservative?"

"I mean both socially and fiscally. I just accept more people than many politicians do. I am not prejudiced, especially against myself." I remember being confused as to her meaning of conservative.

"Are you staying in Bloomington?"

"I live in Morgantown now, but I would like to move back to Indianapolis someday."

"So you will run for councilperson?"

Undeterred

"If I run, I will run for more than that. I figure I have to do something in business first to be able to afford my campaign, so that I don't end up a slave to special interests. Hey, if I run for mayor, you can be the city surgeon general." I laughed at that. She did not.

Dr. Kalen studied me with a strange, distorted facial expression. "You might be better off in science or engineering. There are plenty of career paths and support for that."

"I have an engineering minor."

"Good! That is promising."

"But I do not want to use it." She deflated. I continued, "I can help motivate people to do better for themselves."

"This is a conservative state. Few people want you motivating people." She was losing her temper.

"I think people need a little motivation. I can help."

"Again, we are a conservative state. No one wants you helping people. We believe that people should help themselves within their own group. We help our own people. We don't want to help everyone else."

When I asked what group she spoke of, her disappointment returned. "You could go far in an empirical career path here," she said, nodding. She explained that there were plenty of empirical career paths in Indiana, but I still did not know what I wanted to do.

Even from youth, I've never known exactly what I wanted to do, flipping from medicine to engineering, from the military to politics, from law to business. If only I could combine them all. I've only kept one guiding principle the whole time: the desire to use communication to improve people.

"I think of society as a big group," I told her.

"I'm trying to give you advice," she responded, frustrated. Her face distorted again, before becoming hopeless.

"Thanks for your advice, but I'm fine." I had given up on the conversation, too.

Perhaps she thought the conversation helpful, but it felt like "help" from someone who didn't know me well. I had not come to her office to discuss what job I would be "allowed" to do in Indiana. I wondered if all sales representatives were treated this way. If not, why was she so concerned with enlightening me on my prospects in science?

After that meeting, Dr. Kalen told someone that I was attracted to her. No one else was in that meeting. When I walked out of her office, my supposed love of tall blondes began with little input from me. To make things worse, the town quickly became fixated with a rumored love triangle: unbeknownst to me, Dr. Kalen was dating the KKK grand dragon's son, Dr. Tohm Hrisamolaz.

No one asked if I preferred tall blondes. No one cared. I was black and my words meant nothing. I had never dated a tall blond in my life, nor did I want to date one. It didn't matter. I was condemned as thoroughly as if I had actually hit on Dr. Kalen or said something inappropriate. Her boyfriend took issue with the very thought and decided to hold another vote on me. No one informed me of the accusation. Perhaps they thought I would find out soon enough.

Dr. Kalen's Screening

The Klan decided to get to know me a little better to determine plans of action. A few weeks later, my phone rang. "Tracey, this is Degan from Dr. Kalen's office. Someone canceled for lunch today. Can you make it?"

Of course, I thought. Who would not want the chance to present their products?

When the KKK decides that a person is leaving town against his or her will, someone is officially designated to boot or kill them. The grand dragon and his stewards make the decision to hold the vote, but someone must enforce the outcome. The enforcer can be a colleague, neighbor, or a perceived friend.

Dr. Kalen was chosen to be my enforcer. In reality, she was more of the lure, while her staff, Don and Degan, actually performed the necessary tasks. It was her boyfriend, Dr. Tohm, who informed her that she and her staff would extinguish me for the crime of being a lesbian.

Undeterred

One might wonder how she felt about that, given her high school treatment, but if anguished by her mission, she said nothing to me of regrets. Besides, had she objected to her role, she might have found herself in trouble too.

When I arrived at Dr. Kalen's office, Degan's smile, though broad, left me uneasy. She looked like someone hiding a secret. The KKK was turning up the temperature on their efforts to dislodge me. Calling me in had nothing to do with lunch, and everything to do with gathering information.

"Come on back." Degan's smile forced me to pause.

Dr. Kalen's office was one of the smallest in Bloomington. Two people could not comfortably pass each other in the hallway. I moved to the lunchroom with my gear in tow, but before I could start setting up my displays and materials, Degan said, "Tracey, before we stop working, come on into the lab and treat yourself to a free heart screening."

"What are we screening for?" I asked, entering the cramped lab across from the break room. There was a refrigerator, which held both medicine and food, and a long counter with cabinets for drug samples. Dr. Kalen was performing a test at the counter, but excused herself and put something in the refrigerator.

"Anything that might cause heart issues," Degan answered. *Logical in a cardio office*, I thought. She took my blood pressure, listened to my heart, and placed a thermometer in my mouth that also happened to take a sample of my saliva. While I paid attention to all of this, she also plucked a few strands of my hair.

"Why do you need my hair?" I asked, ducking too late.

"It can identify things in your bloodstream," Degan said.

I only had blood in my bloodstream, and said as much. Degan asked a battery of questions about my food and drink preferences. I confessed to a love of diet soda. Diet Coke or an occasional Diet Mountain Dew were my drugs of choice. The other drugs that she asked about had never entered my body. I did not smoke. I did not drink. I tied my shoelaces. I walked in straight lines. The questions went on and on.

I did not notice, but during my screening, her husband, Don, had disappeared, and so had my keys. I had put them down on the lab countertop, but did not pick them up again.

We went back to the break room. I prepared my displays, with no reason to think about my keys. When Dr. Kalen entered the room, Don still had not returned. I asked about him, but Degan said he had gone to run an errand, which I would later learn included copying my house key. We waited on Dr. Kalen to get her food.

Degan and Don

Degan was normally nosey while we were waiting for Dr. Kalen to finish working and join us, always taking an unusual interest in my personal life. One day, she asked me if I was working for the government or alone. She asked if I still had any ties to the military or with Washington. I highly doubt anyone who had such ties would have answered in the affirmative.

"We don't respect the US government. Military service means nothing until we retrain someone to fight like us." She took a big bite of her food and spoke with her mouth open and full.

"Like who?" I was curious.

"The smart soldiers who want to learn what they can do for us." She wiped her mouth with a napkin and threw it down.

"Who is 'us'?" I asked, unaware that she was a member of the KKK.

"I imagine you'll hear about it soon enough. We destroy people." The remark sounded sarcastic, but I ignored her tone. She seemed bitter.

"I don't really watch the news, or any TV for that matter," I informed her. I worked a lot.

Haley, the receptionist, started talking about local happenings, so I listened in. There had been a break-in in her neighborhood. I started to bemoan that, but Degan jumped in, informing me with absolutely no reservations that Don had been convicted of a felony in California for armed breaking-and-entering. He had been caught in a bedroom closet, because he had failed to note the security cameras.

Undeterred

It was a moment that ought to raise an eyebrow and start a person thinking.

"Well, I am glad he is okay now," I offered with unease. She said that he had turned out just fine and that it was just a phase he had gone through. She then confided that she had accompanied him and shared the felony charges. They had both served time for armed invasion in separate California prisons.

My discomfort peaked, but no one changed the subject.

"What have you done time for?" she asked me conversationally.

"Nothing," I answered, surprised. I did not catch her hidden reference to Jayns's tapes.

"It sounds like you have done time for something." I did not know what she was talking about. "Well, at least ours is no secret," she baited me.

I actually wished that it had remained a secret and started thinking about the specifics of a patient's file. The office has access to the name, social security number, and address of each patient. They know the specifics of their means to pay and their prospects for levying a legal stance. That is a lot of information for a felon to toy with every day in a doctor's office. It was, alas, none of my business, though I could not forget it.

Don returned. He was an overweight man with balding dark hair, who wore suspenders despite his belt loops. He expressed some bitterness for having applied for many drug sales representative positions, but his felony conviction halted any chance he may have had in that arena. He stood by the counter and asked how people in town were treating me, as if he didn't know.

I had had a strange experience recently, so I shared it. My young son and I had been in Columbus, shopping at the mall bookstore, which was part of a national chain. The bookstore clerk warned me not to touch a particular book on mandatory display. I did not note the title, but the clerk told me that the book was about "them," and "they" permitted no one to buy it, even though it was displayed. I asked why. She simply said, "Because it's about us." The KKK ruled that no one buy it.

A group of white teen boys were the only other people in the store, save the clerk, and they started following my son and I around, commenting on everything I touched. I was concerned about my son, so I decided to pay for my purchases and leave. As I walked out, they stopped short of the door and shouted that "porch monkeys should not be out so late after dark." I had never heard that term before.

As I told the story, Dr. Kalen's office staff just listened. "Interesting," Don mused. "Has that sort of thing happened here in Bloomington yet?"

I did not think so, but I was also in shock regarding my Bloomington treatment. The most I could say was that the people in Bloomington were angry people.

"No one writes about us and lives," Degan informed me. "We robodial their number so that no one can reach them. We offer them a figure they cannot resist, and they die after they sign the book over to us, and we take it out of print. Happens every time. We own everything printed about us. The writer dies owning nothing."

I didn't know what she was talking about. I thought perhaps she knew the writer of the book I was not allowed to look at in the Columbus bookstore. In reality, the KKK regularly threatens writers who might potentially write anything about them and their doings. The public must remain blind to their crimes.

The more I thought about Degan going around killing writers, the funnier the idea was. I mused aloud, "Here lies Tracey, writer of a children's book, mowed down by Degan, who now owns not only the words, but also the cute little illustrations." Haley and I roared with laughter, which only vexed Degan more.

A book was a book, I thought. But Degan was serious, and it unnerved me. Drug reps keep it light; I always joked a great deal with my offices. Humor, if only in my own thoughts, got me through the day.

"I didn't expect prejudiced treatment in Columbus, given its distance from Martinsville," I shared.

"Actually, the KKK is right here in Bloomington. After all, it's only about thirty minutes away from Martinsville," Degan informed me.

Undeterred

I was surprised, and I said so. I asked her if she knew anyone in the KKK. She assured me that they were all around me. "Are you expecting them to look different, or something?" she demanded.

I actually was, but I made a joke out of it. "Well, they will be wearing sheets, won't they?" I smiled, indicating that I was kidding. Degan, Don, and Haley just stared at me. They clearly didn't find it funny.

Degan's disgust exuded "We don't wear sheets," she informed me tersely. I imagined that her tone was meant to threaten me, but no warning bells sounded in my head by the inclusivity of the word "we." To my fogged, shocked brain, she could have been saying, "We, as in the office staff, do not wear sheets." And why would they?

Don said something to Haley in a kind of guttural language or code that I did not understand. Haley responded in a similar fashion and he nodded. Don and Degan repeated the display, then all three turned back to me to gauge my reaction. They had been speaking in a KKK code language.

"I speak a little Spanish," I volunteered innocently. "Of course, that wasn't Spanish."

"No. It wasn't," Degan spat harshly. She nodded firmly, becoming more incensed. "White robes are rarely worn anymore, only on special occasions. Things are modern and high-tech now. We also drive cars and not horses."

Now that's funny, I thought, but I was the only one who chuckled. I didn't realize it, but Degan was teaching me that you cannot recognize KKK members by their appearance, and that they identify and greet each other using a special coded language. I also did not recognize the threat inherent in this demonstration.

"It sounded a little like Russian to me," I continued. No one responded.

When Dr. Kalen finally entered and prepared her meal, the rest of us lingered a little longer than usual. After I gave my presentation about my products, Don and I talked about guitar. I had picked up an acoustic guitar while I was pregnant, but eventually holding the guitar became prohibitively uncomfortable. Once my son was born, I was able to take it up again. Now, I drove to Indianapolis to take lessons. Don bragged that he was a pro at guitar and claimed he could play anything by ear. I told him that I intended to play some of the songs I wrote at a local bar called the Wildbeet, and they took an immediate interest, asking for the date and time of my performance.

"How often do you go there?" asked Don.

"Every Sunday. It's amateur night."

"Where else do you hang out?"

"My house." They all laughed, but it felt strained.

Dr. Kalen excused herself. I thanked her for her time, noting that she did not make eye contact with me.

"I told Tracey about our time in California. I think I shocked her about us being young and getting in trouble there." Degan informed her husband once her sister left the room.

"That was a long time ago," admitted Don. To be polite, I asked them about their years in prison. "Felon" was such a big, scary word for me. Don and Degan were strangely fascinating, but I did not gravitate toward them. In fact, I did the opposite, leaning forward just enough to feign interest, but pulling back in the opposite direction, just short of genuine concern.

"What did you learn?"

"Well, I learned a lot about security systems." Don laughed. "In Bloomington I am a bit of an expert on security systems and video equipment. I advise many people on that and real estate."

"Are you an agent?"

"Well, not in Indiana because of the felony. I advise only family and friends. I got caught in California by the security system video."

I asked what kind of security system I should get, and he laughed again.

"The thing about security systems is that they are all good for one thing: they make the homeowner feel better. But the truth is that, if someone like me wants to get into your house, we are going to get in.

Undeterred

The alarm just slows us down." Degan nodded in agreement. They both held my stare.

He went on to explain that if they want to break into a house with a security system, they cut off the power at the service box, preventing the alarm from sounding. The assailant could then use a self-made key to enter the front door without a trace, using night-vision goggles. Mine would be the only power outage on the block, he assured me. By the time the cops came, there would be no evidence of a forced entry. The aftermath would appear to be a suicide, murder-suicide, overdose, or accident. Why bother with an investigation?

I considered that. The words were hard to forget, especially since I had started out thinking that he was talking about the behaviors of robbers, but what he ultimately described was murder. Assassination, even. The fact that a person could shut off the electricity without permission stunned me, but, then again, Don lacked permission to do most of the things he bragged about. Haley sat in silence, glancing at me on occasion with a rapidly disappearing smile. We made small talk for a while longer. Drug reps never cut off a conversation; we stay for as long as we are welcome. I just didn't understand that I had never been welcome.

We eventually bid our farewells and I gathered my material and my keys, which were now on the counter that Don had stood by, rather than in the lab where I placed them. Degan stopped me as I was leaving and foreshadowed that my prescription sales were going to skyrocket. "Don't think that it has anything to do with you, though. You are going to watch sales for your prescription drugs rise. Let's just be clear that it is not you; it's us."

"I don't understand."

"You will," she assured me and waved me away.

Only the criminally astute would summarize my visit to Dr. Kalen as having gone perfectly. I sat with convicted felons while not accounting for the whereabouts of the keys to my house. I provided hair, saliva, and blood samples, as well as my food and beverage preferences, my pastimes, and my schedule. While I was doing a meager job for Pfizer, Dr. Kalen was doing a great job for the Ku Klux Klan.

Bloomington's Second Vote

The Grand Dragon

The Hrisamolaz Family Medicine office summoned me one day a few weeks later. I had never met the requesting doctor because he had refused to meet me on previous occasions, even though several doctors such as Dr. Bando had "referred" me to him. Yet that day he elected to speak to me for some reason. I was excited.

Dr. Francis Hrisamolaz did not tell me that he was the grand dragon of the Indiana Ku Klux Klan. He also did not tell me that his son was dating Dr. Kalen, that they had been dating since medical school, and that he, Dr. Francis, wanted nothing more than for her to bear his grandchildren. No one in Bloomington told me this, but it was destined to become a deciding factor in my life.

Dr. Francis directed me to sit across from him at his desk. I tried to talk to him about my products, but he silenced me with a wave, showing no interest. He appeared to be about sixty or sixty-five years old. He tolerated no new information because nothing new mattered to him. Instead, he asked me, "Why are you dressed like that?" Confused, I studied my outfit and sought clarification. "You have on a man's shirt," he said.

Undeterred

I corrected him, for I had purchased my woman's shirt at Talbots. He probably thought the shirt was for a male because it had cufflinks, but the sleeves' cuffs flared with a feminine red print that matched the red cufflink.

His face resembled a sad rock that couldn't smile. It certainly did not smile for me. He was clearly unimpressed with my fashion choices.

"I hear your birth father was a drug dealer," he continued, as though such a subject naturally extended from women's fashion.

I froze, unsure what to say because I really did not know that myself. In my silence, Dr. Francis took my left arm, which rested on his desk, had me pull back my sleeve, and straightened my arm. When he failed to see what he was looking for, he asked for my right arm. I handed it to him and he repeated the process. I lowered my arm to the desk so that I could look for whatever he was searching for, too. I did not know what I should be seeing; I saw nothing unusual. Neither did he.

"With a history like yours, what do you do for recreation?"

"I play guitar." I did not understand what history I had.

"That's not what I mean, and you know it."

"Sir, that is what I do for fun. I play guitar." He had no interest in my answers.

"Someone like you coming into this town with your ideas is not what we are looking for." He took my left arm and, with his big finger, dramatically poked my skin three distinct times, looking at me. "I'm not a fan. My vote is for my son. I *stand by my son!*"

"I'd stand by my son too. Who is your son?" I was curious.

"Get out of my office!"

"What's wrong?"

"*Get out of my office!*"

Stunned, I sat looking at the floor, then at him. He was not joking. He waited for me to move, and I finally did. He followed me to the reception area and announced to his staff, "Look at her. Recognize her face and never let her in my office again. She just asked me to help her find drugs."

"What?!" I was stupefied.

His staff quickly dropped their gazes from me, and Dr. Francis disappeared back into his office. I thought about pleading my case, but staffers really lack the power to do anything anyway.

I had never met Dr. Francis's son, but another rep told me that I probably wouldn't. Every time she went to his office, his staff checked his samples themselves. You may never meet him, depending on what you carry, she assured me. Sure enough, I had no prescription data for his son.

I called Brian, who had me put in a help desk ticket to get my system corrected. According to my boss's data, Dr. Francis's son, Dr. Tohm Hrisamolaz, was my number-one prescriber. I told Brian about my upsetting encounter with the elder Dr. Hrisamolaz. He reminded me that I was pulling teeth with an unwilling patient in southern Indiana, and sometimes that rubbed people wrong. He reminded me that they have little diversity down there, but they are responding to me in scripts. "Keep up the good work. Make an appointment with this Dr. Tohm." Neither Brian nor I knew that I had just been officially rebuffed by the grand dragon of Indiana.

When I arrived at Dr. Tohmios Hrisamolaz's office several hours later, he declined to meet with me. All of the offices were starting to get in my face again, rejecting my giveaways, yelling at me, denouncing me, escorting me out, slamming and locking doors. I finished my day and dismissed the rebuffs.

Second Rampage

April of 1996 was a dismally wet one in Southern Indiana. The vegetation seemed pleased, but people like me who worked outside were tired of broken umbrellas, dashes for cars, and lawns celebrating new heights. The wind was so strong that I could not retrieve paper products from my trunk without ending up chasing them through the air only to have them settle in a puddle. Arguably, I could have stayed home. Characteristically, I did not. I worked.

Undeterred

There had been several weeks' respite after the initial backlash at me, but I never could understand that it was actually directed at me. I felt like the aggressions were a mistake on the part of the participants, like a bad rumor.

I cruised through Bloomington singing at the top of my lungs one Monday morning, happy to have seen my son over the weekend. I reached my destination, a doctor's office that favored a 1950s drive-up restaurant. The side of the structure faced the street, and a long, wide carport hung over the parking spaces. Turning in, visions of waitresses on roller skaters, chewing gum and transporting burgers and shakes, rose before me.

A doctor dwelled within, and with that doctor dwelled the potential of scripts. He didn't write many prescriptions, but I had adopted a call-on-everyone attitude, since I needed to boost my numbers. I went in with some free hospitality items, hoping that the staff would offer time to see the doctor.

I opened the door, and was immediately greeted by the smell of old people. Before I could advance into the lobby, though, the receptionist, having instantly spotted me, stood up and yelled, "We vote for Tohm!"

I smiled and figured there was a primary election coming up soon. I advanced into the room and greeted her, but she just yelled louder, "We vote for Tohm!" This attracted another woman to come forward from the back office, along with the doctor, yelling, "We vote for Tohm!"

"That's fine," I said calmly, assuming a particularly contentious vote was imminent. "I don't know the candidates here well."

The doctor pointed to the door and ordered me to leave. I had heard that numerous times in the past few months, but it made no more sense to me then than it had the first time. No, I could not bring lunch. No, I could not schedule an appointment. The doctor asked me to leave again.

Assuming he meant I should just come back later, I excused myself with a heavy heart and made a note to circle around and check back in before the day was done. Little did I know that by the time I rotated through my day, I would forget that office and its treatment of me.

I did not connect the Tohm they spoke of with Dr. Francis's son, Dr. Tohm. The grand dragon's son concocted some sort of contest between himself and me for the affection of his blond girlfriend, and all KKK members were ordered to scream, "We vote for Tohm!" at me until I vacated my job, my house, my territory, my entire life in southern Indiana.

After the 1950s restaurant-turned-doctor's office, I went to a glass-structured multi-office building nearby, thinking that, based on its architecture, it would be more modern and civil than the podunk place I'd just been. Unfortunately, even with broad daylight streaming in from on high between clouds, the people in the modern office suffered from the same antique hate. They circled like lazy lionesses surveying the ease of an attack. "We vote for Tohm!" screamed each office in its turn.

It's worth noting that these KKK doctors were knowingly playing this game against someone who was not fully aware of what was happening around her due to a clinical disease. With this kind of cruel mindset, they held all the power in this lopsided battle. If you hate someone for little reason, knowing your prey is unaware of your stalking him or her raises your entertainment level. I learned nothing from their spectacle, and they knew it.

All I could wonder was why everyone was getting so worked up over an election. Did they all think I was someone else? Did I look like another candidate?

Maybe the Tohm they spoke of was a drug rep with a competing product? Brian had told me that I was doing well against my competition. If so, perhaps I would soon be losing scripts in various offices to this Tohm. I did not think to run. I thought only to work harder.

"We vote for Tohm!" I heard it going from office to office. They were back to storming at me, screaming, and pushing me to the door.

"You are not staying this time. We vote for Tohm!"

"Take it up the road, Honey!"

"I'm your Pfizer rep," I explained, thinking they had me confused with someone else.

"We don't want you."

"We vote for Tohm."

I sat in my car and buried my face in my hands, numb to my treatment. My underlying emotions were sadness and guilt for not being able to sell in a given office. Every office was worth money to Pfizer. I started the morning with a deficit. I just wanted to do my job.

I thought through my next steps. Given the previous halt of such behavior, I thought the resurgence was only a minor disappointment. I was by now used to angry faces spewing hate in Bloomington medical offices. I kept on calling on eight-to-ten offices a day, and in eighty-five percent or more, I was met with the same collective venom. Only the message had changed: "We vote for Tohm!"

The KKK believed that I had hit on Dr. Kalen, and they were openly siding with her boyfriend, their leader's son. Everyone knew this but me. I simply thought they lacked command over their emotions, and had dissolved into bad days again. With each new day of screaming, I talked through it, walked through it, until the day was done. At night I forgot it all, sleeping deeply in preparation for another day, another round of "We vote for Tohm."

For old time's sake, someone would occasionally throw in a "Get out of town!" The abuse went on for weeks, months. I went on attempting to do my job for weeks, months.

My Reaction

I found this new behavior especially confusing, given that Brian said my numbers were going up. I was immediately in shock again with this new round of abuse, and I started dropping these experiences from my memory. When asked, "How are you doing?" I did not know how I was doing, so I defaulted to "fine." Each day I repressed more and more. I woke up expecting a great day, because I had no recollection of how bad the previous day had been. This new onslaught was more vicious than the first had been and the treatment had expanded to include restaurants and other public establishments. They were trying to break through my disease to reach me.

I showed up at doctors' offices each morning surprised that people spoke of kicking me out, even threatening my life. I could not understand their behavior, so I just defaulted to work mode and showed them my newest shipment of pens, paper, candy dispensers, or other supplies. Some hurled these back at me. I left these items strewn around, thinking they would appreciate them when their day got better. I asked if I could help them with whatever troubled them. I kept contributing, despite their words or deeds. All we can do in this country is contribute. America can ask for no more.

Focus on the positive, I preached to myself. I visited doctor after doctor who told me that they had "voted for Tohm." Still not knowing who Tohm was, and given that Brian kept saying that my numbers were going up and that I was doing better than I thought, I assumed that my numbers were hurting another antidepressant sales rep, probably one named Tohm. That made sense to me in my PTSD-fog.

Other Offices

I still visited my other cities, of course. They were tranquil compared to Bloomington, which seemed to have strong groupthink reactions to everything, while other towns took things more in stride. No one seemed to care about the Tohm thing in Columbus and Seymour.

I started having problems with my senses, particularly with my sense of smell. People with PTSD can have blurred vision and hearing problems, but smell? That's not normal. Yet I could not figure out why everything smelled metallic, even myself. I bathed as often as I could and washed my clothes constantly, but nothing helped.

My phone calls to family grew shorter. When I got home every night, I collapsed, exhausted. Often, all I could do was grab a Diet Coke and rest. I could rarely remember how my day had been. I also could not concentrate on much. The ceiling and most of the left wall of my bedroom were the only things I could recall well anymore, because I stared at them each evening. When I woke up each morning, I knew where and who I was, but I struggled to recall where I'd been the day before.

I drove to a nearby office and asked to see the only other nice doctor I knew. She peeked out into the lobby and quickly pulled me back into an exam room. The doctor assured that I smelled normal, and not at all metallic. When I doubted her, she said, "Tracey, you are just stressed." I told her the doctors in town were all damning me, but my boss said that I should just press on.

She offered me a topical medicine and told me to come back if it got worse. She did not want me to develop anything serious, like OCD. I knew the term from my West Point psychology class, but I knew that wasn't me.

"You are definitely stressed, Tracey," the doctor repeated. She held my hand, trying to reassure me.

"I have never felt stressed before. I do not feel stress now. I'm fine."

"Did you just graduate?"

"No, I graduated in 92."

"Okay. Where did you go to school?"

"West Point." My answer worried her even more.

"You should know stress."

The smell issue lingered for months.

The Window

Dr. Kalen came up to the window that separated her staff from the public in the office lobby. She normally made a point of visiting with a drug sales rep when we came by to leave products. With a deep breath, she asked me, "How are you feeling, Tracey?" She sounded genuinely concerned.

She clearly didn't want to hear "fine," so I told her and her staff that I smelled something funny. Don and Degan looked at each other, then Don laughed.

"How are people treating you?" Degan asked, as she and Don ate one of the muffins I had brought them.

"Okay, I guess." I felt numb, and Bloomington had blended together into one angry mob in my mind.

They knew better. The town was trying to uproot me to leave.

"Have you met Dr. Francis?" Degan asked.

I confirmed that I had and told them everything about our encounter, including the arm-poking routine. Degan looked at Dr. Kalen, who backed away, shaking her head in disbelief. Arm punching meant something from the grand dragon: overdose.

"Well, that is a little much," Degan said after a pause, waiting for a verbal response from her sister. Dr. Kalen did not speak. Her eyes grew large and she stared past me.

Haley, the receptionist, reminded me that I always looked dashing. She personally liked my wardrobe, especially my cufflinks. I joked that if I really wanted to dress like a dude, I would borrow Don's suspenders. That won me a brief laugh from Haley. Degan and Dr. Kalen had disappeared behind the receptionist's wall to whisper. Dr. Kalen's voice suddenly went up an octave, but I could not decipher her words.

"I don't know how you are doing it, Tracey," Haley said, shaking her head. "I just don't know."

"Doing what?"

"Your job."

"It's easy, really. You would be a great rep because you are nice and have a sense of humor." She lost eye contact with me.

"Have you been to Dr. Francis's son?" Degan returned, pressing on in a firm voice. I said that he had declined to meet with me, which also caused Degan to eye Dr. Kalen, who was still hiding out of my sight. I heard a cry, a soft outburst, but I did not know if Dr. Kalen was mourning or had hurt herself.

"Try again!" Dr. Kalen suddenly commanded from further down the hallway.

Undeterred

"Call on Dr. Francis's son again," repeated Degan. Then she left to console her sister.

If I were a sassy person and had known Dr. Kalen was dating the son of the grand dragon, I would have asked her to arrange the meeting; unfortunately, I lacked information on almost everything that swirled around me in Bloomington. After a while, you stop trying to read the behavior of secretive people. It's better to just be who you are and continue on. That is what I was doing, and I felt certain that, sooner or later, it would work out.

The Son

I checked my hair in the mirror. I sported a wild Whitney Houston look, so I brought it down a notch before heading to the office of Bloomington's top infectious disease specialist. Granted, he did not have much competition in town at this point.

He sat behind a small desk directly in front of the door. Nothing else about his office was memorable, except that his nurse, Trudy, was helpful and kind. He had declined to see me before, but had suddenly changed his mind, according to Trudy, who summoned me. My new numbers noted that he was the number-one prescriber of my anti-fungal in the hospital setting.

I greeted him pleasantly. He said nothing, nor did he smile. He sat behind a desk with so little on it, I gathered that the office was not his. He had short, dark hair with no facial hair. He motioned silently with two fingers for me to sit down.

I shared some clinical information about my products, but his expression rebuked the effort. I sensed that he did not actually want to talk to me. I asked him if he had any success stories that I could learn from. He declined. He asked if I had anything to say to him, but he did not want to discuss Pfizer products.

"You have *nothing* else to ask me?" he inquired. I should have asked why he had called the meeting. I declined.

The fact that he expected someone in shock to ask him something about which they are in shock defies logic and medicine. A great deal of the hate I experienced was not logical.

We sat there in silence and he stared at me with tight lips. There was clearly something that I was supposed to know or say or do that I didn't. There was always something that I was supposed to know in Bloomington that I didn't. Eventually satisfied, he silently motioned with two fingers for me to leave his office.

I walked out to my car, digging for my handheld computer. I recorded a call with no samples given; I addressed him with his title and last name. I wish I had been more curious about his first name, which was Tohm. Without PTSD, I could have made the connection.

Wildbeet

A few nights later, I played guitar at the Wildbeet, which was on the busiest northbound vein of town. There was a radio station across the street that offered to let me preempt my songs. I declined because I was already unsure about my upcoming reception. A part of me asked myself, *if people are hateful, why are you putting yourself out there?* I did not know if all people in Bloomington were as hateful as the ones I worked with.

The club manager, Steve, was always nice to me. He was the long-haired, grungy, how-does-he-keep-a-job kind of guy. He helped me pick out an amp for my guitar before the performance, so I trusted him as being nicer than other people.

I noticed that my food tasted metallic, even my Diet Coke. I grew rather irritated with the cook, and took my plate back to protest. A server told me that Steve was the only one who could make my food. When I pointed out that someone else was at the stove, she rephrased her statement: Steve had given orders that no one else was allowed to make my food.

When confronted, Steve claimed that he'd made my food according to the recipe. He even asked me if I were stressed, which only aggravated

Undeterred

me more. I wanted a new everything and I stood by, watching him prepare it. That offended him and he said he would bring it out to me. It still tasted metallic the second time, but not nearly as much. I ate some of my food, but soon suffered a headache. I thought my performance nerves were getting the best of me. Steve said that he would give me aspirin, and I was grateful. He gave me five. I took one and put the rest in my jacket pocket.

My turn came, and I mustered the nerve to get up on stage and play my songs. The crowd liked it, or at least no one left. I received okay applause. I was both happy and relieved.

Getting off the stage is when I felt it. The stage stood only two feet off the ground, but as I exited, it felt more like two miles.

Steve offered a hand to assist me so I would not fall into oblivion. He led me to the musicians' waiting room, and I sank down onto the couch. Relaxing, I looked back at the stage and thought through my inability to get down. I felt like Steve had saved my life. I waited on the couch for about twenty minutes before getting ready to go. The blonde who had sat down next to me offered me a date, but I had just wanted the applause. Her insistence struck me as memorable, as though dating me was some kind of mission she was on. She knew my occupation, which meant that someone from the offices had coached her. I moved away from her.

As I left, Don, Degan, and Dr. Kalen greeted me. My eyes were blurry and I was exhausted. Don offered to drive me home, but I declined. As I walked out, Steve gave me the money I'd earned, and said that I'd played well for my first time. He went on to say that I must be pretty special to "the organization," because Tohm had a vested interest in making sure that I had a "good time." I questioned that, and he said that Tohm paid top dollar for everything. That made no sense to me, given that I bought my food and drink myself. Tired, I shrugged it off.

What Steve was trying to tell me was that the metallic taste I had detected was a drug he had been ordered to put in my food and drink. The Ku Klux Klan was not above chemical warfare. I just couldn't see it yet.

On the way home, I had trouble seeing the road. That had never happened in my life, so I drove slowly, carefully. Despite being impaired, I made it home, drank some soda, and slept.

The next day, someone called my boss and suggested I was under the influence. Bloomington's medical staff was clearly trying to create a statistic, and they were getting more and more creative. Fortunately, I only had to tell Brian the truth from my perspective to squelch the story. He believed me.

Awakening

I opened my eyes one morning to see my new handgun pointing at my face. I lay flat on my stomach and left cheek, but my head was cocked back to the left. My right thumb and pointer finger were wrapped around the trigger of my handgun up to my first knuckle.

My first thought was, *How did I get into this position?* For a second, my thoughts lulled me into believing that I was in no danger. Of course a soldier would have the safety on. I just lay there, groggy, debating my current view. I felt exhausted and heavy. I slowly unwrapped my fingers from around the trigger, then slid the weapon forward, above my head and away from my face. The safety latch pointed to the 'off' position, which baffled me. Pointed right at my head, in my hands, with no safety. Bizarre.

My right shoulder ached. When I massaged it, the whole area felt sore, but one pinpoint was much more tender, as though I had been injected with something. I rose and felt heavier than my normal self. I walked through the hallway, past the other two bedrooms and bathroom, through the living room, and into the kitchen to get soda for my dry mouth. Something told me to pass through to the rear room beyond the kitchen. The back door stood wide open. Air and sunlight trickled in.

Instantly alarmed, I closed and locked the door as if to stop someone from walking through that very moment. I had walked through the entire house to get to that door. I checked it every night. I could not remember doing it the night before because I could not remember the night before, but my routine dictated that I never failed to ensure it was locked. *What if someone is in the other rooms?* Numb and incapable of feeling the fear of a normal woman, I did not run. I slowly walked back through the rest of the house naked. Other women may have run, screamed.

I checked the other bedrooms. I rechecked mine. I checked the closets. Jordan was with my grandparents, so at least I did not need to worry about him. There was no one else there. I started my shower and picked out fresh towels, even though I had a hunch someone still might be lurking. The noise of the water drowning out possible sounds meant little to me. That is the power of shock and dissociative amnesia for a person with PTSD who rarely avoids aggressors. I carried on.

When I ran my hands over my rear, I found a jelly-like substance on my buttock. It was just a dab, but I had no explanation for it. Groggy, I smelled it, spread it between my fingers, and wiped it away on a piece of toilet paper before flushing. I could not have landed it there. It made no sense. My body felt sore and my brain could not understand it–like being punched to the ground and standing up without remembering the blow.

Mine was a case of being hurt, feeling pain, and not recognizing why the pain happened. Someone had obviously entered my house. Someone had injected a drug in my shoulder to knock me out. Someone had violated my body. Part of my confusion came from being drugged and part of the confusion came from being mentally ill and chronically not able to remember trauma, suffering from habitual memory loss. Mine is a dangerous disease.

I normally stand in the shower longer than most people. It's almost a relaxation ritual for me, soaking in my share of extra hot water. This day was no different. A long day awaited me.

Bottles

My small house was always quiet. I do not watch TV or listen to the radio, so I could always hear every sound I made to break the silence. I spent every evening alone in my house, talking only to my grandparents or mother by phone.

I spent my weekends with my grandparents, or they came to see me, bringing my son. I missed him, but with everyone in town not speaking to me again, I felt certain that my sales revenues were going back down. I could not afford to slow down yet. I hoped for a speedy turn-around.

We bought an inflatable boat to maneuver my ponds with my son. We would go out on the water and fish together, while Papa stayed on the bank. I am glad that we never caught a fish in that boat; it would have taken little to tip us. Papa caught a number of fish, and when my mother came down, she would empty the pond of large bass. She proceeded to tease me that she caught the biggest and best for good eating. I, however, caught nothing but babies. I barely believed the fish existed until my mother and Papa reeled them in.

My grandmother saw them first: Heineken bottles peppered the ground outside my bedroom window. She confronted me, as though I knew their origin. I assured her that I do not sit outside my own bedroom window for Heineken breaks. I checked how fresh they were and found that they weren't aged. I had been in the house for some time, and I had already cleaned the yard thoroughly. The bottles had arrived since I moved in, so someone was standing outside of my bedroom window, drinking. Neither of us said anything further about it.

She threw the bottles away. I played with my son. I knew that Jayns preferred Heineken, but she would have been in hysterics if I told her.

There were times when I had to leave my territory for meetings in Indianapolis. There were no more drug tests. I flat-out told Pfizer that I wasn't taking any more. If they doubted that I worked, given the computer logs of my activity, they could fire me. I just wasn't going to drive that distance to pee in a cup and turn back around. They either understood or conceded, because no one brought it up again.

Brian was the one who had hired me and was my direct supervisor. A middle-aged man with a comb-over, he helped me adjust to civilian work expectations and attitudes. Other sales reps in my district teased that the first thing he did when he got in and out of our cars when we toted him around was to grab a comb and comb the comb-over. I did not notice until they joked about it, but lo and behold, he did.

When he first interviewed me for the position, he told me that there were "small minds in southern Indiana," but that I was strong enough to open doors and bend brains. At the time, I did not interpret this as a race issue, but rather as an education issue. Of course, there are those that would say these things are one and the same. Brian was always encouraging and supportive, and I was grateful to him for that.

During my summer meeting in Indy, he sat down with me to discuss my sales. We looked at my numbers, and even the numbers that predated my tenure in the territory, and they showed that my sales were starting to move astronomically. Degan was right: my sales were through the roof. The doctors purposefully prescribed every drug I had hand over fist, all the while screaming at me as though I were an animal. The question remained, was it enough to relocate me or was I running out of time?

Flu Shot

I left my home early on a Thursday morning to travel farther south of Bloomington than the Bedford/Seymour line in an effort to find new customers. I rarely ventured as far as Salem, Indiana, to search for "friendlies," but the chill in Bloomington, even on a summer day, invited a hunt for warmth. Salem only had a few doctors' offices, but I thought it might be worth my time.

I usually listened to music and practiced my vocals during such drives. The sun, uninhibited by a single cloud, called for an exquisite day. Sunlight made the trees and town brilliant. Warmth penetrated my windshield and windows to toast the car. It was the kind of balmy day that persuaded most people, including most drug reps, to take the day off. I did not.

Had I known the true nature of the people surrounding me, I would have feared the car that followed me all the way from Bloomington to the parking lot of my first office in Salem. Once I parked, a doctor with short, dark hair and a medium-to-tall build approached my car from the front left. It was Dr. Tohm Hrisamolaz. His father, Dr. Francis, the grand dragon of the Indiana KKK, passed around the right side of my car, disappearing around the rear into my driver's blind spot. Thursday was both the Hrisamolazes' day off, but my refusal to leave town had obviously created more work for the two Klansmen. Both were dressed in blue scrubs, just like most of my clients.

I focused on the younger man at my car window. He introduced himself as "Tohm." I did not make the connection.

"Tracey? Tracey Brame, right?" I tried to remember where I had met him. "Yeah, you are my representative in Bloomington. You don't recognize me?" He smiled and acted friendly, and reintroduced himself as a specialist, one of the greatest prescription writers of my anti-fungal. He knew my drugs and knew me from the hospital. He knew other people I called on in the hospital too.

My brain was holding on to Jayns, my treatment in Bloomington, being booted the first time, being booted the second time, the Wildbeet, the intruder in my house, the beer bottles outside my window, and a host of other things no one could draw out of me until my disease let them go. So when he asked me if I recognized him, I responded, "Vaguely. I'm sorry, but your name is familiar. I just have a lot of doctors."

"Surely you know my father here," he pointed to the older man in my blind spot. I ought to remember the mean man that had poked at my arm and screamed in my face that he voted for his son. Unfortunately, though the confusion of my disease, I didn't.

"You work for Pfizer in Bloomington. You're our representative. Our partner office in Indianapolis has done your drug test a time or two. Sound familiar?" No doctor in Bloomington was partnered with a drug testing facility in Indianapolis in the 1990s.

Still, the reference to testing was recognizable. "Oh, I don't go up there anymore. It's too far," I said casually. He must have spoken to Pfizer or Dr. Kalen's office, because I didn't think I had told anyone else about the drug test.

Undeterred

I should have noticed the familiarity, the casual nature of the exchange. He smiled a lot. The hunt is not always abrasive. Sometimes it's fluid, using insider information. You may not think twice about a person, given that they know so much about you or those close to you. It's easy to miss.

"Well, my father and I are coming to you today." Dr. Tohm continued comfortably. "Pfizer shared that you have not had your flu shot this year, Tracey. I'm headed back to Bloomington, but I thought I'd go ahead and give you your flu shot rather than having you come by the office. They are having you come to my office because you seem not to want to go to the Indianapolis office again. Did you tell your receptionist off?"

"I did, because she does not understand how far that drive is. I cannot get back to my territory in time to call on any offices, and so I lose a whole day of work. I can't afford that."

He nodded understandingly. "Well, we don't want you to miss more work. Everyone seems to know you down here. You can take your shot here. Brian called this morning and told us to try you here."

"Brian, my boss?"

"Yes, Brian your boss. How do you like him?"

"He's great."

"Have you been tired?" A doctor in the KKK that regularly terrorizes people certainly knows that people with PTSD are tired after trauma.

"Yes, I drive a lot."

"Well, you can stop driving now that you are here. Have you been feeling a little numb?" I nodded.

For the most part, only doctors know that PTSD shock patients feel numb. We literally cannot gather strong emotions, good or bad, because the shock is too crippling. We may seem zoned out or uninvolved, because numbness overlays the emotions of shock.

"Let's get your flu shot done. I'll need your left arm."

"How do you know I'm tired?" I suddenly thought to ask.

"Tough job. How are you doing at work?"

"Okay. Brian is happy." He laughed.

"A lot of people in Bloomington aren't. They talk about you, eh? Are they pretty tough on you?"

I did not know how the doctors in Bloomington were with anyone else, so I could not make a comparison. In my mind they were growing tired of yelling at me, but unleashing two Klansmen to my car door to clarify their dissatisfaction might have been more telling, had I known the true meaning of the encounter.

He asked me if I knew of another black woman from the area, but I did not recognize her name. He said we had a lot in common, but that she had died in the 60s. He promised to introduce me to her later. I thought it was an odd, figurative expression. I did not know he meant it literally.

In hindsight, I realize that he was referring to a black female sales representative that was killed by the KKK in the 1960s, but I could not come up with her name on the spot. According to Dr. Tohm, she was smart and articulate. His Dad had met her before her death.

I was confused by his talk, and not interested in hanging out with anyone new. Dr. Tohm assured me that she and I would get along; supposedly, we had many similarities. He was set on my meeting her.

"Are you pretty confused by how your offices feel?" he asked. He feigned empathy, nodding and smiling, sometimes broadly but other times with a nod and almost a wink.

A lot confused me. The offices' inability to have a good day baffled me. I was offended that anyone thought that I took drugs, as hard as I worked. I stressed over how to find day care for my son, so that he could come live with me full-time. I overcompensated for my tiredness, because I did not want to disappoint my boss or my grandparents. The beer bottles outside my window completely freaked me out, as did hearing someone walking on my property at night. I focused on the little things to keep myself going.

PTSD patients teeter in confusion at times when we have not fully come out of shock. Doctors, better than anyone, know that. Every moment of the day we unconsciously fight to make sense of the clouds that have formed in our heads. When the clouds part to clearer weather, lo and behold, we figure out what happened to us. The miracle is that we

Undeterred

somehow manage to stay on-task. If a criminal detects that they can push us off balance, as if we are on a teetering bicycle, they will almost always take advantage of the opportunity.

Dr. Tohm Hrisamolaz, the kind son, the keeper of flu shots, the holder of insider information, unrolled a blue towel from the hospital on my car windowsill and administered the flu shot. The needle mechanism was metal and its arm-like structures clanked before and after the shot. I remember his hands moving in a bird-like fashion to mock my going to sleep. He laughed aloud to his father, and a more astute person would identify little about his demeanor as being kind.

What I failed to register was that he and his father were not helping me at all; they were creating a statistic. Dr. Francis was videotaping me and had come closer to the driver's window. Their plan was to film me compromised in an office or two, and then authorities would find me in my car, dead from a drug overdose. Various office staff members would attest to having seen me high and no one would bother investigating my death. They were putting a lot of energy into humiliating and then removing someone. Still, their whole plan was coming together nicely, leading to a deadly end on that ordinary, sunny day.

I do not know how the medicine made me feel at first, but I quickly fell asleep and slept in my car for some time. When I finally woke up and got out of the car, I could not stand on my own. Dr. Tohm generously helped me get into the building by letting me lean on him. I had trouble balancing, but he got me to the door, opened it, and nearly tossed me inside with a wave to the receptionist. She knew Dr. Tohm better than I did. To her, he was the grand dragon's son.

I stood there, afraid to approach the counter, my legs wobbly and also entrenched like tree trunks. The receptionist laughed at me. I did not know it, but I was famous in southern Indiana thanks to virtual communication and a broadcasted picture and video. Everyone in the KKK knew me as having been voted out of the region.

"I don't know what he has going on with you, but you're going to have to get that paper to me for a signature, even if you crawl. I ain't helping you," the receptionist said unkindly.

Needing to give her the necessary paperwork to get my job done, I stepped forward, fell, and finally crawled, slapping the form onto the counter. It was that important that I get the job done. As I stood, the counter actually held me up. She checked samples and the doctor in the office signed for them, after waving at my Bloomington escort.

"You're going to feel a lot better when you leave. I can't figure out what you've been waiting for," the doctor said, shaking his head firmly.

We stumbled to the next office. Dr. Tohm insisted that another office was not necessary, but I insisted. Based on my previous experience in the town, I knew that all of the doctors' offices were clustered close together.

I stumbled into the next office and placed my back firmly against the southern wall to hold myself up. I normally kept my right coat pocket filled with drug rep pens, and my left pocket filled with personal items. When the nurses found out I carried with me the secret pill for yeast infections, they begged for samples and for pens. I obliged, but reached into my left pocket by mistake, producing a few receipts and a tampon for viewing. I was disoriented.

Smiles disappeared. "Try your other pocket, honey. How you feeling?"

"She will feel a lot better when she leaves."

"What's taking you so long to leave, honey?"

"Looks like it's getting too late."

That doctor, who normally did not sign, signed for samples, waving to my escort, who was waiting like a bird of prey at the door. We left.

In a nearby town worked a physician who sold pharmaceutical samples for patients for profit. He would later be arrested, but right now the KKK grand dragon's son stood at my car window, bent on giving me flu shots for free. I feared the aforementioned doctor because he knowingly broke the law. The latter, however, won me over with his concern that I not take ill from the flu. It never even occurred to me that it was summer and flu season was long over; people usually get flu shots in the fall.

Back outside, Dr. Tohm was trying to talk me into a second dose–a special booster shot, he said. Something inside me whispered "danger," and I got in my car quickly. I closed my door just as he reached for it, and

Undeterred

his broad smile evaporated into fury. I somehow found the wits to lock the door. Hearing the click, he punched at the window in frustration. He started speaking through the glass.

I needed the booster, he assured me. He had concocted it just for me. His smug persuasion quickly turned to near desperation. He wielded a metal syringe in one hand while explaining my foolishness to his father, who was waiting expectantly for the final blow. I watched and listened with growing interest from my driver's seat. I was suspicious.

A roster is kept at West Point, for everyone has to have a flu shot or log a reason as to why they couldn't have one. No one in my company had ever failed to get a flu shot in my four years at the Academy. But West Point did not force anyone to take the concoction twice in the same year, let alone on the same day. A booster was unheard of.

The first "flu shot," sent to me by the same folks at Pfizer who did blood draws, seemed completely logical to me at the time. But even to a mentally ill person, the idea of a second flu shot was absolutely disconcerting.

My escort from Bloomington seemed a tad shiftier to me now. Didn't I like the first one, he argued? Wasn't it great? Anyone trying to woo me with "the best sleep I could get in my lifetime" doesn't know me well. I sleep out of necessity, not for pleasure.

I headed to my next office and the Drs. Hrisamolaz followed me, but stayed further back since I had regained my wits more than they expected. When I emerged from my next call, we bickered again.

When I emerged from my final call in Salem, Dr. Francis occupied the passenger seat of his car. His "helpful" son feigned "orders" from Pfizer, my employer. Well, amazingly, so did I. I got in my car and he lunged for the handle, but I had immediately locked it. He punched the window several times.

How important that window was. It separated me from an attempted murderer, but had he broken it, it would have told the truth. It would be much harder to rule my death an overdose or suicide. Had that glass broken, would Dr. Tohm Hrisamolaz claim that he broke it to save me? No one planned for the glass to break and, thankfully, it didn't.

I started the car. We quarreled through the glass mightily, and I left for my last stop of the day–out of town, to his chagrin, and possibly saving my life in the process by sheer accident. On that sunny day, I navigated Pfizer's dark-green Chevy Lumina north to I-135, the direction of the rest of my life. I drove away compromised but victorious, despite the father/son pair's preying on my disease and weaknesses.

There's nothing like a fighting spirit to stall fate for a moment. I still had no idea that I had enemies or had motivated any kind of vote against me. After the first month of trying to kick me out of town, they knew of my mental illness, but they buckled down, insistent on breaking through my disease to teach me a lesson. However, no one, not them, not me, not anyone, could wear down and break through the barriers my illness had erected to protect me.

Could the KKK kill me without the theatrics? Certainly, but the attempt to exterminate me had become entertaining for the KKK voters of southern Indiana.

They now wanted a show. Dr. Francis was videotaping our interactions in order to share with the other members who would want proof of my end. Members I would learn paid a premium for such video access.

Plus, Dr. Tohm, son of the grand dragon of Indiana, and participant of a speculative, but amusing, competition for a girl like Dr. Kalen, needed to make a statement. What better way to do so than to stir up the electronic crowd with a slaughter that combined humiliation with entertainment? To the matador I pranced, guilty in his mind of hitting on his girlfriend, who had turned me in for demise. Only they and their audience thought the game hilarious. I, on the other hand, drove off one "flu shot" richer, suspicious, but still clueless as to why he had nearly broken the glass of my car window.

The thought of purposefully hurting a shock victim who is just trying to spread cheer for a living leaves me speechless. It's like killing a five-year-old for not cooking Thanksgiving dinner.

Well, in shock, I could learn nothing. Yes, I did graduate from the best military academy in the world, but I could not understand the concept of hate in my own country. You certainly cannot break someone out of PTSD. When in shock, our brains will not change on schedule or command. The only thing that leads to change and healing is time.

Sodas

Degan called to invite me in to the office one day when she had a canceled appointment. I took it because Dr. Kalen seemed to be one of the few doctors in town still being nice to me. We made the usual small talk, but everyone clamored to know how I felt. They said they had not seen me in a while, but no one asked me why.

I brought a diet soda with me. I had grown so accustomed to them tasting metallic and bad, that I did not notice that this one from the filling station tasted great.

"How are people treating you?" Degan asked as we sat in the small break room waiting on her sister.

"Fine." I had long since accepted the idea that everyone in southern Indiana was perpetually in a bad mood, so things were as good as they could get.

"How are your numbers?"

"My boss is excited, so my 'Change the World' campaign must have worked."

"What's that?"

I had expensed every version of Eric Clapton's single, "Change the World," in both southern Indianapolis and southern Indiana to send to doctors as a thank-you card: "For every time you change someone's world with Zoloft, thank you." The letters "O-L-O" in "Zoloft" formed a smiley face. My numbers spiked after that month.

"And you think *that* was it?" Degan had to erase any credit I might think was due me.

Changing southern Indiana eluded me. "I like to do something different every now and then," I explained.

Don cleared his throat. "You know, we have noticed that when a town does not want a drug rep, they can do one of two things: run them out of town, or write the hell out of their scripts until they are promoted away."

Degan stared to gauge my reaction. I paid no attention to the stab. Pfizer had slated me third in line for Rookie of the Year, thanks to my growing numbers. I worked hard and received relatively good responses in other cities. I did not recognize Don's insult or the dichotomy between my sales and my treatment. I no longer recalled Degan warning me that my numbers would grow due more to "their" efforts than mine.

"How's the soda?" Degan wanted to know.

"Good," I said, focused on the one I had.

"You still downing them left and right?" Degan wondered.

"How do you know that?"

"You don't remember anything that you say to us, do you?" asked Degan, forcing a smile.

"I see a lot of people. I drink a ton of soda."

"That's perfect," she proclaimed. "Keep it up."

I thought she meant my work ethic.

Missing or Dead

I went to the office of four small prescribers, and they invited me to their back office area to go over my products. They were all new male doctors who talked up the "vote for Tohm" thing. One of them genuinely asked how I was doing. When I said I was doing fine, he denied it for me.

"You are in over your head," he assured me in a low voice, as two of his partners exited. "They will use you like a sex toy and then you will disappear. Maybe you will move. Maybe you won't, but you cannot win this competition."

"I'm not in a competition. I am simply doing my job."

The younger of the two remaining doctors stood and laughed. "You're so outnumbered it's funny." He walked away, tickling himself by chanting, "I vote for Tohm."

Undeterred

The first one stayed a little longer. He was a tall, slight-looking man with a sincere countenance. "She did not do you a favor by putting your name in to this mob."

"Who?" I was perplexed.

"Dr. Kalen."

"What did she put me in for?"

His patience dwindled. He stared at me and even took a step or two in my direction, then seemed to register that I had no clue what he referred to. It seemed to hit him all at once. His mouth fell open.

"This is pathetic," he whispered to someone or something other than me. "You are a lamb waiting for the slaughter. Do you realize what is happening?"

"No." I offered a blank stare. He seemed to be troubled.

"You do not want to get attention in Bloomington," he said in a lower voice. "They intend to hurt you. You will turn up missing or dead."

My PTSD led me to conclude that the doctor was crazy. I wondered if he had bumped his head.

The doctor, informant of my doom, grew tired of waiting for me to understand, and walked away.

Dr. MacTech

I dropped by Dr. MacTech's office, the dermatologist. Once again, she looked more composed than friendly. "When are you going to give up?" she asked me.

"Give up what, ma'am?"

"Well, do you think you are winning?"

"My boss says I am."

"Your boss doesn't like you either, I suspect."

"He loves me."

"That's his decision. My decision is to vote with the crowd. I vote for Tohm."

That hurt. She didn't even prescribe antidepressants, so I asked what Tohm, still a rival drug rep in my mind, meant to her.

"Well, we attended IU Medical School together, same year group, and I personally think that he and she look like Ken and Barbie. He must like the role, because he is doing a number on you. Look at yourself. Why do you have sores on your face? Acne? I think not."

She was the dermatologist. Of the two of us, only she knew that certain street drugs caused open sores to erupt on the face. Perhaps she knowingly diagnosed me as a warning. She seemed to look down on me as much as she spoke down to me.

"He doesn't play fairly, does he? Your life will get better when you quit. You'll feel a lot better when you move. I'd move quickly if I were you." She left the room.

I called my mother at work. She tried to calm me, telling me to call my manager. If I was really unwelcome there, they might move me. Was it worth staying to win Rookie of the Year? At that point, nearly every doctor openly called me to leave town. I would forget by nightfall, but now my mother knew by day.

"Wouldn't it be better if you just left and found someplace where you are wanted?" asked one doctor.

Another would warn, "The hard decision is the right decision."

All unanimously concluded, "You'll feel better once you leave."

Dr. Bando, Jr., son of the IU basketball team physician, flat-out told me that he did not care what Tohm did with me; he would support him no matter what.

I often joked that I was a legal drug dealer, a play on words, given that I peddled a pharmaceutical company's drugs. The joke was funny when I first got to town, but one doctor pulled me to the side one day and asked, "Young lady, do you know that you are up against the primary illegal drug dealer in Bloomington? You are in danger."

Overdose

I drove home, registering failure after failure for the day. At home, I played guitar until I got a headache. I had nothing to take for it. I sat on my bed, holding my head with one hand, and my second, metallic-tasting soda for the night in the other.

I suddenly remembered the aspirin Steve had given me at the Wildbeet all those weeks before, which were still in my coat pocket. Taking two, I immediately felt better, then worse again. I felt sick.

Gayle, a friend of my guitar teacher, called, and I told her that I likely would not make it to her party the next day. She was trying to get me to meet other people and break my solitude. I told her I was sick. She asked me what I was taking and I answered, "just aspirin." She asked what kind, but I did not know.

I called Mama and she wanted to know the same thing: what was I taking? As with Gayle, I could only speak in a whisper. Unlike Gayle, she refused to hang up. She asked me if I needed her to call an ambulance; I must have sounded particularly bad. I whispered no, that nothing was wrong and I just needed sleep. Not aware of my actions, I downed one more aspirin and most of my metallic-tasting soda. I told my grandmother that I was fine and that I would call her back after I slept for a bit. I didn't.

I lay across my bed diagonally, my limbs strewn about. My breathing was uncomfortable and shallow, and my pulse slowed. Blood ran thickly from my nose. It looked as though I was overdosing, but if anyone would have told me that, I would not have believed them. If I could have risen above my body on that bed at that moment, I would have slapped myself with a scream, "You have never sought to get high in your life. Wake the hell up!"

Home Sick

My eyes opened.

Birds sang outside my window, though there were no trees on which to perch. My own room appeared unfamiliar to me. I felt as though a train had hit me in the forehead, smashing my brain and body flat to the bed. I literally crawled to the bathroom and, with great effort, clawed myself upright to the mirror above the sink.

My eyes looked like Jayns's: dark, wild, and desperate. My nose bled. I rinsed dried blood from my cheek. For the first time in my life, I was scared of my own appearance. I felt sick. My hair favored Albert Einstein, leaving me speechless.

I lay back down in bed and called my grandmother, assuring her that I was fine. She praised God with mighty "Jehovah!"s and "Hallelujah!"s that compounded my headache. I assured her that I would stay home from work until I felt better.

My sodas poured flat. I opened three cans, all with no fizz. Curious, I rotated one of the cans to find a tiny dot on the back. A perfectly punched pinhole the size of a needle puncture opposite the drink opening explained the can's lack of carbonation. All three cans had these tiny puncture holes in them, as did the two remaining in the carton. Was someone breaking into my house to spike my sodas? Not to my PTSD shock-fogged brain. As far as I was concerned, I had discovered a distribution problem in southern Indiana.

I stayed home for a week or so, wrenching from the effects of detoxification. Someone wanted me addicted to something. Thoughts of doom overwhelmed me. Nothing made sense. Sheer exhaustion overrode everything. I could barely maneuver, not straying from the fetal position in my bed. When I felt strong enough to maneuver, I noted that my sense of smell was returning, as the roses Mama planted behind my house smelled like roses, not metal.

While I was home sick, I called my mother over and over again. She concluded that I needed to move.

After that week at home, I felt better. I was uneasy, as though I had been through something; I had, even if I didn't fully realize it. I felt lightheaded and unsure, but I was alive.

Brian

Brian thought it only natural that I should need to rest, given my rigorous work ethic. I never even asked for vacation time nor took days off given that I perceived myself as behind.

He did tell me that there were times when reps rubbed doctors the wrong way, to the point that they should be moved. When I questioned him, he said that what a doctor prescribed demonstrated a personal choice or belief in efficacy, a habit. To change that habit, it generally took repeated calls with the same medical message couched in different ways before it clicked. Doctors resisted change as a result of having studied medicine in habitual and repeated patterns. To change habits as quickly as I had, I must have been assertively pushing them out of their comfort levels. How could I tell him that to change habits, I needed only to anger doctors until they prescribed anything to rid themselves of me?

You could rub a doctor the wrong way while getting him to change his habits. Brian told me that there were two types of reps the company moved from a territory: the very worst and the very best. "You are not the worst, Tracey. You are now second in the district. You started out at seventh. You'd be first in two months if we left you where you are."

Instead, he told me to prepare for a transfer. He also reported that he might be moving to Chicago for a promotion. Either way, he would take care of me. I thanked him, but he really ought to thank Bloomington for his promotion.

Leaving

When I returned to work, I hit the number-one prescribers first. I dropped into Dr. Kalen's office, and Don and Degan were circling the window as I came in. Everyone asked how I was feeling, and everyone rudely assured me that I would feel better when I left.

I told them that I was fine, never felt better, which was clearly not what they expected to hear. Still, it was the absolute truth.

I went on, and asked them if they knew why soda cans in southern Indiana were manufactured with tiny holes near the top. All activity suddenly stopped. They seemed surprised, irritated. Don and Degan looked back and forth at each other and at Dr. Kalen. Taking their silence for confusion, I told them I had discovered that my sodas were going flat because they had holes in them.

Everyone agreed that was odd. Degan and Don seemed exasperated that I had made the discovery and they searched Dr. Kalen's face for their next steps. She appeared stupefied as well, looking back and forth between her staff and me.

"What do you make of that?" Don finally asked.

"Well, they were getting flat soon after I bought them, week after week. I did not know why, but I stopped drinking them a few days ago."

Don knew why. He and Degan had worked hard getting themselves into my house with a copied key each week to inject my sodas with something.

"I'm better now," I assured them.

My smile deflated Don. "Really," it was a statement, not a question. *Would they have to start all over again?* he wondered. We stood there chatting amiably, with me not associating them with attempted murder. The KKK generally preferred suicides, overdoses, and accidents, because no one investigated those and made arrests for them. His mind churned through options. A myriad of restaurants around town prepared my lunch or breakfast and I always skipped dinner. His only reliable entry point into my system was poured through a soda can.

Changing the subject, Don wanted to know if I talked to anyone interesting on the Internet. I said I had pen pals. He informed me that Degan's second job entailed getting to know people's computers a little better.

I asked how long she had been doing that. It turned out that that was her other pastime, much like security systems were for Don. Those were their jobs for the "organization": they set up networks so that people had better connectivity and could gather information easily. That conversation introduced me to what would be a major realization in the years to come: that Don and Degan conducted cybercrimes for the KKK. Time would spell out the specifics for me.

Talking to Dr. Kalen's staff was always strange and interesting because, unlike the people who worked in some offices, they all had these

Undeterred

different activities going on. No one else bragged to me about their secondary jobs or activities, but Degan and Don seemed to want me to respect theirs. They enjoyed taunting me; the hunt thrilled them. I asked how they had time for each other, and he said they worked as a team.

"Security systems and the Internet?"

He confirmed that they did it for the "organization." He seemed to assume that I knew who or what the organization was, and assured me that their work was invaluable to many in town. I guessed that that was why they always seemed busy. Degan was often downright harried, and mean to boot. Hanging out in the doctor's office seemed to be a chore for both of them. I could tell they both had greater ambitions. Degan later commented on the low pay she earned in her sister's office.

Degan asked if I had noticed anything different about my computer. I said no. I had a work computer that had great security and a personal computer from West Point that still worked fine. She asked me if I still kept it on my living room floor. I did not recall telling her this, so I asked how she knew that.

"Oh, you chat a lot. You must have mentioned it at one of your lunches." *That would make sense,* I supposed. The computer indeed lay on the floor. She said that I might want to move it before something entered it. I asked her what could get into a computer, and she chuckled, alleging dust or debris.

I announced my imminent move. Relief, but not joy, filled the room. I rarely got this gratifying reactions in my offices in Bloomington, but suddenly people were at least satisfied that I was leaving. Dr. Kalen approached the window again, and she asked when I was moving, specifically. "Soon," I told her. Degan said she would be keeping up with me. On the surface, it seemed like a nice thing to say.

Don smirked, "So, you are passing on beans or corn?" He asked the question, "Beans or corn?" incessantly. He was asking which I liked best with fried chicken. I did not eat a lot of fried chicken, so I never answered. The real question was whether I wanted to be buried in a bean field or a cornfield. He could arrange for another alternative or just pick one for me, since I was clearly too dense to voice a preference. "Is it beans or corn today?" The joke never resonated with me. I ignored it.

"Please give me the date," Dr. Kalen asked gravely. She wanted an endpoint. Was she satisfied with having me gone? I did not ask, nor did I know to.

"Dr. Kalen, I do not know when I leave. I'm going to look at houses in Indianapolis this weekend. I have to sell my house." Don perked up at the potential of new business. When I told him that Pfizer was going to handle selling it, he waved me off and walked away.

"Tracey," Degan called me back as I approached the door. "You have figured out that Dr. Tohm is Dr. Kalen's boyfriend, right? They may even get married. The entire town wants that."

"No, I did not know that," I admitted. "That's fantastic though. I hope they are happy." I meant it; I had no reason to not mean it. I was nothing but happy for Dr. Kalen, and I had zero interest in pursuing a relationship in Bloomington.

A game being played with my life over other people's possible nuptials made sense to Degan and the Klan. To them, a mentally ill black woman who was attracted to other women was interfering with a storybook wedding, but no one bothered asking how that could happen if both individuals slated for the alter were satisfied with their relationship.

Degan searched my face for either confirmation that they had taught me a lesson, or that she had somehow hurt me. "Well, you know that Don recently had an experience with a black woman?" Dr. Kalen was out of sight, but I stepped back into the office since Degan seemed to be confiding something personal.

"No, I did not know that."
"It didn't mean anything."
"To her?"
"To him."

Undeterred

"Are you telling me you're having troubles?" I was preparing to leave Bloomington and felt no tenderness toward Degan, even if she were dealing with an extramarital affair.

Somehow, she seemed satisfied. She was trying to tell me something, but I wasn't sure what it was. She taunted, "You won't begin to remember everything that we did to you."

"What did you do to me?" I was just too ecstatic to be moving to associate Don with the incident in my house involving the jelly-like substance.

"You know I'm present for all his crimes?"

"I thought he was reformed since your time in prison."

She chuckled. Much later, I would realize that she and Don were the ones entering my house, tainting my sodas and tampering with my body to quench Degan's thirst to hurt another. Her having compromised my computer would take center stage later.

Cognizant of nothing, standing there before Degan, I was just happy to be changing territories because Pfizer said so. I waved goodbye and continued on with my day.

Everywhere I went the rest of that week, I made sure to tell all of the angry people to beware of holes in the tops of their soda cans. It concerned me as a southern Indiana phenomenon, since no one I knew elsewhere in the state had such problems. My awareness of the tactic irritated many in Bloomington. Still, I did not want the angry people of Bloomington to be at risk. I cared greatly that their drinks be fizzy, even if they cared little for me.

PTSD can manifest or compound after many different events, including injuries, deaths, accidents, and natural disasters. It also results from demeaning, hostile, or life-threatening events, like being kicked out of a town, stalked, and almost murdered in broad daylight to amuse an electronic mob because you were born smart and articulate, or because you did not know or care that two people were a couple. As bad as my PTSD was from Jayns, my treatment in Bloomington had certainly exacerbated it.

One last issue hovered as I prepared to leave Bloomington. I had watched Dr. Tohm Hrisamolaz and his father, the grand dragon, try to kill me face-to-face. I had repressed the memory, but, as doctors who terrorize people through their social organization, they knew that I would eventually remember. Dr. Tohm's mission changed from driving me out of town to coercing me not to report or publicize his pastime. The Indiana Ku Klux Klan rallied behind him in this new mission to destroy my will to recount what had transpired at their hands.

INDIANAPOLIS, 1997

Kelly

I settled into Indianapolis quickly, which thrilled my family. I knew it would take heroic efforts to move this new territory, so I just studied the numbers and tried to find a logical plan.

Indianapolis's mindset was different from that of southern Indiana. No one cared about my dress. Offices were huge and seemed less catty than those in Bloomington. No one sent you across town to be eyeballed by another person. I had grown so used to the small-town mannerisms that I almost forgot that other people don't act that way.

Kelly, a medical assistant, did not take no for an answer when I said I could not hang out with office staff outside of work. She literally said, "Yes, you can," and told me we were going to an art fair.

My grandmother's voice claiming "No you can't," echoed. The memory of the West Point instructor who asked if I were a lesbian surfaced. Was I? Kelly suspected that I was.

We began dating. I ventured away from Mama's condemnation into something new, my first lesbian relationship.

I bought a house just inside the northern border of Indianapolis. My son had a room that, unlike in southern Indiana, he could sleep in every night. I was home, and we were happy. Kelly visited often. My mother liked her. My grandmother did not.

Dale

I had a new boss, a man round in body and face, who was teeming with a desire to impress and insisted on rehashing my success in Bloomington. Though Dale lived close to me, north of Indy, the rare occasions that I saw him face-to-face were at company meetings. No one came to those meetings from Bloomington because, once again, the company had trouble filling the slot.

Dale had relocated from upstate New York. He considered himself a mover-and-shaker insider who could get things done, and he sought to bring that out in all of us. Movers and shakers reach out to people, and Dale reached out to me every time the regional vice president asked him when he'd last ridden side-by-side with a rep. Whenever he wanted to ride with me, my phone would ring, and fifteen minutes later he would be camped out in my front seat, trying to add value to an otherwise simple process: calling on offices.

One day, we were taking a break sitting in a Starbucks when he asked me how I had liked working with the Ku Klux Klan. I said that I hadn't worked with them and he assured me that I had.

"That is all Bloomington, Indiana, is these days," he schooled me.

I thought it strange that a New Yorker was suddenly a Klan expert. The truth was that my castling had already begun when I'd lived down south, and I could not focus on Bloomington or anyone or anything referencing it. I rarely discussed my experiences down there, and could not even remember what "Klan" meant anymore. Dale offered no sounding board.

He switched topics. "Are you on speaking terms with your grandfather?"

The question did not take me aback at first. I grant people room to be foolish. I told him that my grandparents had visited from the country that very weekend and that we had all had a great time. My son really enjoyed spending time with them.

"I would just think that it would be awkward seeing him."

"Why?" I wondered.

"People have different ways of doing things."

"Like what?" I asked.

"Coping," he offered.

I prefer soda to coffee and I'm not a fan of sitting around in Starbucks, acting as if I like coffee, so I was pretty much ready to go. I had just met this guy and did not really want to have a conversation about coping with him. He did not seem like a psych major. His big plan was to push people to the limit so that he could get the credit. His style was far from Brian's, and Brian's style worked well. The district had done great under Brian.

"Are you ready?" I asked. I felt fine ignoring whatever he was attempting to elude to.

"Am I making you uncomfortable?" he asked, feigning concern.

"No, we are making each other late. Let's hit another office. Let's work."

Concert

Kelly liked going to social events. Young, fit, and attractive, she liked heading out downtown to walk the canal, catch an art fair, or enjoy an ethnic festival with great food. My son usually came with us and we had a good time together. We could not take him to a concert though, so when Lilith Fair came to Noblesville, Indiana, just north of my house, we let him stay with Mommy, a more-than-willing sitter.

Kelly insisted that I not work late the day of the concert. "I do not see why you work late all the time. Most drug reps barely work at all. You have a date on the books to go to a concert. Please, please, take off a little early. It's one day out of 365. You can do it," she urged. She shook both hands to the heavens, irritated.

Tracey Brame

I worried that someone would find out. Plus, once you start slacking off, you keep slacking off. It's as habitual as work, just with the opposite results. As a result, I pulled into my drive long after she did. She was already prepared to leave. I quickly changed clothes, and, though I had not eaten lunch, I forgot to grab anything to eat or drink in the house, and we headed out, my stomach completely empty.

When we got to the concert, we met up with two of Kelly's friends who seemed nice. Kelly and one of them braved the line for drinks. They were all getting a beer, so I decided to try one, too.

When Kelly came back, I downed the beer in gulps. I welcomed the large cup and, famished and parched at the same time, I had much of Kelly's too. I did not notice her growing frustration. I wished that she had bought food and told her so. When she asked why I was starving at that hour, I informed her that I had not eaten all day. She deflated; she had foreseen this.

Singing was not harmful, so I started off the concert in my chair with some numbers of my own. Kelly's anger increased as my volume did. I kept singing. I kissed her in public. But it was when I told her that I loved her for the first time that she accused me of being drunk.

I was having a blast. People seemed to be moving around, so I thought it made sense to talk a little louder; after all, it's good to be heard. I also wanted to walk around and meet strangers. I almost never did that, but it seemed like a good idea at the time.

I lost the opportunity when a concert official kicked me out. We had driven there in Kelly's car, so she had to leave with me. I sang the whole way to the car so she wouldn't feel like she had missed out on the concert. At that moment, I don't think she loved me back, but I sure loved her. She warned me squarely that if I vomited in her car, we were done. I convinced her that I really did not want to vomit. We were home in forty minutes and I went straight to bed and slept until morning.

She rose with the break of dawn, ready to argue. She ordered me to get over my headache so that we might have it out.

"How did you know I have a headache?" I asked, groggily.

"You should!" she yelled. "Don't you get a headache after drinking?"

I confided that I had never been drunk before. I just thought the beers would fill my stomach because I'd rushed around all day without eating or drinking anything, so I wouldn't be late. Perhaps I should have had soda or water. She forgave me and I learned the dangers of drinking on an empty stomach.

Dale, Again

My boss continued to pursue something in our infrequent conversations, but I did not know what. He seemed to know of Jayns's legal problems and asked me if I were involved. Still in shock, I did not recall Jayns's legal problems.

Dale baffled me. He casually mentioned a childhood incident: our male Shepherd had showed me his wiener, and I had retrieved scissors to cut it off. I didn't do it, because my neighbor called my grandmother and alerted her that I was prepared to operate on the poor animal. Mama canceled the procedure.

My boss confided in me, as if to a friend, that he knew that it was impossible to excite a dog. Jayns's tapes must have reached him, too. When I told him I was offended, he berated me, saying that I had to sit and listen to whatever he was talking about. I thought it was impossible to have a decent conversation with him, and I gathered that he knew my ex-husband. I spoke to him less after that.

Dr. Reenie

Only three doctors from Bloomington had touched my life positively. The first treated me, the second treated me duplicitously, and the last treated me well. That final one recognized me before I recognized her.

"How are you, Tracey?" she smiled.

As I stared at her, my brain calculating, I was able to return, "Dr. Reenie. What a pleasure."

She had moved from Dr. MacTech's dermatology office in Bloomington to a more lavish Carmel, Indiana, office north of Indianapolis. She was still a junior doctor, but working her way up. She looked fantastic, and a bit more sophisticated with her hair pulled up and little wispy strands floating freely. Dr. Reenie always offered to sign for my samples in Dr. MacTech's office, yet emphasized that I really needed to have the senior doctor sign. I was immensely glad to see her.

"You weren't the only one," she began.

"What do you mean?" I moved closer to her.

With a lowered voice she enlightened me, "It's not just race, ethnicity, religion, and seemingly everything else. It's also money. In fact, its mostly money."

"Please explain."

"I'm obviously not in Bloomington anymore either, Tracey. They ran me out of town too. They only want 'friendlies' making money there. If you don't join, you don't stay. If you stay, you have to contribute and be a part of the group. Refusing will get you ousted or worse." She looked around to ensure that no one overheard us.

In shock about Bloomington, I did not fully relate to "the group" that she spoke of, but I knew that things were very catty, sometimes mob-like, there. Happy that her move had given me a friendly face to confer with and visit, I asked, "Which office did your husband settle down at?" He was also a doctor.

"Bloomington. He stayed," she told me as I tried to understand the logistics. It seemed strange for married doctors who liked each other to live so far apart. "Their favor outweighed our marriage."

"He'll change his mind," I assured her. I did not understand why anyone in Bloomington did not like her. I had no idea who these people she spoke of were. Still, I privately thought that Dr. Reenie was better off on her own. Her husband had always been condescending to me, appearing to enjoy the misery and confusion that being outnumbered brought to my life. "Friendships are not that deep."

"Trust me," she laughed before she started whispering again. "He's embedded."

I stared.

"The group only shares business with insiders. He is one of them now. That is why I am here. They give you a decision to move. If you don't make that decision, they make it for you."

She hugged me suddenly. "We were all really worried for you down there."

"You were?" I asked, shocked.

"When they ordered you to leave, you stayed and stayed and stayed, Tracey." She laughed, so I did too. "Those of us outside of the group seriously thought they were going to hurt you. I'm glad you are well. You are fine, right?"

"Always." Maybe that was a lie, maybe not. Can you argue that a PTSD sufferer really knows whether or not they are okay when they are in shock?

I was still processing the part where she thought someone had told me to leave. I did not recall that. I did not know to appreciate that she was not one of "them." I just moved on to the next office, happy for her because her new office seemed better and nicer.

In hindsight, Dr. Reenie represents a softer brand of indifference in the US, where someone knows that crimes are committed and that people are hurt, but they do not or cannot see themselves making a difference. They do not participate, but they do not interfere. I credit Dr. Reenie for trying to warn me in Bloomington, which was more than her friends did. Still, removing oneself so as to not witness a crime becomes the most comfortable option for adults sometimes. As kids, we ran and told an authority.

Quitting

I had to travel to Chicago to meet with my regional vice president about an issue, and he referenced Jayns's tapes, just like Dale. He openly bemoaned my having been molested as a child by my grandfather. His words were shear nonsense, and I stopped him right there.

"Sir, what are you talking about?"

"Listen, it must be hard on you. We are committed to helping you in whatever way possible. Just let us know if you need something."

"What?" I was incredulous. "My granddad is fantastic. He'd never hurt a fly."

"I'm confused. Why would you say that he did it then?"

"The question is *when* did I say that he did? I could not have made a statement like that." It was probably spliced together on Jayns's tapes, but I did not know that.

We were in a standoff. He apologized, saying that something he had heard was not what he thought.

I started looking for a different job, and soon landed an offer with a software company. I informed my chain of command in the morning and my phone rang in the afternoon. The president of the sales division at Pfizer wanted to meet me that week. I flew out the next morning.

Ernest was based in Pfizer's New York headquarters. He was African American, brilliant, and influential. He had a stately office decorated with woods and leathers that warmed the room. A view of the New York City skyline came with the corner office. I had seen him loom at meetings, but he seemed like a reserved man, in keeping with his tenure and level of work. He asked me to have a seat as he closed the door.

"You're amazing, Tracey," he said, sitting before me.

"Thank you, sir." I was grateful, but did not know why he'd made the statement. He needed me to wake up in that conversation, but my disease needed me to sleep.

"We have had no one succeed in that Bloomington territory as you did. We could have left you there to win the contest, but it was best to get you out of there. Don't you think?"

"I'm happy to be in Indy with my mother. I'm still trying to wrap my hands around what I have now."

"You can do anything that you want. I hear you write songs?"

Undeterred

"Yes, sir."

"I want to keep you, Tracey. You are safer with us than with any other company, because we specialize in you."

"Black people?"

He laughed, "No, people who have experienced trauma. You sell one drug for that, but as a company we care about the minds and success of people. You will not be judged here. You have the spirit of a fighter. With you, I know one person in Indiana is doing the right thing every day. We can turn our backs on you in that respect, but I will not let the company turn its back on your disease. There is only one problem." He paused for emphasis.

"These audiotapes that your ex-husband is sending our doctors are fabricated. We know it and we can prove it. But we need your help. We will go after him for you."

"I don't know what you are talking about. What trauma? I never made a tape. It's not me."

"Tracey, it's not *him*. Someone is posing as him interviewing you. Your answers are cut and pasted; we have researched it. It is your voice, but it's not you. We know you. We love you. The tapes being mailed have been spliced and rearranged. We need your help, Tracey."

He specifically said "tapes," plural. Since I had not made any tapes or consented to anyone making tapes of me, I felt unaffected by what he said, my PTSD kicking in full force. I could not remember that, at Fort Bragg, Jayns had spliced together tapes of my voice saying all kinds of things, and disseminated them to the 82nd Airborne. My colonels, every last one of them, knew. They still had faith in me because they fought for me.

Ernest asked for specifics about Dale's taunts, which I had made official complaints about. I told him all that I could remember. He then asked me to send him my detail book. A drug rep's detail book lays out the district's official sales message and strategy as determined by the company and supervised by the district manager. We flip through it over lunch conversations with doctors. The federal government monitors what a company can say and show to doctors. I agreed to share mine with Ernest.

Before I left his office, Ernest called my name. When I turned around, he assured me that I amazed him. I thanked him, but with the haze of my disease, I did not know what I had done to earn such praise. I moved on.

Kelly mourned the change. She had dated my job as well as me. I felt like I was getting ready to go through something, so I let her go. I usually went through things alone; it's the only way I knew. With a different person's life, I would never have broken up with Kelly. Hurting her was not my goal. I just knew that worse turbulence lay ahead.

First Insurance, 1998

Recruited, 1998

If you did not meet expectations at the Massachusetts-based software company, our manager cursed you out. Women were not spared. I tried to focus on the specifics of making sales: cold calling, presentation, closing techniques. I enrolled in an expensive sales training course to improve on my own. The software product itself required a great deal of learning, which I loved.

I sold enough my first year to win the national award trip to Hawaii. I took both my grandparents, though Mama had to stay in the room a lot due to her deteriorating health from a virulent lupus attack on her brain. I took her seashell hunting on the beach. She and Papa were thrilled to see the ocean.

My boss worshiped money. No amount was ever enough. We lost people by the droves. Our company recruited talent, abused talent, and leaked talent.

One day, I asked my recruiter how her job worked. If we hired someone and they lasted, the recruiter kept the money. The hiree had to stay ninety days. If not, the recruiter had to return the money. I imagined the profit in that for the recruiter.

"How much do you get paid?"

"Nine thousand dollars," she answered

Interesting. I started thinking about going into recruiting, and began to look at every employee in the software company as a paycheck. I made appointments to speak with recruiting firms to figure out if I should work for others or start my own business. I was honest and upfront about my desire to work for myself. They appreciated the honesty.

One business owner told me that I should just start out on my own. Another told me I should come join him, because he could give me a leadership position and help me develop experience. Both companies were management recruiting franchises. I went with the latter, which eventually took on a non-franchise name, Protist. I explored the possibility of selling my house and moving closer to my new office and a local realtor listed my property.

The recruiting firm was located above a bank in Avon, Indiana. Berk Milhere owned the firm, but he tried to bill it as a woman-owned business to get diversity credit with major food and beverage companies. Mitchel Betard was his Vice President and Lurea, Berk's wife, passed out mail and performed administration work around the office. The office had an outer reception office and conference room, but the employees worked in a bay area in back. There was only one room that the sales representatives could not access, a locked room in the hallway.

I arrived ready to make cold calls, the first and only black person in the office. I matched my first candidate with a hiring company only nine days after my start date. Then I made another and another. I had three sales in less than a month, and no employment contract. Berk asked me to sign a contract so that he could pay me for my work.

I signed it, but later wished that I had not. He refused to honor the promise of a leadership position that he had used to recruit me. He started having new people sit with me to train, but I was not being paid for their production. I refused to train them.

Undeterred

After a couple of months, I talked to the other owner across town that I had met, and he advised me to quit immediately. He and many others in their field knew that Berk did "shady" things to stay in business.

The longer I stayed, the more Berk could say that he'd "made" me. I turned in my two-week notice and Berk immediately invited me to his house to discuss a "leadership role." He harped on the fact that my profit to him appeared to hover at the $40,000-a-month mark. My quitting would change that to zero. He had a vested interest in keeping me.

Insurance I

The more compelling reason Berk wanted me close was because he owed a large debt to the KKK. To help pay off this debt, Berk was ordered to find a way to convince me not to speak out about my treatment in Bloomington. He called himself an "insurance man": he insured that I, the victim, did not damage the KKK's reputation by speaking out about KKK crimes. Many organized crime organizations have such a position, though the names differ.

When an insurance man is called to do a job, he may enlist a family member to help him, though he may choose anyone that he does not mind knowing he has obligations to organized crime. It is not mandatory to involve others, but failing to take the assignment can lead to death. Thus, for the insurance person, it's him or the victim. Once he gathers some kind of information that could potentially "hurt" the victim, he will issue the threat: "Everything we have on you will go public if you open your mouth."

The problem with issuing such threats to a PTSD victim is that many do not recall the threat for years. Indeed, knowing my illness, the KKK used multiple insurance people with differing crimes to dissuade me from believing that my life has equal value to Dr. Hrisamolaz's reputation.

Berk seemed almost disorganized about accomplishing his mission for the KKK. The day I was supposed to come by his house, he invited me into the locked room in the office, the only room off-limits to the sales force, at the end of the workday. There was a conference table, a few chairs, and a safe with two drawers, nothing more. Berk and Lurea showed me the contents of the upper safe compartment: countless stacks of wrapped hundred dollar bills. When I turned back to Berk, he stood behind a camera with a red dot blinking, pointing a gun at me. He poked me with the gun two or three times, as if to make me jump back in fear. I didn't. I went into shock.

He then asked me to count out the money. Lurea placed handfuls of bills on the table. There was too much to count. He made me sign papers, some of which were duplicate carbon copies. The top layer of the carbon copies had rectangular boxes at the top or bottom of the page, in between which I was supposed to sign. He kept saying, "Don't touch outside the box."

Obviously, Berk and the Klan wanted a person in shock to seem liable for signing papers without knowing what they were signing. When the exercise was over, I slept in my car. I was exhausted. I would have gone home, but Berk had invited me to his house to discuss my promised leadership position.

When I arrived at their house that evening, Berk and Lurea were not there yet, nor were Mitchel and his girlfriend, whom I was told would be there as well. When the four of them eventually showed up, they invited me in through the garage, where a white, fairly beaten-up van sat parked. Berk made me sit in the driver's seat. The van was old and lacked bucket seats. It was a stick shift. He held a gun on me and forced me to touch the steering wheel, clutch, and signals. I went deeper into shock.

He clearly wanted me to appear to have driven the van somewhere. Nobody asked me, but I could not, nor can I now, drive a stick shift.

We went into the house and gathered upstairs in the recreation room, where Berk started talking about real estate insurance fraud. He discussed how to scam insurance companies by hiding items for owners and staging break-ins around town. He had apparently done this to raise money early on to keep his company off the ground when family loans ran out.

It was hot and I drank a diet soda. Lurea had picked it up for me because she saw me drinking it in the office all the time. They would not let me open my own cans, but rather brought it to me already opened in the other room.

I wanted no part of their conversation, but it lasted absolutely forever. Berk called me into the closet of the recreation room and lifted a mounted coat hook on the wall. Behind the large hook were more stacks of one hundred dollar bills. The wall was filled with money. I was speechless. He asked me to touch it, but even in shock I knew I had touched enough money that day. "Are you interested now?" he asked. I repeated my answer: no. I would rather leave his company than work under the table in a way that could get me arrested.

The Klan, I would learn, prefers to stack its cards in its favor when hurting someone. "We can prove this, or we can prove that." A lot depends not on what they can prove, but what the victim will believe they can prove.

Berk considered what to do with me. I finished off my soda, which was spiked. I passed out at his house, and woke up at mine.

Voyaging, 1998

I awoke in my own bed the next morning, remembering only bits and pieces of the previous evening. My memories were garbled: Berk driving my car to my house; a **BOB & TOM** radio show sign along the highway; Mitchel sitting behind Berk; pulling into my driveway; Berk carrying me in to my house; another car pulling in behind us. I remembered cameras flashing, men talking, laughter. These memories meant nothing to me.

I did recall my readiness to quit, but I did not recall anything coherent about the previous evening. Unable to decide on how to discredit a shock victim, Berk had orchestrated a smorgasbord of accusations, one of which surely had to stick.

I still held a lot suppressed in my subconscious memory: Jayns's rape, Bloomington's oustings, and a host of smaller arrangements by the criminals involved. I was quite sick, having not let go of anything through recall. While not true of all PTSD sufferers, my own pattern releases events in chronological order. It is classic operational inventory: first in, first out. Nothing had been released yet. I hoarded terror. Understanding Berk would have to wait.

On Monday, I drove across town to pick up my belongings from the office. My calm, determined demeanor struck a nerve with Berk. As I started packing my stuff, he called me into his office with Mitchel. We sat at a small table by the door. Lurea closed and locked the door behind her as she left, leaving the three of us alone for the second part of the insurance agent's job: first there is the harm, and then the threat. Berk's plan was to hold the "evidence" he had against me over my head.

"What are your thoughts now?"

"About what?" I asked, obviously having no recall of the events of the weekend.

"About your job."

"I am not training people for free in a commission-only job. Commission-only means I work for me, not for your employees. I'm not training them without compensation. Plus, you have built up a core business with consumer product goods and beverage companies. I want to work in information technology sales. You don't do that."

"What were your impressions of last week, and specifically Friday?" He seemed irritated that I held onto the same stance as before, but I remembered everything surrounding the trauma, forgetting the trauma itself. Trying to teach someone to fear you while they are in shock is useless. Only a few things bled through from the night at his house.

"I'm great at recruiting. I am not going to learn insurance. I've no interest." The insurance presentation stood out for certain, as it had been cloudy, hot, and boring.

"It's lucrative, Tracey. I'm *inviting* you in. Count Friday as your initiation."

That meant nothing to me. I repeated my position of no interest.

"There are two types of insurance. The first type of insurance is what I showed you last Friday. We help people earn insurance funds. We help people."

"It's a scam. I want no part of it."

"It's not a scam, Tracey! No one gets hurt. There's a lot of money in it."

Someone did get hurt, but I refrained from arguing. Everything I remembered confused me. "No interest. I can make money within the law." Of that, I was sure.

"So *you* are looking down on *me*?" He was getting more and more vexed, and he looked at Mitchel in disbelief. "Your *best bet* is to stay here, under me. In fact, your *only* bet is to stay here."

"Your only bet was to keep your word. You're a liar. With my leaving now, you can't claim much in losses. You don't deserve a good employee."

"You don't deserve to be as smart as you are," Berk shot back. They both laughed. "I cannot believe it."

"Believe this. I am going off to recruit without you. All you care about is money. Nothing else. You have zero scruples, but you want me to work hard for you. I'm not interested."

He lost his smile. "Your husband is a bad guy, but I have completely trumped him. I am seriously *peeved* off that you are not giving me credit for how much I have done to ruin you. If you knew, you would sit at your desk and do what the hell I say. Whatever he did to you has made your brain do this . . ." He widened his eyes and passed one hand in front of his face, signaling that my mind had been erased.

"I got creative and screwed up your entire West Point reputation and your future. That was me having fun with you while you were 'out.'"

"Sleeping," chuckled Mitchel.

"Influenced," corrected Berk.

Without any kind of reference to or memory of what they were talking about, I dumped their statements from my mind. They did not make sense to me.

"Listen, it's sad about your husband, but if you recruit outside of this office I will sue you because you signed an agreement. Who cares how

I got you to sign it. You're not getting out of it, though I might not do anything about your house. I am worse than your husband," he spat with anger. "Right now, this instant, I am *peeved* that you don't know that I won." No one laughed.

I did not understand. "I'm peeved that you think that just because I am in my twenties I am going to reconsider and keep working for you. That's what's unbelievable."

"You made enemies in Bloomington, and I guarantee you they're formidable. You are lucky to be alive. You may still meet a bad fate. Might want to check who the next blonde is dating."

Dumbfounded, I asked, "What blonde?"

"Well, was it wise to try and date her? Pick another blonde next time." Both men laughed.

"I have never dated a blonde in my life."

"Yes, but you wanted to."

"I have *never wanted* to date a blonde in my life." There was no way to ignore my tone.

He lost his smile. They both did. He studied Mitchel for a second and sucked at the gap in his front teeth a bit. He seemed to be baffled. "Tracey, I don't know what to tell you. Someone down there hates the hell out of you." His new smile was only a smirk, as if he were actually sorry.

I reassured him that I would recruit. I guaranteed him he would not see a penny. I placed my key to the office on the table and went to gather my stuff.

As I left the office, Lurea called after me, "Hey, Tracey!" She smiled. "I was wondering something. When you were at West Point, did you have that big streak of gray in your hair?"

In recent years I had developed a gray streak, possibly from stress. I chose not to hide it with dye because it made me look older and more professional.

While I was passed out Friday night, Lurea helped Berk take pictures of me in my dress uniform from West Point, which hung in the coat closet of my house. They posed me, drugged and in shock, in various ways to discredit my education and person. They clearly hadn't considered that the noticeable grey streak in my hair was recent, let alone that I had put on some weight since leaving the service. One would think that if Berk were going to mastermind such a plan, he would have thought to touch up the victim's roots. He seemed to be winging things.

Instead of telling Lurea to jump in front of a moving train, I simply said no. I had no grey hair at West Point. She seemed disappointed.

Berk called after me again and assured me that he had moved the money from inside his walls and safes. He had also cleaned the money wall with a special chemical so that no one could tell that there had been money there. I did not remember the money. I did not care what he had cleaned, so I turned away and did not look back.

Berk was mostly interested in preserving my revenue stream. He loved money, not doctrine. By referring to the KKK as "them boys," he denied membership, but his paying job for the KKK included taking compromising pictures and videos of me and wiring my house.

Insurance men are not KKK members. The insurance person commits a crime to erase his or her own debt to the Klan. They are instructed on how to carry out their assigned crimes and if they are caught, they are to deny KKK involvement. Failing to do so can cost them their life.

The Klan took the "evidence" against me from Berk, right down to the pens that he had me use to sign papers, to assess whether it was persuasive enough. The Klan reserves the right to doctor the final product further, if need be.

Their logic was that, if I were mortified by the prospect of exposure of my "misdeeds," I would not write a book covering my experiences and treatment in Bloomington. Either because their "evidence" was not believable, or because they knew I was mentally ill and did not cower perfectly by Klan standards, they decided to issue multiple insurance threats against me.

Free, 1998

I opened my own consulting company.

"Get after it," my mother ordered over the phone to motivate me.

I hit the phones. I quickly found completely new people with whom to do business. It took only nine days to seal a deal. I did not look back.

I was free.

Amber, 1999

I really don't cook. I simply can't. Growing up, Mama cooked while I had studied in the dining room with Papa, worked a puzzle, or harassed our German shepherds or ants on the back porch. I made peanut butter-and-jelly sandwiches. I aced homework. I did not cook.

Nothing changed. My son and I ate in restaurants continuously. We had no problems with money. We enjoyed plenty, and I saved most of it because I am thrifty.

I did not mingle socially much, but suddenly I had the chance to date a stunning person. My own age, Amber was a thin, feminine woman. She practiced an Asian religion, wore braids attractively, and valued all things outside the norm. She'd had some issues as a kid that made her tastes eclectic. I thought her one of the most interesting women that I had ever met.

We were at her house one afternoon and she was teaching me to play the drums. She had large African drums that were visually pleasing. Her one-bedroom apartment was tastefully decorated, but her books attracted me the most. She was a psychology graduate student and books on depression, bipolar disorder, and PTSD reminded me of my training with the army and Pfizer.

Tired of me testing my memory on each subject, she darkened the living room to show me her newly installed soft lighting. We ended up in bed. I had been with no better.

I found myself thinking about how often we could see each other, given my work and her school schedule. Amber plowed through graduate school. I really respected her endeavor to reach her goals. I like that in people, though there are others who will tear you down for striving.

She wanted to discuss a theory that she had learned in school. Given the topic was her choice, not mine, I said, "Go for it."

"There are no victims," she said. "People ask for what happens to them." This was one of those statements that made me need to adjust myself so that we were no longer touching.

"What is this?" I asked.

She explained: "People are quick to blame others for what has happened to them, but in reality they are partially or fully to blame for all that happens at all times."

"What about crimes?" I asked.

She said that people placed themselves in harm's way, thereby contributing to whatever crime befell them.

Oh my, I thought, looking around for an exit. I did not think that she would expound, but she did.

"Take this open window," she said. I glanced around behind my head. The wood frame suddenly seemed uncommonly close to the ground. "If someone came in through that window, we helped them by leaving it open. Get it?"

In my head, I retrieved my clothes. I dressed and jumped out of that window. Mindful that she thought like a psychologist in training, I tried to understand that theory as part of other developments she had not yet learned. My repressions were still unknown to me, but I had the wits to question, "What about rape?"

"A woman who is raped more than likely did something, strolled somewhere, somehow to get herself in a bad position. She essentially asked for it." Amber stood to go to the bathroom, perfectly naked, perfectly bronze, and perfectly desirable to most perfectly seeing men or women. I lost sight of her.

Aegean Sea, 1999

My mind wondered back to Greece with Jayns. What if I, a 'victimless' soul, had wondered far from land with him?

Greece's Aegean Sea is crystal blue. It lines the country's east coast, giving sailors a great playground in which to frolic between islands off the mainland. Sunshine only accented the trip, and Jayns and I had plenty of daylight. We rented a small sailboat on the coast because Jayns insisted. He steered the boat using the tiller and rudder and I aided as he instructed, but did not really understand how I helped. His instructions, though seemingly playful, were not clear or interesting to me. I feigned attention.

I had not wanted to go sailing with him, but he begged as if I were offending him with distrust. Adept at academics, his knowledge of this small vessel impressed me. At some point I left him in the front of the boat and rested in the back, or stern, portion. The boat came to a rest.

He joined me. I listened to the water and studied the mainsail. How far had I sailed from home?

"Do you love me?"

I hated such questions. We were not getting along, and he wanted me to profess my love for him every given moment. "Sure."

"You don't say that like you mean it."

Here we go. I looked around, but could not see any other boats nearby. They were out there, but far enough away that we were sufficiently secluded. That made this conversation all the more painful.

"Say you love me like you mean it because . . . I absolutely hate you. I hate dykes. I hate smart rear-ended winches that think they are tough. I don't want my wife to have a job as good as mine," Jayns spat.

Staring at the wood on the boat, I could barely look at him. At West Point he had been so sure of himself. That had not changed. What had changed was who he was. I could barely tolerate being this close to him. Since I had arrived in Greece, I liked the times when he left me alone to work on post the most. Greece was fine. My being with him in Greece was the problem, and yet my visit lasted for a few more days. I wanted to go home.

He began touching me, an obvious way to turn me off. I leaned away from him, toward the adjacent seat, and when I did he slammed my forehead with the fire extinguisher that all Greek sailboats are required to carry. I tried to adjust my focus, but felt my legs and buttocks being lifted and thrown overboard. I entered

Undeterred

the water headfirst, rolling over to beg someone kinder to help me. Only Jayns leaned over the side of the boat. His image was mobile, as the light waves engulfed me. My efforts to scream brought water rushing into my mouth and lungs. His image darkened as I sank. No one heard me. No one saw me. I flailed.

My eyes opened and I gasped for air. *This was not my fault. I did not ask for it. Thank God I did not go sailing him. He had asked a hundred times.*

"Where are you at right now?" Amber lay back beside me, staring, gauging my distance from her and her self-blame logic. What I did not know was that self-blame is a common symptom of PTSD, as is irritability and anger, none of which were part of my expression of the disease. All I could think was that *something* was not my fault. People go through things, but constantly blaming the victim, in my opinion, was unacceptable.

How could someone with the best sexual moves have the very worst pillow talk? Why lay there any longer? Why were my clothes still off? How could I bolt without offending her? I could dive out the window naked and run. Had I asked for this moment too? God help me.

I suddenly remembered something I had to help my mother with. Best to get dressed...

Amber didn't understand my hurry. I lacked the ability to explain it further. I ran. She called me twice in the future. I ran from those calls too. I was not aware of my status as a victim, but discounting my reaction seemed foolish. I ran.

Gayle, 1999

When I arrived at Gayle's office, she gave me a tour of the middle school where she provided guidance counseling. Kids strolled through the hallway, not listening to the speakers overhead, repeating their message for emphasis. Gayle and I walked slower than the crowd, but we eventually made it to her office. She was a tall woman, with a boy-cut hairstyle, brown hair, and dark eyes. I was used to seeing her in jeans and a T-shirt, but I noted that she wore a blazer, turtleneck, and decorative pin for the office.

Guidance counselors earn their own offices. Hers was comfortable with a table, chairs, couch, and desk. I debated where to sit, but she tugged me to the couch. She loved trees, and the art on her walls celebrated them: strong trunks, full branches with colored leaves, wintery stand-outs braving the cold. Every season accommodates trees.

"They outlive us ridiculously, these trees," I said, pointing to one of her posters.

"We live life as much as we want to, though" she responded with a wink.

I faced her, obviously bothered by something. We did not know each other well, but she had made gallant efforts to socialize with me when I was in southern Indiana. I was often busy, and sometimes felt uninterested in hanging out with the team of women in her life. She sat as the matriarch of much, while I tend to prefer smaller crowds.

I told her about Amber's theories as though they were just something that I had heard about in passing. Gayle smiled.

"Struck a nerve, eh?"

I denied it, but she laughed. "Nothing sways you, but *that* struck a nerve?"

We discussed it. She did not rebuke the theory, just put it in context, drawing conclusions more softly. The theory outlined issues of availability and awareness. Children were not at fault, nor were those who lacked power or agency in some way.

She brought up southern Indiana. I had not talked to her since the night I had taken the "aspirin" that Steve had given me at the Wildbeet, and wanted to back out of the party she was holding the next day. She asked me again what I had taken that night.

I repeated the answer I had given her at the time: just aspirin.

"What else?"

"Nothing. Aspirin, Gayle."

Gayle studied me and then smiled. "I thought you had taken something else. You were short of breath. You sounded almost like you were overdosing."

Undeterred

That bothered me, as it lay outside my realm of thinking and doing things. I rebutted her assumption: so far as I knew, it was just aspirin. I wondered, "Well, if you really thought that, why didn't you take steps to save me?"

She smiled, slowing shaking her head. "No one can save you, Tracey," she said. "You have to save yourself."

REVISITS, 2000-2001

Cybercrimes, 2000

Once you leave "KKK territory," as they label it, they have to keep in touch with you. The Klan has to make sure that you won't reveal what they did to you, so they have an insurance person threaten you. Pictures and videos did not convince them that I would not eventually get better and write a book, revealing them and their tactics. Specifically, Dr. Tohm Hrisamolaz was not satisfied that he had sufficiently threatened me. I was in shock when he and his people were threatening me, and there was no guarantee that coming out of shock would make me compliant with KKK wishes.

Unsure that it has successfully deterred you, the KKK continues to touch your life. These "revisits" help them gain new information and ideas to determine their next steps.

The KKK is no longer a group of old men riding around on horses looking for something or someone to burn. They are bigoted people with cell phones, Internet access, and other technology, who stay connected and rally with each other in person or online. Cybercrimes and the reselling of cybercrimes are a major KKK illegal pastime.

Undeterred

I worked day and night during this period, and I earned a lot of money to prove it. One day I got an instant message on AOL. It was Degan.

I asked how she had gotten my email address. She thought I'd given it to Haley or left it with the office. I knew that I had not given it to Haley, because Haley was attractive and I would have remembered that. We went around in circles about how she had found my email address before she insisted that I meet her and Dr. Kalen for lunch. Degan correctly gathered that I would not meet her alone, so she invoked her sister as a lure. Not recalling the harm I suffered in Bloomington, I agreed to meet them for lunch.

We met in a newer Bloomington restaurant near campus, a non-franchise location that only locals would know or love. Four-leaf clovers were prominently displayed around the restaurant. The decor was heavy on wood, and was comfortable. Numerous TVs lining the area above the bar drew midday drinkers, but we secured a single table away from others. Degan said the food was gaining popularity as she seated herself, placing her purse beside her to get comfortable.

When the waitress came by, Degan announced that I was paying for her lunch. I was surprised; licensed practical nurses (LPNs) can afford to eat out, so I wondered if she were in financial distress. Why would she demonstrate that distress in front of her sister and employer? Dr. Kalen firmly told her sister that she would be paying for her own lunch, if she ate at all.

"She'll do it," Degan said, alluding to my pliability due to my mental illness. Naturally, I would feed someone who was hungry if they asked while I was in shock, but Degan was treating me like I was dense.

"Not while I'm sitting here," said Dr. Kalen to her sister. Then she turned to me and said, "We're not eating." Seeing Dr. Kalen alone with her sister would remind anyone of why Degan was jealous. Dr. Kalen was thin, smart, and kind, while her sister was the opposite of those characteristics. Anyone with or with out an illness could sense it.

Degan had many questions about my recruiting work, so I explained the basics. She claimed to have already seen the expensive websites used for information technology recruiting, my specialty. She wanted to know more about revenue: what were the yields on different types of skill sets that I worked with? It appeared to fascinate her, yet I was suspicious. Dr. Kalen sat quietly.

"Tell me how your conversations go," insisted Degan.

After the waitress brought our drink orders, I offered some basic answers to her questions, giving generalities about conversations you would have in recruiting or consulting. I did not want to say too much, because my sales calls were a key piece of my work.

As I talked, Degan kept starting and stopping me. Her purse clicked with each start and stop. I thought that through and then asked, "Degan, are you taping me?"

Dr. Kalen's attention piqued, she said her sister's first name as a question, as if begging her for an explanation. Degan fumbled and squirmed before finally admitting that she was taping me. At that moment, both Dr. Kalen and I realized that her presence there was merely a ploy on her sister's part to draw me in. Dr. Kalen was visibly disappointed in her sister.

"Why?" I was curious.

"A friend of mine is thinking about entering your career field," Degan explained. That "friend" could be none other than Don, her husband. "He knows a lot about your websites, but doesn't know what to say. I was hoping that you could help him."

It was an awkward moment, mostly for Dr. Kalen, who lowered her head in embarrassment. She looked like she wanted to disappear under the table and escape. She whispered something about my memory improving over time, but Degan did not care about my memory then or in the future. She cared about herself. She assured her sister that when I got my memory back, no one would care about what I could remember.

Degan claimed that her friend had access to my websites, too. "Why pay thousands for them and not know what to say?" she argued.

Undeterred

Degan and Don clearly did not want to waste away serving in Dr. Kalen's office forever. They felt the money was not enough. One might note that Dr. Kalen gave Degan and Don jobs after they got out of prison, but Degan's tastes required more. She and Don made it clear to me during one luncheon that they needed to make more money before they could retire. I wondered if Dr. Kalen knew how eager the pair was to leave her practice, but I felt uncomfortable warning her.

I gave Degan some ideas to share with her "friend," but I wished that she had been more forthright. I questioned how her interest in information technology developed. She reminded me that IT was her "other job." It's what she did for "the organization."

"What organization?" I asked.

"Greater Bloomington," was the answer.

Dr. Kalen loathed this admission, pushing her water away. Her sister helped monitor information technology–computer networks, equipment, and access. When I questioned what she meant by "access," she referred to what people do or do not look at online.

The real reason Degan had made contact with me was to further the KKK's cybercrime interests. Many of the people hurt by the KKK are monitored through their computers as a means of control. Degan and Don had long worked together to enter people's homes and place a bug-like software in their personal computers. This allowed them to see whatever that person was doing, making sure that they do not do anything to jeopardize the KKK's secrecy or power. They sometimes even turned the feed from a computer into a livestream for Indiana Klanspeoples' enjoyment.

They had done this to me when I lived in Bloomington, entering my house with a homemade key and installing their spying software on my personal computer. Degan could see what I saw when I surfed. Her "friend" was not paying thousands of dollars to gain access to the same IT recruiting websites I used; she and Don were stealing access from me. The KKK spies on people for lots of reasons.

When I questioned Degan about viewing options for the kind of "access" monitoring she described, she became squeamish. She could lock and unlock websites for video and Internet preferences and streaming. The more she talked, the more I got the feeling that the people being watched were unaware that they were being watched.

I was clearly growing suspicious, so she started painting herself as some form of investigator, vigilantly watching over members of her "organization" to see who viewed what. When asked why members would want that kind of supervision, Degan said that members wanted to see who or what they wanted to see, but they had to pay to view premium crimes. According to her, all the people she viewed were fine with being viewed. I asked who would do that, open themselves up for view like that, and she just maintained that they "*appear* to enjoy themselves" with a sly grin.

"They *seem* to be having a good time to me," she repeated to Dr. Kalen, laughing with her tongue out. Then she gave me a knowing smile that was hard to decipher. She did not sound or look believable. When I asked if she only spied on group or non-group members, she said the software and equipment worked for anyone.

Watching her swirl her soda victoriously, I should have asked why she knew the trade sites that I frequented. Also, why would her "friend" have those sites, but lack a clue as to how to communicate with those on the site? For a nurse to dabble in these issues made no sense to me. For people to need supervision and permission to move around videos and Internet materials didn't strike me as logical either. I could not fathom anyone granting permission to be viewed by Degan. I should have asked a lot more questions than I did.

Dr. Kalen abhorred this conversation, thinking it too overt given the secretive nature of the KKK. Calling her sister's name again and again was her best method of halting Degan's bragging. Only Klan-friendly people should have been privy to Degan's talk.

Degan did not care about such secrecy. "Tracey is *ours* now, Kay," Degan reminded her sister in a whisper, as though I could not hear her. She clearly believed that whatever Berk had garnered against me for the KKK gave them some form of control over me.

Undeterred

"We can keep up with her through her family," she went on. "They are close, unlike most of them." To Degan, "them" referred to homosexuals, not blacks. Some homosexuals have estranged relationships with their families who disown them for their orientation. Degan felt this was a bonus in her favor.

"Stop this," begged Dr. Kalen, also whispering.

"Who do you know in my family?" I wondered. A better question might have been, "How am I yours?"

"Well, you have a son." She laughed, but it left me uncomfortable.

Dr. Kalen buried her face in one hand. "Degan, Degan, Degan," she muttered, angry at how overt her sister was being.

"You don't know my son."

"Well, I can get to know him." Her tone rankled, and she nodded for emphasis. The mechanics of such a thought seemed awkward, given her age. I met Dr. Kalen's discomfort equally, though the full hazards transpiring escaped me.

"What are you doing?" whispered Dr. Kalen sternly.

"Helping Tracey understand that she had better not say anything."

"Anything about what?" I asked.

"What we did. What I do. I generate a lot of money for the organization."

Degan realized the value of her words more than I did. I just stared blankly. I simply thought the organization she spoke of was Dr. Kalen's office not connecting Degan's "greater Bloomington" comment earlier. There could be no other organization from my perspective, and who besides them harbored great interest in that? The whereabouts and doings of Dr. Kalen's nurse and office manager were not important to me. Degan was trying to impress upon me that she held greater importance than just as Dr. Kalen's nurse. It mattered little to me. Such things do not impress people with PTSD.

Bored by the direction the conversation had gone in, I asked if anything new was going on with them. Don had sold a house, despite having been previously convicted of a felony. I thought it odd, given that a felon could not get a license to sell, but Degan laughed that away, saying, "The punitive action for selling houses with a felony in Indiana is so minimal it's worth the crime." I did not find that funny; it was memorable.

Degan bragged that Bloomington doctors were trying to get his armed robbery felony thrown out so that he could get his real estate license and legitimately walk in and out of people's houses. As it was, Don continued to enter houses at will. He expanded the Klan's reach using ladders to set up video cameras in high places in target houses. The video was then fed to Degan for a profit. Degan boasted, wanting me to remember, but her sister wanted me to forget.

Degan invited me to come see Dr. Kalen play tennis one Thursday. She played in Indy routinely. I thought, *Okay, maybe someday.* Dr. Kalen was rumored to be excellent on the courts.

I didn't know not to offer that I had run into Dr. Reenie in Indianapolis. Neither Degan nor Dr. Kalen appreciated the announcement. Not knowing their trepidation, I assured them that she was fine, and was as nice as always. Neither sister was impressed.

Degan told Dr. Kalen that "Indianapolis might not be big enough after all" and worried that Dr. Reenie and I were "too close for comfort." I did not understand those statements, but she meant that "banning" two people in the same professional field to Indianapolis in such a short period of time was not wise. We might talk to each other about our treatment in Bloomington and discover some truths uncomfortable for the KKK.

Degan wanted details about my conversation with Dr. Reenie, but like most people with PTSD-induced shock, I lacked details in that moment. She asked if Dr. Reenie had mentioned a lawsuit. I couldn't recall, but I did not understand why she would. They were afraid that Dr. Reenie and I might join forces and file a lawsuit of some kind. The significance of our meeting was not apparent to me, but Degan concluded that Indianapolis was too small for us both. One of us had to move.

Not long after, Dr. Reenie stopped working at the Carmel, Indiana dermatology office. I never saw her again after my lunch with Degan and Dr. Kalen.

In a later conversation over the phone, Dr. Kalen apologized for Degan's taping stunt, knowing that even when it had been revealed, I had not been fully cognizant of the danger I was in. "I do not believe in taking someone's business or livelihood. You deserve to make a living," she said. Once again, Dr. Kalen set herself apart from the mentalities around her despite doing her part to set me up for a second vote. I had been right about her, to the extent that she could be nice.

To my knowledge, I had only given Degan advice, but Dr. Kalen knew otherwise. Her sister and brother-in-law were perched in her office on a daily basis, monitoring my computer and those of others, irritated by their stations in life and determined to try out other people's fortunes. My advice was more than a suggestion to act; in their minds, it was a license to steal.

That conversation hurt me a great deal over the next year. My loss of income was immediate and financially ruinous. One client noticed that every time I sent something, someone named Don Fletcher from Bloomington had sent the exact same suggestion moments before me. "He is somehow beating you to the punch," he told me.

Before Don and Degan started stealing clients and business out from under me through their access to my computer, I was making nearly $300,000 a year in my late twenties. Don and Degan reduced me to $40,000 by year's end, sitting on my electronic shoulder, stealing my sales, profit, and potential for themselves, while also stunting any basis for the KKK to extract money from me later.

Shock, 2000

One spring day, I arrived at work feeling uneasy. I locked the bathroom door in my office and studied my face in the mirror. Nothing was out of place or unusual. I went back into my office, but still had a strange sense of foreboding. As I rounded my desk, I hit the floor, collapsed.

When I woke, night had fallen and my office was dark. I was weak, not sure if I'd live. I could hear my breathing, but I could not move my body. I lay heavy and exhausted. Monterey flashed before me, the sea lions, the cops. I felt the pressure of Jayns on top of me. His face repulsed me. My eyes danced back and forth as each image came and went. I could not stop the images. I felt my heart racing, but I could not move my limbs.

People with PTSD don't feel much. When life's bullets fly, we intercept our share mentally or physically, but we keep walking the field until our bodies break down, at which point we wonder, "why did my body break down?" It's not always clear.

The next morning, with great and singular will, I reported to my old middle school as I had in my youth. I needed to speak to Mrs. Angel.

"You're coming out of shock," Mrs. Angel assured me, after I told her what was happening, the usual song in her voice changed to a grave tone. She ordered me to go to the Veteran's Administration hospital, because they specialize in cases like mine. "Darling, you are a veteran. You belong to them. Run, don't walk. You're theirs." She offered me a warm smile and a hug.

The VA assigned me to Jewel.

Jewel, 2000

When I got to Jewel's office, I could barely sit up in the waiting room, which was filled with comfortable furniture, army memorabilia, dim lighting, and soothing music. All the patients were like me–they needed comfort. There were several places to sit inside Jewel's office, but I chose the couch since it was closest to her. She offered help, and I wanted to be close to her.

When you store major issues, as I had for years, eventually you have to shed something to make room for more. I had been amassing a lot–West Point, Bloomington, Berk, the theft of my company. My brain had decided that it was time to let go of Jayns. First in, first out.

Jewel was in her late fifties. She was short and petite with brunette hair. She dressed older than she was, with scarves and comfortable shoes.

Undeterred

When she arrived at work, her job was to focus on me and people like me, not herself. She knew before I did that I had been raped. The flashbacks left me numb, glazed over, and dazed. The rape was a new piece of information to me. Jewel's job was to help me cope, so she covered the basics first.

"Do you smoke?"

"No."

"Drink?"

"Rarely."

"Meaning?"

"I had a two drinks two years ago at a concert."

"Drugs?"

"No."

"Many people like you self-medicate. If you can steer clear of that, your chances of maintaining your functionality greatly increase."

"I don't self-medicate," I assured her.

"Then you should be able to keep a clear head and learn yourself and your disease better. You will be a great candidate to know if you are in need of help while in treatment. Sobriety and drug-free living will compound your success." She paused, waiting for that to sink in.

"I don't self-medicate," I repeated. The term was new to me.

"Financial problems?"

"It seems I can no longer complete business deals," I confessed, not knowing that Degan and Don were stealing my deals.

"Compulsive buying, now or in the past?"

"No."

"Are you working?"

"Yes."

"Thoughts of hurting yourself or others?"

"I don't care enough to bother," I chuckled. She didn't.

"Are you sleeping at night?"

"Sometimes," I answered, but at that point I was reliving the rape day and night, which was what had brought me to Jewel's office. A lack of sleep hinders a journey to good health, and I slept without consistency or depth. She promised to address it.

"Do you have blackouts?" she asked me.

I repeated that I did not drink, and she educated me that black-outs were not always liquor-related. Recalling the gaps in my memory from Monterey, which had still not entirely returned, I was uncertain. I did have periods of missing time that remained unaccounted for, but I did not know if I had blacked out.

Not everything floods back at once. Some PTSD sufferers cannot remember anything of their trauma at all, ever. I recalled a great deal about the rape itself, but it did not raise memories of more than itself at first. Facts surrounding the West Point doctor's physical exam, the hospital, and other hidden details trickled in slowly, separately, their own brand of horror.

Bloomington was not even a candidate for recall at that point. Having a counselor to help sort through the flashbacks and serve as a sounding board benefits the patient. A prying boss such as Don, or criminals such as Berk aid little. They peruse the psyche to take a trinket for their meddling acquisitiveness, but the patient functions best without the untrained thirst for gossip. Jewel was always a consummate professional.

My memory under trauma is delayed. I am calm, almost numb, in the face of bullets flying, but I may not remember them for years. Jayns's offenses took nearly ten years to resurface in my mind. Jewel's job was to help me remain functional in a society that had little tolerance for, or knowledge of, my plight. I needed to somehow recuperate without burdening my young son, who just wanted to play with toys, or harming my income potential. I also needed to avoid the traps of psychopaths, who often preyed upon people in my position and situation. However, without having healed fully, that would prove difficult.

I began a plan for healing in the year 2000. I distanced myself from many people in order to gain some space. Jewel quickly became an important woman in my life, and I loved her dearly.

"Tracey, do you know what is going to help us get through your disease?" she asked me at one point.

"No," I responded carefully.

"You."

"Okay," I agreed, seeing where she was going with this.

"You have to take care of yourself. Given your intellect, I see a lot of strength in you. I can tell that you will make the right choices to stay on the path. We have a long journey to make though, and nothing will speed it up–not more appointments, not more talk. We have a journey ahead and you and your mind are leading in point position."

PTSD feels like drag on a ship, slowing your progress. Boats in similar waters carry different drag, depending on the shape and composition of the hull. No two people are alike in how their PTSD presents itself. Your senses may be affected. Perhaps you cannot see faces or distinguish between competing sounds. You may be stunned, stumped, or rendered speechless by the smallest things that may not have been a big deal in the past, but now present challenges as you wade through life's waters to catch up with where you might have been, had the terror not occurred.

Eventually, Jewel primed me for the truth about PTSD: in the days before the Affordable Care Act and Obamacare, it was a medical insurance killer. My insurance company promptly dropped me and, without the military medical records that Jayns stole, I could not get military insurance. I needed civilian group insurance.

"Who provides group insurance?" I asked Jewel.

Her answer was short: other companies. My days as an entrepreneur were over. I looked for a job. I was no longer free to work for myself.

Jewel also prepared me for another truth: without the medical records Jayns had taken, I could not be classified as having a service-connected disability, and would have to pay out-of-pocket for my treatment for the rest of my life. Even group insurance might not cover treatment for PTSD. Paying out of pocket promises to bankrupt most people with PTSD, who end up choosing self-medication instead. Homelessness from medical debts and other financial encumbrances could become possibilities over time, all because Jayns had chosen a strange souvenir in the form of my medical records. The Indianapolis VA enrolled me in their financial program that assisted sexual assault victims, but I would lose the program's financial privileges if I moved.

None of this bothered me. Nothing bothered me. I was numb.

Most of the time, when not focused on a mission or project, my mind went blank, incapable of feeling fear, danger, or trepidation. It was the same feeling that I had in Bloomington and at Berk's house. I accomplished my daily goals despite this. Understanding my diagnosis helped to curb confusion and other nuisances, but only time would dispel the terror and my reaction to it. In the meantime, I just carried on.

Mama

Ridding my mind of Jayns's hate crimes made room for me to deal with my grandmother's death in 2000. She lived to age seventy-six, but mentally reverted to an elementary-school level at the end, combating lupus's attack on her brain. She fought my son mightily for his Halloween candy, and I struggled to explain to him why he should let her win. She didn't go from door to door earning his stash, yet she flagrantly stole every piece of candy he had. The continued theft presented issues until she passed away, taking much of life's sweetness with her. Her death floored me. I just wasn't ready.

She looked gorgeous at the funeral. The ceremony was packed with those from the church who loved her and Papa. Papa had taken care of Mama from high school until that day. Other women threw themselves at him once she passed, but he never acknowledged them. He remained a one-woman man, a stand-up guy.

After Mama's death, I wanted to run. Jewel warned me against making a move too soon. She pointed out that when you take your problems with you to another place, you arrive somewhere else with all your problems unsolved. That made sense, so I continued to look for work locally.

I put my house on the market again. I prepared myself to earn less money, anticipating change.

Gillian, 2000

I met a stunning musician from Bloomington named Gillian. She was a few years older than me, refreshing and interesting. She demonstrated an unequivocally superior gift at playing the guitar, and I trekked to Bloomington to visit her a few times. She could make a guitar sing any song that she wanted, either through rhythm or lead. She bragged that her lead capabilities were orgasmic, which might have been true for some.

Gillian liked to drink. I said nothing about it because it really was her business, not mine. Beer quenched her thirst more than other beverages. I tasted and disliked the beer that she had favored, so she bought me white wine, or "girly juice," as she labeled it. She would teach me riffs on guitar and give me advice. My playing was so inferior to hers that I treasured anything she explained.

Gillian was the first person I had ever met who got drunk around me. We were friends, so I mentioned my concern. Jayns had been a closet binge drinker, but Gillian outright loved her booze. The difference for me was that, with her, I knew what to expect. She harbored no secrets. We had a blast together.

One night in Bloomington she had about five beers, while I had two and a half glasses of wine. We played guitar and laughed over my mistakes. When she asked if I had ever had more than two glasses of wine before, I denied that I had. As I kept plucking at the guitar, I heard her playfully sing, "You're a wuss."

"Why?" I asked.

"Wait for it . . ." she instructed. Shortly after, I ran to the bathroom and violently expelled my stomach's contents. She cackled at my pain. Indeed, I was a wuss. That night was the second and last time I ever got drunk. I know my limits and I'm not a drinker.

One time Gillian announced that she was coming over to my house in Indianapolis, and I stressed out because I never had alcohol at home. I knew I had to have something. I went to the liquor store and walked up and down the aisles trying to decide what beer to buy. The clerk said I had a lot of choices, but a few are safer than others. I bought something flavored with chocolate, enticed by its originality. I assumed four would do.

When Gillian arrived, she immediately wanted a beer after the long drive. When she found out that I had bought chocolate-flavored beer, I thought she might explode. Yes, she drank them, but they were the wrong kind and there were too few. I didn't like them either. She found it in her heart to forgive me.

While lying in my room later that day, she asked, "What is that hole in the wall over there?" I had not noticed it before and did not know.

"Look," she ordered. She pointed to an embedded screw left by the owners before me. I saw it as no big deal.

"It's a huge deal." She exited the sheets naked, sleek, and attractive, tossing her dark mane behind her. She examined the screw more closely.

"Why, Gillian?"

"That's how they get you, Tracey." She explained that in Bloomington, all the rich professionals were in a group that used videos and streams of footage to bully people in and out of town. It sounded ignoble.

"They hate certain groups, but they love single women. They use disreputable information to control and recruit people."

"How do they get information?"

"They enter your house and leave no trace. No one knows how." I knew how, I just could not access the memory. Gillian continued, "They set up bugs and cameras to monitor you. They know what you are looking at on the Internet. They can see your browsing history and see what you view in real time. And it starts with a hole in the wall."

She walked the perimeter of my bedroom, examining everything carefully. She seemed worried beyond my ability to comfort her.

I asked, "If it's in Bloomington, why are you worried here in Indianapolis?"

Undeterred

"They are here too, Tracey." Her tone plowed impatiently past my ignorance. "They want more and more influence, and they have a goal to completely penetrate Indianapolis. Trust me on that."

They wanted to control minorities, reminiscent of slavery, she explained, but they would also cross Caucasians that competed for their professional interests or did not follow orders directed by the organization. Immediate targets satisfy revenge, recruitment, and entertainment. Members can subscribe to chosen feeds to watch who is "captured" unknowingly.

"They love single women," she explained. "If they can wire one up and share her over the Internet unbeknownst to her, they do it. They like keeping tabs on your Internet activity. They see exactly what you see; therefore, they know your likes, wants, and desires. They control you with anything they can get to embarrass you."

Had I come out of shock about what had happened in Bloomington before about the rape and Jayns, I may have recognized the echo of Degan's words in Gillian's fear.

I questioned Gillian about the point of such behavior, and she snapped, "Control, Tracey! They know that a woman will do anything to not be seen in a bad light. Husbands protect wives. Well . . . sometimes husbands in the group sell their wives out by getting them to commit adultery on tape."

"How?"

Gillian was becoming exasperated with my lack of knowledge. "Look, you sold a few pharmaceuticals. *They own the pharmacy!* They have drugs that will make you want sex, illicit drugs, or even death."

Thoughts started forming. "Of course, she would have to leave town," I mused.

"Of course." Gillian said the victim would leave if she knew what was good for her. Bloomington and Berk's treatment of me hinted in this direction, but both remained buried deep.

"So, some people use drugs as a habit, but from their view it's merely chemical warfare of sorts," I interpreted.

She nodded. "They control the drugs in Bloomington. They can heal you or kill you."

I lay there, thoughts parading through my mind. Flashbacks fired in my brain.

"What do you call them?" I asked. "The group, I mean."

"You don't call them anything. You hope they don't call you," she chuckled, falling back into bed having completed her inspection of my room.

"They must have a name, Gillian."

"Everybody!" she laughed darkly. "In Bloomington, they are called 'everybody.'"

Gillian had a side business that kept her in regular contact with wealthy Bloomington folk. One day when we were talking to one through the window of my car, the contact asked casually why Gillian brought N-words into the neighborhood.

Gillian laughed the comment off uncomfortably. She had an open beer in her hand that prevented us from driving away until she finished it. Still, driving away from a comment like that would not have made it un-said.

On another occasion, neighbors around Gillian's workplace called the cops on us as we sat in a lookout area of the lake. Gillian left my vehicle to deal with the officer on her own. When she got back to the car, she cursed southern Indiana as backwards. I rationalized that a strange car is always questionable, but Gillian said it was about color. "And it ain't the car's color, either, Tracey."

As she lay in my bed that day, she realized that even Indianapolis wasn't safe from "them." She got dressed and left. I was losing her.

Still, Gillian's comments had jarred memories that I needed to share with Jewel. The flashbacks had started flickering.

Berk Flashback, 2001

Berk pounded the table in his office, threatening me. The rest of the office surely heard it. "What I have on you is convincing!"

Undeterred

I just stared blankly at him.

"Why do you leave your house unlocked all day?" Berk asked.

"My son has trouble getting the door open when he gets home from school."

"Hmm. Well, that explains it, but that's not going to be a comfort in the future."

Mitchel pushed up his glasses with a smile. "Kind of makes all that work to get a key a waste of time," he laughed.

One day while working for Berk, my keys had disappeared from my desk for half a day. Berk had taken them and had copies made, and Lurea brought them back when he was done, saying that he found them. I learned that women should never leave their keys lying around an office.

"My son is stranded otherwise, and I live in a nice neighborhood. We're safe," I said, ignoring the comment about my keys. My disease failed to make me question why my keys or the lock on my house were an issue for two men who lived and worked on the other side of town from where I lived.

Mitchel fixed his face in a pensive way and looked to Berk for guidance. They did not care if my son lived or died. "Maybe with someone else you are safe," Berk smiled.

"Yeah," chuckled Mitchel.

Berk changed direction again. "Do you keep your West Point uniform in the entryway coat closet?"

"Every West Pointer has their dress uniform."

"How do I know that?"

It's not a hard thing to guess, *I thought. I have always kept my West Point uniform in the coat closet. Who didn't?*

"Why can you not remember anything?" Berk demanded, angrily. "I don't even have a gun right now. If I so much as wave a gun at you, your brain shuts down. When will you remember all the things that I have done to you? I have great, convincing evidence that will bury you. That's what insurance is. My job is to ensure that you will keep your know-it-all mouth shut. If you open your mouth, the damage to you will be formidable. I cannot do my job if you can't remember my work. Who can get through to you to let you know that your life depends on knowing that I've won?"

"Tracey," Mitchel interjected, "do you have money problems? I see you work like crazy here. What's so urgent?"

"I'm one-hundred percent commissioned, so I need to move fast."

"So you are having cash problems?"

"No. When I bought my house I had near-perfect credit. My score topped 800-plus. I won a national trip at the software company, and I placed third in line for Rookie of the Year at Pfizer. You're the ones trying to keep me here. I have money. I just don't like to spend it."

"Over time you probably are going to develop a reputation for having money problems," Mitchel predicted.

Berk nodded.

Confused, I asked, "How?"

"It's just going to happen. A lot of single mothers have money problems. Maybe that is when you will find out that I won," Berk assured me confidently.

Mitchel corrected him, "A lot of black, single mothers have money problems."

Berk nodded in agreement. "Very believable. Mentally ill to boot," he continued.

"I'm not mentally ill. And I am going to sue you if you touch my credit. I have great credit."

"You can't prove credit over time," Mitchel informed me.

"I sold you out to the boys down south," threatened Berk. "No one down there is going to give a damn about you or your credit."

"Yep, wrong color, wrong race. Just wrong," Mitchel said, shaking his head with a smile. Both men laughed.

"Don't think it's just Tohm in Bloomington, either. He took everything, but your ownership has been transferred down south. That's the chain of custody. Good luck negotiating your freedom."

"Down by the river . . ." giggled Mitchel in song. "Slave South!" He rocked his head from side to side.

"How far south have you been?" Berk wanted to know. I did not answer. I did not understand the conversation. According to Berk, his chosen destination for me lacked court cameras, unhampered juries, or judges. He repeated, "Tohm's going to choose your jurisdiction. How far south have you been?"

"Slave South!" cried Mitchel again. "You won't enter politics now."

"Well, I'll vote for you if I agree with your politics," Berk said.

Undeterred

"Yeah, but the South will make all the decisions," Mitchel said, laughing. Berk started laughing too, leaning over as if the laugh hurt.

"Tracey," he turned serious again, "you will have to excuse Mitchel. He is in training and has a lot to learn. But seriously, Tracey, your best bet is to get your head straight and hit my phones." He stared at me from behind round glasses with gritted, gapped teeth.

I said nothing, since I did not understand the conversation. There were people on the other side of the door trying to conjure a commission check to feed their families, while in this room two white guys in khakis were talking like this. It made no sense at all.

"We may even let you keep your house," Mitchel chided.

"You have nothing to do with my house," I pointed out.

"Then why did you sign? Why the hell did you sign?" Berk spit out. "This is what pisses me off, Tracey. You have no ability to protect yourself. You are officially insane. You don't have the sense to take care of yourself. I'm offering you a deal!"

Such persuasion.

"You can probably keep your house because that one is not convincing, but I have other, more convincing stuff on you. Your husband captured your voice. I got you, all of you. That's what insurance is! I beat Jayns! I perfected ruining you!" Berk crowed.

I perfected a blank stare. It seemed like he had lost his mind.

He pushed up his glasses and glanced at Mitchel. "You," he pointed at me, "you don't even know what's wrong with you. Honestly, neither do I, but trust me, while the KKK will kill you, I'm the nice guy in this. You need to be convinced," he pleaded with a warm smile, "I'm the one who is giving you a chance to make money. Your best bet is to stay here." The smile disappeared again.

Jewel on Berk, 2001

Jewel asked, "Do you remember seeing the gun, Tracey?"

"No." At that time, I did not, but my memory had also blocked Berk making me sign a lot of papers in his office before I went to his house. He had a gun then. I just could not remember it yet.

Berk was trying to make me think that he could take my house from me, but for a criminal that would have serious legal ramifications. My family and friends would be alerted. Berk's efforts to harass me were simply haphazard and poorly laid out.

"The gun hasn't come back to you yet." Jewel told me that PTSD had four main symptoms. Reliving the event in flashbacks, as I was experiencing with Jayns and Berk, or nightmares, which I never experienced, was the number one symptom. "The gun is the part that you are still blocking."

She asked if I avoided places, people, or words that trigger thoughts of the trauma. When I said no, she said we would have to watch for that. "If it does not happen at all, we'll have another problem."

According to Jewel, PTSD sufferers may experience negative changes in beliefs, summarizing situations, people, or places as inherently bad. I was not doing that. Some people with PTSD are jittery and keyed-up for another traumatic event. I couldn't be calmer.

"We'll continue to keep an eye on how you express your disease."

"Everyone will know before me, right?" I asked jokingly. Jewel chuckled. I often joked about the state of my disease.

"Berk is not a good person. You are better off for having left that office. That situation just promised to get worse and worse. Congratulations for not staying. Berks come and go for post-traumatic stress victims. Other business owners probably know him as a criminal, and he has a wake of victims, I assure you. Still, whatever he is doing in insurance does not concern me. You, however, do. Whether it's with Jayns or Berk or Bloomington, my concern is always you. Are you sleeping?"

"Yes," I answered honestly. Jewel had given me something to help.

"How are your thoughts? Do you have thoughts of confronting Berk or Lurea or these other people there?"

"No."

"Getting to Jayns and Bloomington would require travel, but since Berk is local, please know that confronting them is never a good idea. Okay?"

"Okay. It's not a problem," I assured her. I really had no desire to confront anyone. The truth is that confronting an insurance person is a waste of time, since relieving the debt they owe the Klan is worth more than telling you, or anyone, the truth. There is safety in their deceit.

"Let's work on your techniques for when you are drifting into shock. How do you feel now?"

"Fine." With PTSD I always felt "fine" or numb. I could not tell the difference between the two anymore.

Jewel's motherly voice stirred me from my shock. Only one other person, my mother, could do that. The VA had paired me perfectly with her.

"Jewel, why do you think Berk would talk to me in such a manner and yet tell me to keep working for him?" His behavior still seemed strange and illogical to me.

"Tracey, he is a psychopath who didn't think through his modus operandi with you, so he tried many different things. That's why you didn't get a free touch-up to your roots before putting on your West Point uniform. They get better with time. You may have been his first victim. Trust me, he would love to run your life."

"It's a free country," I said, smiling.

"They don't want the country to be free, not for you. They can almost smell vulnerability, and as a person with PTSD, you are extremely vulnerable. If they wanted you to be free, they would leave you alone. If they accepted reality, they wouldn't create their own." As I thought about that, she made notes.

"We'll have work to do when that gun comes back to you." Jewel helped me with scores of flashbacks over many years with so many instances of terror stored in my memory. We set my next appointment.

Cybercrimes, 2001

Degan called. She invited me down to Bloomington for lunch on a Thursday again. We met at another Irish establishment off Kirkwood in an old building with a green awning that looked like it had been built in the mid-1800s. I arrived and seated myself, declining her request that I buy her meal. Looking around at the establishment and seeing the rich decor and high prices on the menu, I noted that Reagan's tastes in restaurants and free food had grown more expensive over the years.

Only she attended, as Dr. Kalen could not make it. If she had told me that up front, I would not have come down. I had no interest in catching up with Degan. Still, we chatted and it quickly became apparent that her only interest lay in my business and my computers. She made an odd reference to not being able to "see" me anymore. Her blind spot was the source of my lunch invitation.

When I inquired as to the meaning of her concern, she defaulted to saying lamely that my having moved away meant she could not seen me anymore, but I had been gone for some time by then. Didn't I have more computers, she wondered. She remembered "seeing" three attached to my server. Where were they?

Someone without PTSD would have questioned how she knew all this. I told her that my computers were packed up in my garage because I was waiting to take a regular job, and I no longer ran my company on PCs. I had bought Mac computers.

"Oh, well I cannot see anything on Macs. They have added security," she grumbled, growing perturbed.

"What can you see on PCs?"

"Everything you can!" she snapped, wielding an angry tone, then lowering it with a smile for a passing waiter.

When I had been using PCs, once Degan was virtually logged in, she could see and maneuver on her own between the three computers that I owned. They were all connected. PCs can become long-term slaves if particular software is installed on the hard drive. Macs are designed to resist this kind of cyber attack.

I did not see value in staying in a conversation about the benefits of Macs versus PCs. I liked Macs for different reasons than what she disliked them for. That someone could not break into my computer had

Undeterred

not factored into my decision to change hardware at the time, but it was good for me all the same.

"So, you are not recruiting anymore?" Degan asked, increasingly and visibly annoyed.

"I'm a consultant," I told her, smiling.

By switching to Macs and making it so that she couldn't spy on me anymore, I had also turned off her and Don's ability to steal access to those lucrative IT subscription websites. They also could not see any documents I was reading or the contact I was emailing. Degan's fury continued to mount, but I did not know why.

I remembered our previous conversation with the tape recorder, and, hoping to change the subject a bit, I asked, "Who loads the software on computers so that you can spy on people?" The question won me a stare.

"Think about it," she spat.

Thinking about it didn't help. I couldn't understand why modern people would willingly offer themselves up for viewings. It was disturbing, like some form of violation.

"How's Don?" I asked with cheer.

She glared. Was he the answer to who was loading the software for her? Finding out that I had abandoned the PCs, Degan abruptly stopped talking to me. She seemed unwilling to tolerate me any longer. I had no not wanted to see her either, so I didn't mind.

Before I walked away, she suddenly remembered that Dr. Kalen was playing in a tennis tournament that night. She advised me to stop by the tennis facility and say hello. I had no idea where it was. She rattled off instructions and, since it was on my way out of town, I decided to stop by.

Tennis, 2001

There were few cars in the parking lot of Bloomington's Tennis Facility when I arrived, so I assumed the tournament must be over. When I walked in, Dr. Kalen was playing with three men. She played well and I waited in the hallway until she was done.

She came over after the match and complained of a contusion in her knee, for which she wore a bandage. I offered my condolences and wished her well. The others trailed after her from the court, possibly heading toward the showers. She invited me to step outside the front door, where we talked for some time about things of little importance. She did not know that Degan had invited me to lunch, which struck me as odd since Degan had invoked her sister's presence to get me to come down. There was also no tennis tournament this evening, she told me. Strange. *Degan must have gotten the date wrong*, I mused.

As in a previous conversation, I expressed concern that Dr. Kalen's patients' personal data was open to felons. As before, Dr. Kalen told me that in the Bloomington community, Degan and Don were not considered suspicious. She could not explain Degan's computer viewing network, but she felt safe, as did the community. This included Don's entering houses with a pre-made key. Bloomington had no problem with a felon posing as a realtor. I never brought it up again.

As we stood talking, one of the men she had been playing with walked by and greeted her. "Good-bye, Tohm," she said, but then quickly returned her gaze at me. She was suddenly more serious.

It was getting dark and a storm brewed with threatening clouds overhead, so I thanked her for her time and turned to leave. I had paid little attention to the brief exchange.

She called me back. "Do you have friends in Bloomington, Tracey?"

"Yes." At least I thought that I did.

"Do not make any more stops in Bloomington tonight. Do not visit anyone. Listen to me." Her voice was methodically slow, her head nodding to emphasize her words. "Go. Home."

"Why?" She had become so serious so quickly that I felt uneasy.

"Get in your car and drive straight to Indianapolis. No stops in Bloomington. Get out of town."

The last sentence registered more than the others because it echoed the past. I began trying to process her language but found that I couldn't.

Undeterred

I heard the words "get out of town," but my ears distorted the phrase. It resembled the last phone call I had had from Jayns. I tried to hang on to the meaning her words, but Dr. Kalen was losing me to shock.

I broke eye contact and studied my shoes, trying to work through her commands. Staff in the Bloomington offices had screamed at me. They spit words at me. They pushed me to the door. Dr. Kalen never did any of that, and yet here she was, expelling me from Bloomington with less venom or force than her peers had ever used. Hers were the same words, but with a deliberate, even, kind tone–smooth and direct–which stumped me.

"Why?" I managed to ask.

Slowly, she said, "Tracey, you won't make it. Your friend won't either. It will look like an accident or a murder-suicide. Get . . . out . . . of . . . town."

She lacked hostility. Her voice was almost a whisper, "Tracey, think of your grandparents."

"Murder . . . Get out of town. . ." I heard it again. *Pentecostals do not commit suicide*, I thought. I felt embarrassed as I stood there, staring blankly, wondering what to do. She waited, watching me. Even she could not tell if the words had sunk in to my PTSD-stricken mind. I gazed back at the grey tennis facility to my right. My view passed through her to the parking lot on my left. I noted that there were only three or four cars remaining.

The word *murder* stunned me coming from Dr. Kalen's mouth. Her calm voice uttering such a harsh word reminded me of the other people in town who had called for my life vehemently. She did not threaten like those people who viciously commanded, "Get out of town." Her voice saying those words, though benevolent in purpose, did not make the message sound more humane. My mind and body toyed with entering shock and existing shock.

I stood, stuck in my thoughts, trying to figure it all out. As I counted the small stones near my shoes, she waited. I glanced up at her. She did not frown. She did not speak to me with disdain like others did in Bloomington. She stared at me without disgust, just with a seriousness that asked me to wake the blazes up. She repeated something. I watched her say it. She was asking me to save myself. I felt exhausted.

I tried as hard as I could to pull my thoughts together. She tolerated my disease, my self-induced ignorance, my struggle. No one had treated me for my experiences in Bloomington, not even Jewel, since I was not yet awake to the abuse. Consciously, I had no historical reference to associate with her words or tone. With not even half a smile, she squarely repeated, "Think of your grandparents." I heard her voice say one more word: "Go."

It finally registered. I smiled with the awakening. The sky formed darker clouds. "It's a free world, Dr. Kalen," I said, acknowledging her request for me to leave, but not the history it had churned up in me. I simply tried to lighten the tone, which was like me.

"Not here," she said, shaking her head. "Don't stop anywhere, Tracey." She smiled slightly and purposefully commanded again, "Go."

"I'll be back!" I lied, but I needed to save face after mentally scrambling as I had. Maybe she did not know me to be clueless. I had a feeling she did. She held my stare as I backed to my car.

I thanked her instinctively.

Still, I did not think twice about the black car parked near the exit of the facility, waiting for me. The driver waved me past him. I paid no attention to the direction that he drove in after I turned toward Indy.

Dr. Kalen told me to not stop anywhere, but she knew her boyfriend Tohm was going to follow me after having seen us talking.

The dark drive home proved long and rainy. As always, I listened to the radio as I cruised, joining in to sing my favorite tunes. Intently focused on the traffic ahead, I headed around the city to get to my northeastern home. The rain abated when I was midway around the 465-highway loop.

Stepping out of my car in my driveway, I saw the black sedan behind me quickly make a U-turn and come back with a lowered passenger window. *Probably needs directions*, I thought. I approached the car, ready to offer assistance.

Undeterred

It should have been clear that I was squinting right into the barrel of a gun with silencer. "Stay away from my girlfriend," called the faint voice of the dark-haired male driver.

I stepped toward his car, put a hand to my right ear, and asked, "Excuse me?"

"Stay away from my girlfriend!" he repeated with more agitation.

I politely told him he had the wrong house and walked to my door.

I certainly do not suggest that anyone step toward a gun and claim hearing problems, but when you loiter in shock, you may miss a whisper.

Aventis and Jewel

Aventis Pharmaceuticals offered me a pharmaceutical sales rep job in Bloomington in 2001. Every company is always looking for a sales rep in Bloomington. Brian said that unless you hire a small mind to work with small minds, the two sides wouldn't stick. Bloomington had a problem with sales reps not sticking.

I took the position disinterestedly until I tried to report to work the first day. Something about being dressed up in cufflinks and full gear triggered a feeling that I was in danger. When I hit the open road down Highway 37, flashback after flashback warned me to not take the job. I reversed my direction from Bloomington and told the manager, "This won't work."

I went straight to Jewel's office. I suddenly recalled that when I had bumped into Dr. Reenie in Indianapolis, I had told her that I'd taken treats down to Dr. Kalen's office. She thought that was a horrible, dreadful idea. When I said that Degan had kept in touch with me, she thought that was an even worse idea. According to Dr. Reenie, when you leave Bloomington they are supposed to leave you alone. I still glowed as a target, thanks to Tohm.

As I waited outside Jewel's office, flashbacks lit up my brain like a lightning storm. I could see things and hear conversations that I might have remembered before, but I saw them in a different light, finally recognizing a reality of which I had been previously unaware. Everyone was hateful, save a small handful. They talked to me like an unwanted animal. It was clearer than ever before.

I understood that Dr. Kalen had turned my name in for some kind of ceremonial vote, but I did not associate that with the town's turning on me the second time. I just knew that she had submitted me for something, but nothing good ever came to me from it. Other doctors assured me that Dr. Kalen was not my friend. I recognized the connection between the offices and their poor attitude to me, but I did not understand the source of their anger or what if anything I had done wrong. Much of it still made no sense. Why would she want the town to hurt me?

The offices were hostile, mob-like, and suffering from groupthink, calling firmly for my dismissal and death. Dr. Kalen's staff would talk to me about leaving before it was too late. When "We vote for Tohm" failed, every office would repeat, "You'll feel better when you leave," instead. Doctors and staff alike ridiculed me with every visit. I just did not get it, and robotically did my job. Delivering prescription samples, milk shakes, drugs, pens, and cheer is a poor comeback, but I returned every day to do it again. Meanwhile, whatever was being put in my sodas continued to build up in my system, making me physically weaker and more tired.

"What concerns me most is that your memory learned nothing," belabored Jewel. "You demonstrate amnesia."

"I do not."

With a smile, she said, "Oh, yes you do."

"I know where I am."

"Yes, you know that well."

"I know who I am."

"You always know that." She bit her lip, thinking about how best to explain. "When a PTSD-sufferer knows what happened to them, they avoid it immediately upon recall. That avoidance would dictate that you not stay in Bloomington more than a month under your previous circumstances. You stayed longer than a year. That tells me that your brain dissociated itself from the immediate terror, pulling you away from the danger mentally, but leaving you in physical danger, carrying on as if it were not happening or did not happen at all. This is called dissociative amnesia. It can happen in a second, but that lack of memory opens you up to unspeakable danger.

I defended myself with a weak, "I didn't know," which made her smile wider. She knew that I did not know. What I did not know was always my greatest danger.

"Do you know who does know?" Jewel asked. I shook my head. "Doctors, Tracey. Doctors who chose not to help you in Bloomington, doctors who join hate groups like the Klan, doctors who terrorize other people as a pastime," she said without losing eye contact with me. "They know.

"There is a strand of PTSD that allows for your memory loss, but dissociation can stand alone without PTSD. Regardless of which you have, Tracey, you are in the right place now with us. When you freeze instead of going into flight or fight, you are endangered even more. It's involuntary, but you are saving yourself now. I am so glad you are here.

"There is little difference between the people you are running into; they rape others of their lives, they steal potential, and they fictitiously label themselves superior. To them, you represent more than your weakness; you highlight their fears. They are afraid of what you can do, despite where you came from. You, to them, are not supposed to exist."

Now understanding my reaction to going to Bloomington, I explained to Aventis that some offices were flagrantly, pervasively cruel to me. My proposed manager, in turn, contacted Bloomington doctors that he thought influential, to determine if I were telling the truth. Since approximately eighty-five percent of the doctors in Bloomington were KKK when I was there, Aventis's query more than likely fell into their hands. Upon confirmation that I was telling the truth, Aventis changed my assignment to Madison, Wisconsin. I made preparations to leave Indiana, Jewel, Mommy, and Papa.

Mommy, 2001

Mommy worked at Walmart in Indianapolis. The bench outside the market-fresh entrance of her store became her office during her breaks. We conducted a lot of counseling right there. I paid with hugs.

"Why do you think I did not die of an overdose in Bloomington?" I asked her one day. "They were so very evil. Steve, the guy at the Wildbeet, said that this Tohm guy wanted me to have a good time, but that was not true; he was trying to kill me."

"Drugs don't play a part in your personality," Mommy assured me. "You have never wanted to get high in your life. As for why you didn't die, it wasn't your time, Tracey. Someone tried to play God, and they failed."

Thinking about the personalities I had met over the past few years, I mused, "Anyone different from them is considered lesser or farther from God."

"That's their opinion. It's not what the Bible says. That's what is hurting the country now." She paused, thinking about the world around us, the county we lived in. "We have more Hispanics coming through this store than ever. People who hate those who are different cannot reverse this country to yesteryear through their hate."

"They can if they control them with menial jobs and don't pay them," I mused.

"How can they not pay?"

"I don't know about you, but I'm not making enough." We both laughed at that.

"Well, you are getting to go to Wisconsin and have a big adventure," Mommy reminded me, teasing.

"I do not need big adventures."

"I wish I could run away," she said, "and take you with me."

"Wherever I go, you are always welcome. I don't want to run away, though. That new place may not have anything better to offer. Plus, what do I have to run away from? I have no fears."

She twisted her mouth and snickered, "Listen to you talk."

Tohm Hrisamolaz, 2001

Leaving Mommy's job, I pulled into a Shell gas station on North Meridian Street, just south of the Interstate 465 loop around Indianapolis, to use the restroom.

Undeterred

It was always busy, since no competition lasted on other corners of the intersection, and it only had a single-stall bathroom. A blonde woman had walked in to the lady's room ahead of me, so I leaned against the window waiting for her to finish. A guy strolled out of the men's room on the other side of the hall and, seeing me, took issue with my presence. He rushed at me suddenly, sending my brain into protective-mode.

"Hi," I greeted him preemptively.

"What the hell are you doing here?" It was Dr. Tohm Hrisamolaz, the grand dragon's son, in shorts, T-shirt, and baseball cap, the very same clothes I was wearing. I thought he might punch me.

My mind perceived my danger, and I shut down. I could not recognize him. All I could think was, *How furious can one person get with another for going to the bathroom?*

"Well, you go to the bathroom over there, and I go over here," I began, explaining the obvious.

"I look better than my photo online, don't I?" he asked.

I had no idea, but started perusing the salty snacks brimming on the shelves facing me and conceded my ignorance, "I would not know."

"You have looked me up. That's a young picture online. I've lost weight," he added.

Confused, I turned to another aisle, this one containing all the sundry items that one would not think they would ever need: decks of cards, motor oil, etc. Why would I look up a stranger from the gas station? How would I know to? Was he crazy? How long did it take her to pee?

He leaned in to me and whispered, "She sucked my dick last night."

"Great," I said unenthusiastically, not knowing who "she" was. He began describing the experience and it set in that I did not care. What man walks up to a stranger in a convenience store to tell them about something like this?

"You are never, ever going to have her. I will kill you first."

"I just want to use the bathroom when this lady leaves," I said, trying to ignore how close he had moved to me.

"We voted you out once, but tried to be understanding that you had PTSD, you mental case. But when you hit on her," he pointed to the women's room, "we had to erase you. You chose to be the way you are, you freak! We hate you people." He neither yelled nor whispered. He thought about what he could say to hurt me next.

"Your statements make no sense," I told him evenly. How could I hit on a woman that I did not even know?

He told me several times to go to another restroom. I pointed out that this Shell station only had one.

"You can forget talking to her!" He worked himself into a frenzy.

"Why are you so hostile about my using the bathroom? Is the men's room open?" I tried to find a place for him other than beside me, raging in my face. He seemed to be filled with hate.

"As a matter of fact, the men's room is open. I suggest that you go there. It's fitting for some*thing* like you."

The ladies' room door opened and, seeing or hearing us both, the inhabitant slammed the door shut again. He met that with laughter. "She won't even speak to you."

"I get that a lot in the bathroom." I sighed calmly; I really had to go. The station lacked another women's facility.

"You will never work as a senior drug rep in Indiana, because I will tank your numbers across the state! I'll tank you no matter what, until you wish you were dead." He laughed.

He knocked on the door and called, "Honey." The woman emerged and he walked her to the front door while shielding her face from me with one hand. I felt sorry for her.

I headed to the bathroom. When I finished I bought some gum and soda. My new enemy, or my old enemy, returned to taunt my purchase. He claimed that the brand of gum I chose evidenced what N-words bought. He nodded, as if psyched that I had heard him use the word.

I looked down at the green pack of chewing gum and wondered how Doublement Gum could be N-word gum when all the twins in the commercials were white. The clerk asked me if he could help me. Confused, I handed him my chewing gum choice and a Diet Coke.

Undeterred

"You're an addict. I taught you to drink Diet Coke," the crazy man declared with gritted teeth. Speechless, I paid and headed for the door. I had started drinking Diet Coke when I was about ten years old at a family picnic. Where was he then? Was he mad? Who was he?

When I stepped through the door and looked back to hold it for someone else, I noticed that he had left the line to follow me without purchasing anything. "You're not a West Pointer around here, just a filthy N-word."

I held the door for him. "Come back and I will kill you," he said. The threat fell on unwitting ears. I did not know where he was from, but if I needed to use the bathroom again when I was in the area, I supposed I'd return to the gas station.

"I should have killed you when you were there. Come back, you common N-word," he spat. "Please come back. You are going to wish you were dead when we get through with you, I assure you." With no historical reference in my brain, save the pack of gum and soda, the threat seemed senseless.

I walked to my car and prepared to drive away. He shot a finger at me like a gun. I shot one back like a bird.

He swirled and spat, "Disabled veteran my ass! Fuck you!" He turned and continued to his car.

"I'm not disabled," I said under my breath. In my mind, I wasn't.

When I pulled out of the gas station, another driver Dr. Hrisamolaz was traveling with took issue that I'd split up their two-car caravan. Dr. Francis, the grand dragon, was driving the second car and objected mightily with hand gestures. I drove on to Meridian in the opposite direction as them, promptly forgetting the experience.

The Logic, 2001

That night, Degan called. According to her, I had put my life at risk.

"Really? How?" I asked, not understanding her greeting.

"He is in line to be our next grand dragon." They had tried to be patient with me while I lived there, according to her, but I had to be careful and show more respect for them.

He who? I wondered. As she spoke, I figured out that she was referring to the angry guy in the filling station who did not want me to use the restroom. How did she know that had happened? Often she knew what I looked at online or what I chatted about. I believed her to be omniscient.

"That was Tohm! Tohm Hrisamolaz!" she scolded me. "They were coming back from their house up north." She lavishly described how luxurious his second home was. I did not care. I was trying to place this Tohm person with my PTSD-fogged mind.

"Tohm, the Prozac representative?" I thought aloud.

"No, Dr. Francis's son! How could you miss him? How could you possibly miss *her*?" By "her," she meant Dr. Kalen.

"Well, I have only met him once, I think, and I never got a good look at her. He even made disparaging remarks about her." I told Degan what he'd said about oral sex. She claimed not to believe me. Even if I had heard him right, it was just to make me jealous, she explained. Nothing like that could have occurred, given what she knew about them.

"Trying to make me jealous of what?"

"Because you like her," she said.

"I like who?"

"Dr. Kalen!"

Silence ensued as I tried to calculate her meaning. "Why would I get jealous of her or her boyfriend?"

"Good gracious," Degan fumed, exasperated.

"Your sister is a nice person," I told her. "Nice people are hard to come by. They don't approach me and talk about their oral sex escapades. What are you really contacting me about?"

"He proposed to her last night. We were all hoping for a big storybook wedding."

That meant nothing to me. Of course I would be happy for someone's wedding, but why would I care about a stranger's wedding to a former client? In the same vein, I also did not care that she had rejected

Undeterred

him. Degan's concerns were real to her, but I would not have been going to the big wedding anyway.

"Tracey, did she call you?"

"What?"

"How did you know she would be there at that filling station? They were coming from his place up north. Tell me she didn't call you. Tell me she wasn't trying to meet you."

Even with PTSD, I recognized how bizarre this question was as it fell from Degan's mouth. Why would she be investigating whether or not her sister had made a call to meet me? I sensed danger. The call was probably being taped, because few people would trust Degan's words.

"Tracey! Did she call you?" she repeated.

"Nature called me, Degan. I took a bathroom break. It can't be a crime."

"I will let him know that you said that she did not call you. He will always take care of her, even though he has to marry someone else. He will eventually be our grand dragon."

"He who?"

"Tohm!"

"'Grand dragon' is a funny term. What is that?"

"Our *leader*!" She was losing patience with me, though she was the one who had placed the call.

"Leader of what?"

"The *organization*, Tracey! Goodness, do you listen?"

I did not know the organization of which she spoke. Amnesia asked me to let the word go. The call did not last much longer than that.

Before hanging up, Degan warned me that they were in Indy a lot, taking care of their business. Their mission was to take over more and more of Indianapolis, until they controlled the entire state of Indiana. She asserted that they controlled or influenced just about everywhere in Indiana except for slumbering Indianapolis. I had no idea of whom she spoke. The conversation was memorable for what I did not get out of it.

I told her I had to pack for Wisconsin. Years after Bloomington, I was still hearing about the man whom I thought was the Prozac rep.

Jewel on Tohm

"They punished you for being gay?" Jewel marveled, shocked.

I said nothing.

"What did he mean by 'erase you'?"

I had no idea.

"Tracey, do you even know what you did or said to her, or what was perceived that you did or said to start this?"

"When? In the bathroom? I didn't speak to her. I barely saw her face."

Jewel chuckled at me often. "Never mind, Tracey, never mind." She complimented my timing at the gas station. What were the chances that that meeting could have happened to anyone else? I was an interesting patient for Jewel.

"There is this, though," she continued. "Do you see a connection between Jayns's problems in Greece and what transpired in Bloomington. Isn't that family Greek?"

"Two things, Jewel: I'm not trying to be a sleuth. I'm just trying to get help with PTSD. Second, do we really want to give Jayns that kind of credit? I don't." We did something we did often: we laughed.

What an interesting life I lived, just moving around breathing.

"Did you ever speak to her alone?" Jewel asked of Dr. Kalen.

"Yes. She once grilled me about my employment goals and political orientation. She tried to push me into empirical science as though that were a place where she and others would like to see me. Nothing I said pleased her. After that conversation, I supposedly liked blondes, towering blondes. Namely her."

Jewel noted, "No blondes, no giants." We both found that hilarious.

I repeated, "No blondes, no giants." It was like an oath. "They tried to break my disease manually over their knee," I observed.

Undeterred

Jewel mused, "That would be a totally different science of medicine."

"Almost empirical, even." I smiled.

"Goodness. Imagine if all we psych specialists had to do was spit on a person and say 'you're healed'?"

We laughed.

"I have a disease, Jewel. My prescription isn't a swift kick in the teeth."

"Tracey, I know." She sobered up, as did I. "Trust me, I know.

"My disease does not baffle me, nor does it define me. The treatment I got from people who knew I had a disease–that was baffling and defining."

Wisconsin, 2001-2003

Responsibilities, 2001-2002

In 2001, I moved to Wisconsin for Aventis Pharmaceuticals, and so did Jayns's tapes. The weather horrified me in Wisconsin. I had a small SUV, but the snowy roads stressed me out tremendously, and each night I feared I would not get home. I worried about my son, my sales, the remote offices, and much more. My partner, Colby, who moved from Indiana with me, exhausted us both with complaints about the hours I was keeping.

Several doctors in Wisconsin warned me against writing a book as I made my daily sales calls: "You had better not hurt us." It was a strange threat coming from a doctor who was not helping our company scripts. Another warned me that my encounters in Wisconsin did not have to be so friendly. Still another assured me that Wisconsin was not far from Indiana in politics or persuasions. None of these statements made sense to me, so I ignored them.

I blazed through my responsibilities without external cues, but inside I felt haggard, and rushed to keep up with my missions. Had Bloomington not abused me, Wisconsin would have been a cakewalk. I had come out of shock about the rape, but the daily abuse of Bloomington and the attempted murder swirled in my subconscious. With PTSD, the more stress you take on, the more likely it is that you will push out a memory that you are still harboring that terrorizes you.

My Shock, 2003

I came out of shock about a lot while I was in Wisconsin. The timing irritated my supervisor, who lost me to doctor's appointments far away from my sales targets, but I still did the job, driving long distances daily. Until, that is, I ended up in the hospital.

It started with being unable to sleep. We are restless when coming out of shock. I kept remembering a man with a gun in a dark vehicle outside my house. The memory was of Tohm Hrisamolaz outside my Indianapolis home a few years earlier, but I kept checking outside our home in Madison, Wisconsin. No one was there. I would go downstairs, all the way down to the basement, clearing every room I passed in military fashion. In the basement I checked all the windows and doors. Only our Christmas tree stuffed in a box looked menacing. I returned to bed.

One morning, while Colby, my partner of three years, was getting ready for work, I sprung up. I told her that we had to leave the house because someone was outside with a gun. I was animated, panicked, running for the door. She, half dressed, tried to calm me. I was stronger than her though, and I pushed past her, rechecking the house despite her protests. My son was sleeping. Our rooms contained furniture, but no other people. The garage was still. The Christmas tree in the basement remained in its place.

"I'm taking you to the hospital," she concluded. I tried to go on my own, but she refused to let me. She drove, after my son walked across the street to school.

Colby was the perfect partner for me in a lot of ways. My personality and strengths focused on securing shelter, food, drink, and transportation for us. Colby's personality and strengths turned all that I secured into a home. She was my height with short brown hair that I once cut myself to save money, winning me wrathful stares from her family. She caught me and stabilized me without question during every up and down I experienced.

In the passenger seat, all I could think about was how easy it would be to break into our house. I could do it myself. We were not safe. Where was Jewel? Though far away, Jewel held the belief that I needed to trust the people I was currently seeing at the Madison VA. I tried to help myself. I couldn't.

I said nothing to Colby as she drove, but I could hear and see the flashbacks forming. For Dr. Tohm Hrisamolaz to reenter my memory, he would grab, pull, and drag Bloomington conversations and harassment, along with threats on his behalf from Berk, forward in the process.

Berk Flashback, 2003

In 1998, Berk had pointed a gun directly at me in two of our conversations in order to coerce me to sign something or do something. Berk's job for the Klan was to scare me into submission, but I am my grandparents' child and a West Point graduate. I'm not one to be in awe of a criminal. He made me sign papers, just like Jayns had forced me to say words. Among the papers Berk made me sign, he claimed that one of them gave him possession of my house. He bragged of selling my reputation to the KKK.

Hurting people is a source of entertainment for men in the KKK. They hold certain prejudices, among which is that idea that minorities are prone to drug use and will do anything for money, and that all women are whores. They brew hate through these stereotypes like a distasteful soup, and they drink of it as though it quenches their thirst. When they hurt someone, they speak in these terms and ideas, not because they know they are true, but because they wish they were true.

My flashbacks persisted.

Berk used one hand to smooth his beard and mustache. "Now, Tohm Hrisamolaz didn't use a gun to orchestrate that flu shot. Tracey, you are just

Undeterred

mental as hell. No one knows why, and God knows you need help. However, if you breathe a word about anything that happened to you in southern Indiana, you will be bombarded with degradation, pornography, and, ultimately, death."

"I have never been in pornography."

Berk slammed his fist on the table and reminded me, "We don't give a damn about what you've been into or will be into!"

"Well, I do. I don't even own pornography. How are you going to say a West Pointer who is doing as well as I am slipped into pornography? West Pointers don't go into porn. We help people. That's why I do well in sales."

"You are sick as hell right now. You are no match for the KKK. They hate you. They will follow you and humiliate you at the leisure of their viewers. They certainly do not want your help. Indiana does not want your help. Take the hint!

"If you are dumb enough to sell your story, you will be associated with pornography. First, it will help the KKK make money off what I did to you, because I am smarter than you. They may hate you, but them boys are going to make money off of you if at all possible. They love money. Even with that brain of yours, you show potential. It's amazing." He laughed, but sobered up fast.

"Second, they will punish you for standing up. No one wants you standing up for anything here. In this state, the KKK is God and you are damned. Take the hint."

"She can't remember the hint," laughed Mitchel. "You were just another black chick without a husband who couldn't manage her money. You were desperate."

At this moment, two things were true. First, I was still not aware that I had been booted out of Bloomington. Second, I could not access any reference to the term "KKK" in my memory. It was simply gone from my vocabulary. Berk sounded insane to me.

He described how all of the Indiana Klan people had voted against me via computer. *How could they vote for or against me? I wondered. I had not even run for anything and I was unsure whether I would ever run for political office,* but Berk insisted that the votes against me had already been tallied. "You're desperate, both of you," I said. "You are the one borrowing money from Lurea's family to keep your doors open. You need me more than I need you."

"Where is your pride? I can describe every shirt you tried on before coming to work last Friday. Now, how do I know that? How do we know the last time you took a crap? I helped them debase you. You cannot win," he shot back. "The information that I have on you is designed to destroy you someday. If you talk, the KKK will destroy your reputation. If you do well, expect to share your earnings with them. Every time you file your taxes in Indiana, Tracey, the KKK knows how much money you are making, where you live, and where you own property in the US. They will determine what of yours they want and they will take it, with or without your permission. They monitor people, Tracey, and they will monitor you.

"The KKK runs this state from top to bottom. There are tens of thousands of them crawling all over the place and only one of you. You cannot hide from them; Indiana is their world. You got the attention of the wrong people. They screw with people like you. You will always be inferior to them. You are greatly outnumbered. You will never get your life back."

"I have my life now," I said. "And as for my pride, you can't touch it. Regardless of your wealth versus mine, you are the worst person. I'm better than you in sheer fortitude."

"You no longer have your good name, let alone your life," he assured me. More insanity. I thought he might have a drinking problem, but Mommy's test–checking his pupils–failed.

"Listen, there are places in this country where Bloomington will own the judge and the jury. They will decide if you are into pornography. You need a lot of money to fight the KKK, Tracey. Your family is poor. There's no sympathy for the likes of you.

"We don't care about you in general," he pointed back and forth between himself and Mitchel. "We care about our client. Tohm wants your mouth shut about him and his father, and he's worried that your West Point degree may make people believe you. He really wants you dead, but your case got messy down there. You are only alive by accident. And now, no matter what you do, they can trump you by destroying your reputation; so be quiet.

"We don't care that you are mentally ill. God only knows how your sick brain talked you out of that second dose. You're like a lucky, little cockroach that scurries away over and over again. They were threatening you daily for months, Tracey, *trying to get you to leave town. Day after flipping day for over a flipping year! And yet you managed to live! They usually do not try to kill people. They don't want the body count, but Tohm got fed up with your dumb ass!"*

The Drive to the Hospital, 2003

Colby cursed the traffic as the car came to a standstill in the rain. I was fascinated by the trickles of rain gathering volume as they found easier ways to traverse the window and pool at the windowsill.

My thoughts, however, remained on Berk.

If you raise your voice at a mentally ill person, they do not hear you better. Immigrants don't understand English better that way either, but nevertheless people shout at them as if that were the answer. It's not our ears that fail us. The problem is not misunderstanding English; it's the synapses in my brain not firing correctly to allow me understand connections. If I do not have a memory due to PTSD, I cannot make sense of what is said referencing that memory. It truly is nonsense to me.

Screaming at a person with PTSD does not make your reality real to us; it makes us dismiss the conversation faster. Until we recall the terror, nothing about it registers. For years, I did not know that the KKK of Bloomington had thrown me into shock day after day after day for months on end. I did not recall a man trying to take my life for a woman or his honor. Planting conversations for the future doesn't make them sensible, now or later. The memory will come back much later without help from the perpetrator, and we will process it in accordance with how we were raised or trained, not the way a criminal preconditions us to.

The Second Berk Flashback, 2003

"So here is how it's going to go," Berk continued. "You are going to say nothing of what happened to you in Bloomington, or you are going to die. I will kill you myself before I give back my insurance pay, plus interest for however long it'll take

for your sick brain to wake up over the next ten to twenty years. So, if you ever want to talk about what happened in your pathetic life and the injustices thereof, you come on back to me. I'll listen. I'll also kill you. You will stand down, shut up, and lose. Life is not set up for someone like you to win."

"Life is not set up for me to win, and yet I'm running circles around your employees," I retorted. "You are threatening to kill me in one breath and begging me to work for you in another. How can anyone take you seriously? Maybe you are mentally ill. I certainly am not."

"Life is not set up for you to win," he repeated, ignoring my statement. "That's all. I honestly don't know if you are going to live."

"Oh, don't write a book either," Mitchel added, keeping his chuckles flowing.

Berk begged, "Please wait until we are all dead. Please don't make me read your demented thoughts before I kill you. Before you think of writing your story, remember this: your life is no longer your story. It barely exists after being erased like this. And when you market your book, we'll see it first. If it gets popular, the KKK will own your name. Trust me. You have no idea what you signed. To be honest, I'm not sure either." They both snickered.

"Seriously, people you could use as witnesses will disappear. IU won't have a record of them. No one will help you. When the Klan in Indiana stands up against you, no one, white or black, will stand up for you. Everyone else knows better except you. I cannot believe that they left you alive.

"That's why I'm here. Tracey, no one wants to hear from you. God help you if you are too sick to figure that out. Your voice no longer exists. It's called being erased. You grew up playing by the rules. The Indiana KKK doesn't play by those rules. They make their own up as they go along.

"Listen to me," he ordered and waited until I met his eyes. "No one wants to hear your side of the story. It's over." He waved a hand through the air. "For now anyway," he looked down. "They just hate you so much. They have a special list for people like you. I don't know if you are going to make it." He shook his head without a smile.

"You're insane, Berk." He certainly sounded like it. I did not understand the words he spoke, but I understood his sloppy delivery. "You make me sick, spitting and yelling over this table. Your insurance business is as ill-conceived as your

Undeterred

birth. One second you are threatening to kill me, and the next you are asking me to bring you $40,000 a month in profit. You can't make up your mind. I'll make it up for you."

The conversation with Berk proved one of the strangest in my life, with him trying to wake me, and my mind trying to remain asleep. The Klan had probably considered approaching my other employers as a way of getting to me, but they were not Hoosier-based. Pfizer hailed from New York and the software company from Massachusetts, neither of which were exactly Klan-friendly locations. Berk, who dabbled in after-hour projects that sometimes left him with broken bones and forced Lurea to make nervous explanations for him, was perfect for their needs. This was why Degan kept up with me, waiting for a more opportune employment environment for all parties involved.

The VA, 2003

Colby drove to the wrong hospital; I needed to go to the VA. When we arrived at the regular hospital, I was placed in an examination room for nearly an hour. I remonstrated. Why were we still there? Colby said that they were checking on something. She did everything possible to keep me in that exam room, but I successfully pushed past her. A cop and a nurse were at the end of hallway. I demanded to go to the VA hospital, and the cop took me to Madison's only veteran's facility.

Insurance II, 2003

A stranger visited me at the VA hospital two or three days after my admission. He said his presence was "courtesy of Tohm," and threatened not only me, but also the wellbeing of my partner and my son. He introduced himself as a local businessman from Madison, but warned me that I would not remember him so much as the reason that he came.

A person not in shock would quickly infer that this man was my second "insurance agent," Berk having been the first. He did not announce that he had a debt to the KKK, but his behavior and the threat referencing my expected compliance revealed the truth.

It started casually. He explained that someone from the district attorney's office was trying to do me a favor, and that I should sign a piece of paper to prevent charges, severe charges, against me for having caused harm to my partner.

I denied the accusation that I had ever laid a finger on Colby. I grew up with a man who never touched my nagging grandmother. From him, I learned that the trick to staying with a woman was to let her be right in everything, but, if you were the breadwinner, lead on those issues that you knew were essential to your combined economic wellbeing. In our relationship, I was the breadwinner. Colby was right about everything, and I kept my mouth shut.

We argued. He correctly pointed out that I had pushed past my partner at the other hospital. He said that the people who witnessed "the fight" were prepared to testify against me in court. I argued that there was no fight. He insisted that people seen and unseen heard a fight and saw me push past her.

"Sign this," he demanded, frustrated, and slapped the document before me.

The document admitted to "domestic abuse" on my part, for pushing past Colby to leave the civilian hospital room. When I questioned the term "domestic abuse," which was highlighted, he casually said that it was a general term. I had the sense to know that it was not a general term in Indiana, and so I doubted that it was in Wisconsin. He assured me that I could not stay in the hospital without signing the form.

We both raised our voices and argued for some time. He claimed that my partner was waiting to sign it as well. If she signed it, I could stay in the hospital. I wondered why. In 2003, homosexuals in a relationship could not affect each other's stay in a hospital. I left the room to ask my doctor what to do, but she said that she did not interfere in the legal matters of patients. Hers was an odd response, because doctors do not normally permit legal people to harass their patients.

Undeterred

My visitor and I argued again, and he grabbed a hold of me, saying he would not allow me to leave the room again until I signed. We almost came to blows.

I was tired and wanted to lie down, so I signed the document, worn out from verbal roughhousing with the insurance man. I would address his methods in court later, if need be. He held the sheet up triumphantly and said that though I would never see him again, I would live to see that paper again and would regret it.

While this was going on, someone else had informed Colby that if she did not sign this same form, I would be yanked from the hospital and jailed. We both signed the document under duress, so I dismissed it as having no legal standing.

The form was an admission of guilt for something that I had not done. Had it been filed, it would have been a serious legal black eye. The KKK hoped that I would take seriously their efforts to threaten me. Of course, this is a psychological tactic that can only work if the victim first thinks they are inferior, and then believes that they have no recourse against the lie.

Before the insurance man left the hospital, he warned me that the Klan could only use the signed document if Colby were dead, since they could have no witnesses. The message was clear, at least to him: it's up to you to keep your mouth shut.

But for me, that statement sounded like static; it meant nothing to a PTSD patient like me. The specific threat of pinning domestic violence on me meant even less. I had grown up watching my granddad quietly sit through skirmishes; he was teaching me that women are the head of the household. Mama took care of us. Papa provided. No one was ever hurt. It was a negotiation, and I followed these same principles in my own life now.

Perhaps the hospital could find a place for this insurance man, I thought. He was clearly teetering on shocking, illogical thoughts and conclusions himself.

He waited for his threats to sink in and affect me, but I said nothing. The possibility of him murdering my partner to use his so-called evidence did not even enter my mind. If they waited forty years for her to die, I reasoned, why would anyone care about this little sheet of paper? Perhaps I thought for too long, because he nodded at me, "Your reaction tells me that she is not the one." My reaction should have told him that a person dealing with PTSD could not care less about his message. I was relieved when he finally left.

Due to my nonchalance, the KKK rightfully doubted that their second attempt at insuring I would not talk had worked at all. Still, that little piece of paper would show up in my life again.

In hindsight, that scene could not have happened if I had been in the Indianapolis VA. A victim and a patient, I was in need of treatment, more and better treatment than what I was receiving. I had no interest in writing a book. The Klan had no interest in leaving me alone.

Still, these tactics assured me that it had a way for one chapter to call on another to finish a job. When people pack up and run, they only exchange their last oppressor's backyard for their next aggressor's front porch. Three truths emerged from that visit. First of all, the KKK felt that Berk's insurance against me was not good enough after all. Secondly, I did not take the new insurance person as seriously as the Klan needed me to, which meant that this had not worked either. This could only mean one thing: a third insurance effort loomed when I was least expecting it.

KKK Intent, 2003

I had never been sicker than I was in Wisconsin. Colby, weary of my constantly asking why she signed the insurance man's document, broke up with me while I was in the hospital.

The doctor who did not dismiss my strange visitor spent most of my stay asking me to name the man that was in my flashbacks. Her fervor to identify him made me uninterested in helping her. Doctors don't normally want to discuss the names of criminals more than they want to assess their patient's well-being, unless the criminal's name is more

Undeterred

important than the patient. Moreover, there was a solid year of abuse and abusers from Bloomington. How was I to know which one she wanted to discuss? I was released, having kept my conversations with her at a minimum, and went back to work.

In making sales calls, several distinct Wisconsin doctors reminded me that the information regarding Bloomington's damnation was national, not just limited to Indiana. Degan had bragged of their organization being high-tech; they were. They were able to stay in touch with members around the country, and had a national registry of those that needed to be kept an eye on.

It's the modern form of control and terrorism. A person can move and start over, start a business in another state, interact with new people, and, if they are members, those people can pull up the KKK entry for you online. The national database prefaces your arrival to every new place you go. Moving on command can be an exercise in control, depending on how much fun the group has demeaning you. They want you to never be as free as you were before they targeted you.

Many memories revisited me during my time in Wisconsin, and not having Jewel to help made things more difficult. I turned inward, often sitting on my porch listening to the rain, as I had during my childhood at Mommy's.

For a PTSD patient, flashbacks flood the rooms of our brains. Sometimes they are intrusive, sometimes not. They start out as a pencil sketch. By the time ink colors the sketch in permanently, they might as well be imprinted in stone, repetitiously invoked by new or different triggers. We recall exactly where we were and what we were doing when the horrors began. We know who hurt us. We know how. Those who harm us, thinking that our illness will exonerate them, forget that they created our memory delay through terror as easily as they created the terror itself. It all comes back clearly in the end.

To the KKK, "erasing" someone means taking away their potential via death or some other means so that they cannot be a threat in the future. It's what combatants do to their enemy when sweeping through a town, trying to round up or kill men and boys. Soldiers double-shoot a dead body with an extra bullet to ensure the deceased are indeed dead. KKK insurance men are that second or, in my case, third bullet to control the victim's will to stand up.

Organized crime insurance also sullies the victim's story, since the insurance perpetrator who delivers the threat will loudly deny any association with the KKK. That perceived distance allows the KKK to take cover from blame, to castle as if innocent.

Jayns in Wisconsin

With time, Jayns's tapes arrived, and my Wisconsin manager hinted that he wanted me gone. My time in the hospital had already alerted the company that I was less than perfect health-wise. Now Jayns's work gave them reason to think my problems were self-made. I, like anyone else carrying a primary drug that was not covered by managed care in Wisconsin, was doing just doing okay.

My manager quoted Jayns's tapes, asking questions that I found beneath me to answer. His last words to me were "I hope you are telling the truth. Otherwise yours is a complete waste of a life."

Mommy, 2003

I called my mother one day as I was preparing to leave Wisconsin for a new job in Indiana. I loved talking to her, whether by phone or on her "office bench" outside Walmart. I was still angry that Colby had signed that paper, and the fact that we had split up over it probably kept it in the forefront of my mind. Sometimes you call your mother to rile her up on your side, and that was just want I needed that day.

When I finished explaining my side, she was silent for a long time, then announced, "She loves you."

"Mommy, I am not lying. She might as well have testified that I hit her."

Undeterred

"Something happened," Mommy allowed, "but that woman loves you. I know she does because she acts as though your happiness is her primary goal. She loves you."

It was my turn to be silent.

"What did they say to her to get her to sign it?"

I did not know. I explained that a man had told me that I would go to jail if I did not sign it.

I felt exhausted. Long drives and taking care of my son and the house alone left me drained. Mommy let me hang out on the phone brooding.

"Mommy, do you ever feel like your superwoman powers don't work anymore?"

"Honey, women never lose their superwoman powers. No one can take those away from you. Your gifts are what made all these people hateful, but your gifts are what make you, you"

"I feel stuck, though."

"You are not stuck. You are just struggling. You were born with wings. Whenever you decide to fly, you will."

Return to Indiana, 2004

Retaking the Queen

In chess, there is one specific way to retake one's queen after it has been captured. If the feeblest piece, the pawn, can successfully cross the game board, escaping death along the way, it can resume play as any previously lost piece. It's a grueling journey, given that life permits only one meager step each turn. But if the pawn makes it, it can return as the queen, stronger, faster, and more dexterous than ever.

Every time the KKK has tried to destroy me or humiliate me, I have resumed play. I refuse to permanently surrender my queen without a fight.

Back in Indiana, I worked for a specialty pharmaceutical company called Odyssey, which was headquartered overseas. My new manager was a man named Maurie, whose leadership was as inspiring as Brian's. He and I were a great match because he wanted me to work, and I wanted nothing but to work. Under him, I took my Fort Wayne territory from tenth in Indiana to number one.

In life as in the Bible, Pharisees line your path, laughing at the strengths God bestowed on you. They hate your potential more than your face, because you look like anyone or everyone, but you think, speak, and smile like only you can. They celebrate your wounds, especially those they cause.

Undeterred

The Pharisees that I met in my new territory were once again KKK doctors who, recognizing my name, had rude slights for me once I entered their offices to do my job. Some asked if I had learned my lesson. Others threatened me, referencing something about writing a book. One refused to meet with me because I showed "no gratitude." Lingering in shock, his words meant little to me. He kicked me out of the office.

Every other piece outranks the pawn, a simple, lovable scout. Yet only the pawn's feet, when shuffled from end to end along the board, can bring the game's dead pieces back to life. We have a duty to recapture our queen, giving her a second chance.

I was highly successful in my own second chance at my new company; so much so that Maurie relocated me to Indianapolis. Then I took that territory to first place in Indiana, and seventh in the nation, too. I garnered these numbers without the Klan or anyone else boasting that they had inflated them for me.

Maurie nudged me forward for two years, until the company abruptly went out of business. No one expected the closing; Maurie and the rest of our staff were equally shocked.

My family as well as my co-workers entered a dark time and finding a new position proved difficult. My self-pep-talks started out positive, but wavered if not supported by a person with sound advice. I was very glad to be back in Indy with Jewel as my guide.

I leaned on my mother and Jewel for counsel a great deal during this period. Terrors flooded me in flashback fashion, and Jewel and I had a lot of work to do. She knew well the kinds of personalities I had run into; some of her clients were not victims, but rather perpetrators, a group that rarely seeks treatment unless forced by the legal system.

Papa, 2006

Papa passed. We were given time to prepare and, unlike with Mama, I used that time wisely. For several weeks I came over every day and gave Papa a close shave while going over the sports page with him or sitting through a Pacers game. I fed him his breakfast, despite Saint Vincent's

Hospital being more than willing to do it for me. I savored my time with him and said my goodbyes. He gave me advice until he was unable to speak.

I was grateful for the benefits he had received from Eli Lilly. His generation enjoyed the kind of retirement that the rest of us will never know. Lilly's underwrote my childhood nourishment, my safety, and my shelter through compensation to a man good enough to take care of his family. He was grateful to have had the job. I was grateful to have had him. It was a full circle of gratitude.

Papa was the best man I'll ever know. He helped others and did not hurt anyone; his was a splendid soul that I loved immensely. We could barely fit the cars into the cemetery when it was time to bury him. Everyone wanted to say goodbye.

Leasing, 2007

When my grandmother had died back in 2000, I caved in grief. When my granddad died, I felt rejuvenated. He always kept a positive outlook on my prospects and motivated me to be my best.

I had been at my best when I owned my own company. I researched possibilities and decided to start a leasing company. I still needed group insurance, so I worked odd jobs. Leasing sets up a payment system for expensive corporate or municipal equipment, so that money flows more easily than it would using cash. I flew to New York to one of the best leasing agents in the nation and took classes under him on commercial leasing.

What I did not know was that, in Indiana, the Ku Klux Klan runs the leasing business. Black businessmen tried to warn me, saying things like, "Girl, you takin' on The Man," "The Man" being a black colloquial term for *a* or *the* white man or men. Having always been a minority, there has always been a white man somewhere.

Even the only other black lease broker in the state named Timmy grabbed me by the arm during a function my first year in business and assured me that I would not make it. I wondered how he made it. "Every card in the deck is stacked against you," he cautioned me. He reminded me of Jayns. I demanded that he unhand me.

With such a welcome did I quit? I ignored every warning available. Besides, I had a great plan.

Mommy, 2007

I drove to Mommy's "office" and waited outside on our regular bench until she came out for her break. Our regular mother-and-daughter meeting convened.

People were stealing from the store, she told me. The cosmetics were statically taken by middle-aged white women, but she had a sneaking suspicion that the coats and hats were going to the large number of Hispanic people who would come in without a coat and leave wearing one. That was her theory at least, and Walmart was researching the matter.

"I bet the Asians are taking all the light bulbs," I said.

"Tracey, I'm serious!"

"Have you noticed that the Islamic folks are just leaving the rugs on the floor, all pointed in the same direction?" I continued, jokingly. We giggled.

"You are nuts," Mommy said. She was right, of course, in so many ways, but she laughed at me all the same. "What do Asians have to do with the light bulbs?"

"What do Muslims have to do with Walmart rugs?" I asked. "Nothing. We define each other as groups, not as individuals with the ability to think for ourselves."

She lit a cigarette, nodding.

"Why do you think a woman would want me to be kicked out of town or murdered in Bloomington?"

"Who did?" Mommy asked, surprised. Spirals of smoke curled above her head. I wanted my mother to stop smoking.

"Just a cardiologist in my old territory," I explained. "I was nice to her and to everyone else. Another doctor told me that she was the one who turned my name in to the group."

"Were you friends with her?"

"I wasn't friends with any of them."

"Why did the cardiologist say she turned you in?"

"She never told me. According to the other doctor, I hit on her."

"*Did* you hit on her?"

"No, I don't recall thinking that way about anyone in that town. I mostly only talked to her with her staff in the room. We had a one-on-one appointment once where she asked a lot about my upbringing and goals in life. She said that Bloomington was all that she had ever known. That struck me as odd. I encouraged her to travel."

"None of your goals that you discussed included your dating her?"

"No."

"*Traveling* with her?"

We both laughed. "No," I assured her.

"Did you date anyone in Bloomington?" she wondered.

"I had drinks once with a blonde nurse. She invited me out, but she got sloppy drunk and asked me repeatedly to go to her place for the night. I didn't want to stay in town, so I refused. When I dropped by the hospital later, she gave me the cold shoulder because she was embarrassed. She told me that she had not wanted to go out with me in the first place, that it had been some kind of order. She said 'they' were in an all-out effort to get rid of me. Her manager told me to let it go. According to her, I did not want attention in Bloomington. It would never fare well for me."

"Well, that's an interesting one-and-only date. Please tell me you have let that go."

"I'm driving back tonight to see how she's been," I joked. We laughed.

Even years later, I did not realize that that one date was a ploy and that the blonde nurse was a purposeful lure. Dr. Kalen had alluded to the possibility of a murder-suicide when we were outside the tennis facility.

Undeterred

The possibilities abound with the most casual shift in reality. There is no better word than *dangerous* to describe what it's like to be in shock among hateful people.

"Maybe, given the doctors there, getting you out of Bloomington was their nicest gesture, Tracey."

Mommy waived at a co-worker leaving for the day. The woman waved back and called, "Bye, Miss Nancy." She was a thin white woman who alone was senior to my mother at the store.

"Be good, Betty," Mommy called back to her. Betty had a slow gait and a face too aged to be as deeply brunette as her hair was dyed. She had a tough time greeting folks, let alone doing anything else in the store. "She's been really sick," Mommy offered as an excuse. "I brought her some of my chicken noodle soup yesterday." The woman soon disappeared behind traffic.

A younger associate arriving to work also saluted Mommy, "Afternoon, Mama Nancy."

"Hey Donita," smiled my mother. To me, she said, "She's pregnant, and that is gonna be a cute baby. Watch." When your mother is sweet, you share her with many.

I waived at Donita as I had Betty, but continued with our conversation, "But death, Mommy. They voted to kill me!"

"Was that the doctor's decision or theirs?"

"She started it."

"Maybe she did. Maybe she didn't. Maybe her boyfriend forced her to turn you in. His dad *is* the grand dragon. Men carrying that type of hatred find it hard to turn it off, even for their women." She exhaled smoke. "He would have enjoyed hurting you more than she would. There are people who enjoy pointing fingers so much that even they can't tell what's true anymore."

She paused, then asked, "What was this woman like?"

"She's extremely tall, probably six feet or more, and extremely blonde."

"Extremely blonde?"

"Yes."

Mommy did not always comment on her nerdiest child's life. We laughed and joked, but I often stumped her. Sometimes the best response she could offer was to exhale her cigarette smoke in silent thought.

"Tracey, you know race is a big part of the landscape here."

"Tell me about it," I agreed. "You do not have to endure hate daily for it to start feeling regular. The hater wants you to stall and trip. If you don't, they stall or trip you anyway."

"And if you do, then you are *guilty* of stalling and tripping," Mommy laughed. "Someone like you having 'a gait problem' is typical, once you're assigned one."

I watched cars slow as they passed by and customers mosey in and out of the store. Mommy sat thinking.

"What color were her eyes, Tracey?"

"Whose eyes?"

"The Bloomington doctor's."

"I have absolutely no idea, Mommy."

"Then I have no need to hear any more about the incident."

We sat there, me with my head down and her taking drags off her cigarette until Mommy said, "Let's go back inside. It's going to rain."

Insurance III, 2008

The first two insurance attempts against me were not successful. The KKK may believe that a picture, tape, or paper would destroy me, but I think that the "evidence" they hold displays the KKK's nature more than mine. Up until 2008, I was not interested in falling in line and believing myself inferior or debased when hounded by insurance men that I was not even conscious of. The KKK, therefore, unrolled their most effective weapon against women.

In this form of coercion, a man targets a specific woman to date. His mission is to have sex with her on tape. The sex can be consensual or not: the KKK does not care. The tape will then be used to blackmail

Undeterred

or coerce her. In my case, the threat was to warn me not to expose Dr. Tohm Hrisamolaz and his father as attempted murders.

A man assigned by the KKK to target a woman tells a different version of the truth from her. That's his job. He'll call, but say that he met her at a bar. According to him, several of his friends "who know her well" referred her to him. He'll say they all frequent the same bar. Countless white men will line up in court or the media to defame her if she speaks out.

It's a totally different story from what actually transpires. From start to finish, the process is stacked against an outnumbered woman. His words will be designed to casually discredit and demean her publicly, while downplaying the KKK's involvement.

He will convince her to come to a hotel room, which will have a hidden recording device already planted, for the purpose of intercourse. If they arrive at the same time, he will enter the room alone briefly to turn on the device, and then immediately let her in.

She will not suspect a thing.

The final step is to get her to legally consent to the usage of the sex tape that she didn't even know she was starring in. This is done in a car with a recording app on a smart phone for several reasons: it changes the venue and the story, and it yields better acoustics. The KKK-appointed male will assure the woman that he will tell everyone that they spent most of their time alone in his car, not the hotel, because the car sounds more distasteful for the woman. She will consider her prospects and cave to KKK control or humiliation. He will try to find a way trick or coerce her into saying that she consents to his using his videos online. That will be the first that she hears of such videos, since they were not apparent in the hotel.

Jock Roman, my insurance person, said the process targets young females who drink and do drugs, or who obviously have mental illnesses, through sequential steps, with the hope that their compromised state trips them incurably. If the insurance person can secure her "consent," her reputation is lassoed into the male-dominated, multi-million dollar porn industry. The threat of exposure through the Internet constantly looms so that she feels that she has little to no options.

The consent conversation is so important that the insurance man wears an ear bud in his left ear, not easily seen by the passenger. Jock showed me his earpiece to demonstrate that someone else was listening and instructing him in what to say. He explained his unusual forthrightness later. The trappings of the car exchange being as important and thorough as they are, my guess is that the mystery listener is familiar with the law and any verbal loop holes through which the woman's words or tone may slip. After the car scene, the rouse is over, and the woman is trapped.

The specifics of how it transpired in my case were quite different than the plan.

Execution, 2008

When Jock first called me, it was to work on a real estate deal for a hotel he owned. I had never worked in commercial real estate, nor had I marketed myself as such. He could not remember where he received my name and number.

Physically, he was taller than I and claimed to have played football in his youth. Bald, he had a brunette mustache, broad build, and a middle-aged midriff, and he joked with gentile sarcasm. He had several properties in distress, and he thought that an infusion of money in one in particular would allow it to survive, but he needed to find investors. I thought a couple of my clients might be interested or at least be able to make a few suggestions, so I told him that I would help, despite my inexperience. After we started working together, he asked me to go out with him.

I made an appointment to consult with Jewel. I had not dated anyone, male or female, since my partner in Wisconsin. After taking care of someone for several years, and having her essentially declare that I had abused her in some way, I was hesitant to enter a relationship again. As a result, I had lived a singular life of hibernation since Wisconsin.

Undeterred

I announced this possible change to Jewel: "I'm going to date a man." The statement came at the end of our session, and it shocked her. She gripped her pen tightly and gritted her teeth, trying to pick and choose her words carefully. She knew I had not dated a man in sixteen years.

"What if Jayns was just the worst choice ever, and I actually like men after all?" I continued, justifying my decision. "Did you ever think about that, Jewel?"

"Oh my, Tracey," laughed Jewel, "did you ever think about that?"

She composed herself and asked me to identify the man I planned to date. I told her his name was Jock. She wanted his contact information, and I provided it.

"So this is a controlled study to see if Jayns was an isolated case?" Jewel hypothesized. We both laughed, but she concentrated on accessing my comfort with my own decision. "Do you remember seeing a man naked?" she asked.

I didn't. I had been honest with Jock, and had already told him about having been raped at West Point. In response, Jock assured me that he was not built to rape a woman. I did not understand that, and even Jewel wrinkled her brow when I told her.

I knew that Jock's ex-wife had insulted him with the assurance that both of his kids were not even his. He considered the ridicule "vicious," and Jewel explained that that was a frequent claim of a woman who wanted to hurt the man in her life. I would soon learn the raw truth of the allegation.

Jock and I went out a few times while working on his project, and one day he asked me to go to a hotel with him. I asked him why we did not use one of his two houses, and he said that during the split with his ex-girlfriend, she had gotten the smaller house. I thought it odd that an ex-girlfriend would get a house, but he refused to discuss it further, save conversation about her working at a museum. The larger house had an HVAC/mold problem according to Jock that needed a few more weeks of work, so he was staying in a hotel for the time being.

Tracey Brame

The hotel was just north of the Indianapolis city border in Carmel, the wealthiest area of the state. Upon entering the room, one walked past the bathroom on the right to a king-sized bed with nightstands and lamps, all also on the right. Past the bed, on the same wall, was an upholstered bench. A long table supporting a TV and a lamp was on the left wall, with a mirror above it.

When I knocked on the hotel room door, Jock was already inside. The KKK wants the man inside first to turn all the cameras on. They have a camera dedicated to the door to prove that only the man and the woman, not themselves, were in the room. They also have hidden cameras focused on the bench and the bed.

I was not prepared for Jock's body. Once he removed his pants, I sat quietly as he began explaining the reality of his anatomy. I stared at what looked like circular scar tissue, a flattened lump of flesh. I imagined, with less knowledge of male anatomy than some, it to retreat backwards into his skin rather than protrude outward. I felt embarrassed, but maybe my embarrassment was for him. I took deep and shallow breaths and tried to think of words that could help in the moment.

When I made eye contact with him, his face was twisted in shame. I thought he was holding his breath. With a wave of his hand like Vannah White, he whispered unconvincingly, "There is enough here to have fun." I considered that, but glanced down at the floor, studying the carpet. The room was becoming nauseating warm.

Jock assured me that he had experienced successful sexual encounters in the past. His intimate partner had to hang from his shoulders while his knees pointed at a downward angle from the side of the bed to create as much surface area as possible for the woman. Then his partner bounced to accomplish possible penetration or even self-impregnation. It sounded more like a way to fall and pinch a nerve in one's neck.

Still sitting in front of Jock with misgivings, I contemplated my departure. He, reading my reaction, suggested I go to the bathroom to rinse my face, and I did so. The room had grown increasingly hot and dizzying. Despite being half naked, I considered escaping to the hallway.

Undeterred

Jock did not threaten me, but he had not been completely honest, either. I left the bathroom to retrieve my clothes and suddenly the room became dark, with no light whatsoever. I stepped toward the door, but could not leave half naked, so I felt my way around the bed. That is where he lunged at me.

I screamed. In the dark, Jock's voice shushed me. It was a calm voice, serene. "I'm a businessman," he said, "I am not going to hurt you. I have a daughter." His right hand entered my jeans and wrapped around my left hip to suspend me from behind while he turned the lamp on with his left hand. The room lit up again.

I went into shock. Jock went into motion.

Shock victims may stiffen their limbs at the moment of the trauma, and I did so at this point. Jock fought my unnaturally outstretched arms, indicative of complete shock, throwing them over his shoulders repeatedly because they would not stay, whispering for me to bend them if possible.

Jock climbed on top of me, faking penetration, and whispered, reassuring me, "I'm not inside of you. It's just pretend." He posed me in different ways on both the bench and the bed. He coached me to take certain positions, making it look like he was actively having sex with me. At one point, he jumped up and changed his shirt, most likely in compliance with unknown orders. He built up a sweat, audibly and visually feigning excitement on top of a woman he felt nothing emotionally or physically. Anyone watching would have thought him a masterful lover.

While I laid there in shock, his face appeared and disappeared as he changed positions. Each time he made eye contact with me, he whispered, with sweat beads standing out from his pink skin, "It's just pretend." His abrupt and repeated body weight pounding on top of me left me unable to catch my breath at times, unable to think my way through the situation, and unable to leave if I reasoned to do so.

I tried to sleep as much as I could once he was done. Shock is exhausting. He side-stepped awkwardly when on the long edge of the bed, the side facing the table, lamp, and camera, but walked normally once he passed this point, which would tell me later that he was protecting himself from a frontal view with the camera.

While resting I heard Jock say that Tohm and the doctors in Bloomington did not want me to write a book. Specifically, "they did not want to be represented as white supremacists."

When I saw Jewel the next week, I described what my disease allowed me to remember: his body's shape and the inverted rocking motion that his ex-wife and girlfriend probably went through to get pregnant or penetrated. The prospects of him or me holding my weight for such exaggerations frightened me. What if he dropped me, and I pinched a nerve in my neck?

Jewel looked up from her notes, probably not envisioning the acrobatics any better than I could. Placing her pen down, she asked, "How are you doing?"

I assured her that I had not tried to impregnate myself. I confided that I went to the bathroom to rinse my face, because the room had grown dizzying and warm once he showed himself and, save for being half naked, I considered escaping to the hallway.

I could not volunteer anything else. Missing from my memory was everything that happened after I left the bathroom and went into shock, and neither Jewel nor I knew what my brain blocked. I could confidently assure her that I did nothing to humiliate him, which she, having expertise in male egos, thought was best.

Missing also was the car component of the scheme the next day, where Jock tried to get me to verbally authorize the KKK to publish his videos online. The goal in the car is to harass the woman into giving consent. If she is still drunk, high, or in shock, the gamble should pay off.

The experience, what I could remember of it, convinced me that I had no future with men in general. I continued working with Jock professionally. Being in shock means that, not only can the mind with PTSD-induced amnesia not tell a therapist what happened, the victim also cannot tell herself. Thanks to my usual expression of the disease, I did not avoid Jock; he actually pulled me closer because he had a different scheme yet to unveil.

Undeterred

Jock's Insurance, 2008

When someone goes into shock, there is usually a witness, even if it is only the person who caused the trauma. Likewise, there is usually someone invested in trying to pull a person out of shock for his or her own reasons. In my case, Jock was invested in awakening me to his unlawful actions. He knew the details of his crime, and he desperately wanted me to know them as well: what really happened in that hotel room, his motivations, and his potential gain.

"We have to work together," he said to me one day. We were sitting at a table in a quiet restaurant less than a week after his exploits. He drank scotch almost exclusively around me, and he was doing so at that moment. I sipped a Diet Coke. Contrary to what he said, we did not have to work together, because I was discovering that finding financing for his hotel was impossible. Jock was not speaking of the hotel though.

"Listen," he said, sipping his drink, "I have absolutely no incentive to help you if you do not wake up from shock within five years. You cannot sue after five years. If you do not sue, there is no lawsuit. We need a lawsuit. How do people come out of shock?"

I made him explain what he meant by "shock." In my opinion, I wasn't in shock, couldn't even recall the word's meaning, and lacked data points in my memory to make sense of his words. In shock, with no memory, and no instinct to avoid an aggressor, I had no ability to grasp his conversation. With many an antagonist, I'd be in serious danger.

"You go into shock, Tracey. You forget things. What does it take to get your memory back?"

If only it were that easy, as if all it took were an exorcism, a ritual to be performed, and he, having hurt me, could benefit. I was speechless.

"I didn't rape you," he bargained.

I felt incensed by his assertion. I had not accused him of rape. When Jayns raped me, I woke up feeling mutilated on the inside for a week. I felt nothing like that in reference to Jock.

"Legally," he lowered his voice as two women sat down nearby, despite the nearly empty seating section, "you cannot claim rape, because I will walk for that."

Why is he speaking of rape? Why is he talking this way?

"Visually," he continued, "*they* all think that I raped you, but only you and I know that is physically impossible."

I focused on the fizz in my soda, mini rivulets of condensation vertically diving for the napkin beneath my glass. I tried to recollect the "they" of which he spoke. If I could access the Monterey experience in my memory at that moment, I would have realized that a man bragging that he did or did not rape me was not a safe man. My brain refused to connect the dots, though. I studied the Diet Coke's carbonation and said nothing.

"Damn, if I can't reach you…" he trailed off, gritting his teeth and sipping scotch to soothe his anxieties.

I regained eye contact with him. He sounded crazy. I had not been raped. I had no plans to sue anyone. He had a tiny penis. I wondered if every woman who saw him naked went through this conversation. My confusion abounded.

"You can claim that I behaved inappropriately with a mentally ill person behind closed doors," he said. "That is the only case you could make."

I stared at him. *How can he call me mentally ill?* No one can look at a person and know if they have PTSD with dissociative amnesia.

"I cannot reach you while you are in shock," he repeated, dropping his eyes. "We'll give it time." He seemed dejected. "I hate these assholes. You have great reason to come out of shock."

He was giving me time, but I did not fully understand his words. *Shocked about what? I tried to be outwardly indifferent to his body. What else could I be shocked about?*

The rule about insurance men is that they cannot be a member of the KKK. Jock was Catholic, and he complained mightily about the KKK members at his golf course who were heavy-handedly harassing him about the money he owed them and the Klan.

Undeterred

Jock was so far in debt that he had to cancel a few of his golf course memberships in anticipation of filing for bankruptcy. I hoped he dropped the golf course with the insulting Klansmen, since he hated them so much. Hopefully, he was at least that smart.

Jock complained about things every time we met. He complained if his scotch was not perfect, he complained about the government, and he complained about people who complained about his favorite talk radio pundits. I eventually grew tired of his complaints, but I kept in mind that I only had to see him on occasion. On each occasion, I had to tell him that there was no funding for his hotel.

Jock's Persuasion

Jock called other meetings, under the guise that we were friends or that there was something new to discuss about the property. Little changed with me: the property was just not financeable. I went to say hi, to get out of my office, or just to chat, but there was no attraction.

Sometimes I still had trouble hearing what he said. When you are in shock and someone forces a conversation about the trauma you are in shock from, your brain blocks the message. The brain does not want you reminded of the shock, so like a heavy-handed parent, it translates the worst information into noise. I experienced that with Jayns during the phone call where he taunted me about raping me with the beer bottle. Jock teetered on the same offense, but with a different mission.

"I'm sorry," he said one day. We were in his office off of Michigan Road on the west side of Indianapolis. The building was so close to my mother's Walmart store, I mostly went to this meeting so I could see her afterwards. As I stood in his starkly decorated office, I studied my car in the sunlight outside his window. I needed a car wash.

"You are sorry for what?" I asked.

"Everything that happened in the hotel and the car. You did not understand what I was asking you to say in the car. It's obvious," he sounded sincere.

I looked at his desk, and noticed his bottle of scotch sat close by. "What are you saying?" I asked.

"I do not know why these guys hate you so much, Tracey." He shook his head sadly.

"Who?"

He covered his face with both hands in disbelief at my naiveté and spoke, "The guys at the golf club... they made me do this. I regret the day I borrowed money from them." He recounted his mission: he could repay his debt by humiliating me on camera.

A commercial property specialist with no knowledge of psychiatry, Jock said that he was specifically instructed on how to make me go into shock. Once I was in shock, Jock was supposed to have sex with me on camera. He gave me all the details of the operation: the hidden cameras in the hotel room and in the car, the need to get my consent to publish the videos online or, at least, to get me to say enough to cut and paste my consent together. He asked me if I knew a specific doctor in Carmel who had orchestrated the crime on behalf of Tohm and the KKK much like Dr. Kalen was in charge of her employees in Bloomington. I did not know the doctor.

"I am involved in this because I have a huge debt to them, but you are a target because they hate you," he finished, peeking at me from behind his hands, then crossing his arms on the desk. He put his pen in a holder, and stared at me.

Thanks to my disease, my ears just heard senseless chatter. The more detail he gave, the less I heard. *I should tell my mother that my hearing is going bad again. Not since Bloomington have I had such problems.*

Jock could not tell the Klan that he could not penetrate a woman seated, prone, or standing up, so he faked it. He hoped that because he had not actually raped me, I would come out of shock before the statutory limitation of five years. Then, we could co-prosecute the Klansmen and testify for each other, trap his golf course enemies in a lawsuit, and earn a "retirement" thanks to the FBI's witness protection program. Tangled in his financial problems, Jock was well ahead of me in bringing closure to his crime.

Undeterred

In shock still, I was not that far alone. He sounded insane. Shock victims are always the last to know what happened to them. To me, he just had a small penis, but now he was talking about golf buddies, Klansmen, and retirement. Confused, I could only declare that I did not want to retire with him.

"You won't," he shot back. "We will each have to agree to not talk to each other, or the FBI will retract our retirements completely."

He poured another scotch, "You don't think that a Catholic man would dare wear or wave confederate flags at a camera, do you? I'm Catholic, Tracey. That was humiliating for me."

I said nothing. I had no recollection of what he was talking about. Insurance men wear confederate flags, scarves, shirts, or dragons in the videos, not to flaunt their own allegiance to the Klan, for they are not members, but as a form of ridicule and humiliation. It is a punishment for them, too. Jock could recall and despised the buffoonish actions he performed. I could not.

He lowered his voice. "You stand to gain more than I, but you have to wake up."

I didn't wake up. He called me over and over and we went out infrequently, always after some persuasions on his part. We went out to eat, to get drinks, and even to a shooting range. None of that wakes a person up, no matter how friendly you pretend to be. He tried valiantly at each encounter and, after his bankruptcy in 2009, he tried even harder to shake me from shock.

"I'm ready," he laughed at one point. He was 55 years old and unsure if he could rebound after his financial woes. He had lost the hotel I worked with him on, along with several other properties. He did keep a Bloomington business deal, because he felt his "connections" would help.

I disappointed him at every meeting by recalling nothing. "You realize that you are not the normal target for this kind of treatment?"

"What treatment?"

Jock rolled his eyes. "The kind of women they are taking to these hotel rooms are drinkers or druggies. Your illness makes you go into shock, so they tried it on you." He laughed to preface his next statement: "They think you were raped because I faked it pretty good." He smiled with upheld hands, giving himself all the credit.

I said nothing. He went on, "Assume it's consensual for a second, just a second. If she is snockered out of her mind, or if you are in shock, is that really consensual? Someone could disappear while incapacitated in one of those hotel rooms." Were there multiple rooms and ruses set up? He held my stare for emphasis, waiting for his prophecy to sink in, and then continued, "You escaped something. There is no way a shock victim can negotiate the landmine they created for you, but we can work together and get a little revenge for the both of us."

I did not want to hear anymore. He sounded like someone on TV, trying to sell me something I did not need. As I was leaving, he took out a picture of his daughter. "I'm not for hurting women. I do not want anyone hurting her," he said, showing me the picture. "We have to keep talking, but we can only talk to each other."

I complimented his daughter and, remembering his ex-wife's insults, tried to note whether or not she looked like him. I did not respond to his comment about us needing to talk to each other.

"There is money in this for you. I'll call you soon."

I headed toward the door.

"You need time. I get that, Tracey."

People with PTSD need time? More like years. If only he knew my history with Jayns, he'd know his "talk" seemed like screeching rambles. Eventually, I would only speak to him by phone. Once I entered graduate school, we did not speak much at all.

Out of Shock

When I finally came out of shock seven years later, I pondered Jock's bodily challenge. His participation in a dating ruse perplexed me. I needed Jewel's wisdom, but she had retired. My mind raced, cycling through fear, worry, and guilt. "I should have known" when he called me out of the blue. I had no experience with real estate. My business card said real estate, but that was for a specific government loan with lower level properties. How did he get my card? "I should have known" there was an agenda. "I should have known."

Every KKK crime I have endured was about control or humiliation, rather than logic. This third insurance against me speaking out was no different. To keep one person from writing a book, why would you introduce her to your criminal methods that might potentially entail kidnapping, sex slavery, and trafficking? How important is the book? How deep is the hate?

Upon awakening to what happened, I went to the police. The sergeant explained that, since the five-year statutory limitation on prosecution mark had passed, they could do nothing about Jock. She also told me that having a penis of only three or four centimeters precludes one from being charged with rape. She concurred that improper behavior with a mentally ill person was a better charge, but that was also only prosecutable for up to five years.

If my lingering in harm's way allows me to shed light on these tactics for others, then parents may give one more specific warning of danger to a daughter from Indianapolis's northern suburbs teetering on the wild side. I am not the usual target for such operations; young, white females are. Still, the woman is out-numbered as much as I was by men who believe that, because they are white and wearing business suits, they will trump her youth and compromised situation.

I was fortunate not to be physically hurt. Perhaps Jock's build was a shear blessing. God looks over us in small ways.

Insurance

Berk, my first insurance person in 1998, once laughed that if I wrote a book and included him, no one would believe me because the story would be too fantastic. He reiterated that all he would have to say was that he is not a member of the KKK, and prevailing opinion would conclude him innocent. Many businessmen confuse a suit and tie with a badge of honesty. When the victim encounters multiple KKK insurance people, putting them side-by-side is good for comparisons and emphasis.

All three insurance men failed to seek help from the FBI upfront out of fear. Jock, unlike Berk, was not a criminal by nature, yet even he complied with the KKK. Instead of getting help beforehand to stop his crime, Jock's logic led him to seek help after the crime, since he would not have actually raped someone, as ordered. He expected that his victim would save him.

Being white offers no shelter from hate. The insurance agents were all white. Most victims of the hotel operation are white. The logic goes beyond race, and presumes that a few are essentially better than all the rest of society, who are unworthy of consideration. Thus, those who harm them do so without compunction.

The KKK has not used their insurance against me, though there have been repeated threats. I am supposed to fear members of the Klan, who feel bolstered by their numbers, eluding the law while bullying other citizens. I am supposed to fall silent to protect the reputation of Dr. Tohm Hrisamolaz and his father, the grand dragon. Unlikely to write a book before the KKK's actions to silence me, the insurances, threats, and illegalities actually encouraged me to pen their methods, to let our country understand both the prevalence and illogic of hate crimes and coercion in a state like Indiana, which has no law against hate crimes.

The victim is not unbelievable. The after-hours banter of bigoted criminals, set on pampering their interests and exacting perceived debts at the expense of others–that's unbelievable.

Jayns's Tapes, 2009

Jayns's tapes were unbelievable as well, though they resurfaced again and again in my work life as he stalked me electronically. I finally brought them up in a San Jose court in 2009. He was living in San Jose at the time, and, chronic with nonpayment of child support case, he was forced to appear. I asked the judge to block my personal information from Jayns.

I explained that my ex-husband had taken to crack at West Point and had begun taping all of our conversations so that he could cut and paste them into something more sordid for his listening pleasure. He had sent these tapes to my employers and clients. Pfizer had them. Berk referenced them, as did others. Some promised to keep the tapes on file with their legal department.

Jayns panicked. Apparently he had government customers, so he threw a conniption in the courthouse hallway, demanding that I recant my statement. I said no. He offered more money if I would drop it. I refused. Finally, he had to write a rebuttal. It was two pages long.

To paraphrase: "I, Jayns C. Jhomes, Jr., graduated from West Point and served in the army. As an officer, I once talked to high school students about West Point. I started going to church a few times. She can't prove it. Make her prove it."

He never denied that he made and distributed the tapes. He just castled behind the walls of the legal system. No one loves diving for cover more than the king. There is safety in hiding. Moreover, the castle trades places with the king and fights for him. All Jayns had to do was point to where he wanted the law to focus, and the institution kicked in to cover his wrongs, while I was left in a tug-of-war with the federal government to obtain his locked records so I could get the disability benefits I deserved.

Castles in chess can only move horizontally and vertically. They can't make a diagonal move. Imagine that: the castle, or institution, fights in a straight line for crooks who can't walk a straight line within law.

I found Jayns's reactions curious, until I remembered that his apartment had been tapped. When the federal government tapes conversations, the federal government owns those conversations. He probably had to sign over the rights of those tapes to the federal government. Had he committed more felonies by tampering with government property? Without due cause to open Jayns's official military records, the federal government's tapes protected the rapist, not the raped who was missing medical records or being bludgeoned professionally.

I raised the issue of blocking my personal information from Jayns only to make the judge consider my and my son's privacy. But by doing so, I halted Jayns's illegal tape-mailing activity. From that point on, I never had another manager bring up his fabricated tapes. He had been sending them for fourteen years to reduce my employment prospects. Fear of exposure is a true motivator for some kings. Criminals only take credit for their work when shielded. They may leave a mess, but they hide when the light shines on it.

THREATS, 2010-2012

Jashon's Threat, 2010

Insurance threats are arguably more dangerous than other, more personal threats from individual Klansmen. When a group hates someone, individuals feel obliged to show distaste too. While I was in Bloomington, scores of individuals threatened me when they were trying to kick me out of town. The Klan switched to insurance threats once I left Bloomington. Two separate threats by Klansman once I returned to Indianapolis stood out more than the passing comments I had experienced in Bloomington.

In 2009, I was a leasing specialist with my own company, serving as the middle person between banks and commercial customers in finance transactions. No other minority leasing agent in town was doing business with municipalities in central Indiana; the transactions simply did not exist. The City of Indianapolis had not leased anything in nearly twenty years when I approached them, asking if I could handle the leasing of their vehicles, computers, anything. City representatives assured me that they did not lease anything. If Indianapolis could not buy equipment with cash, they would do without. I had my work cut out for me.

Waiting to buy with cash meant that the city could not buy as much property each year. If they could not buy new property, they had to rely on aged equipment, which was prone to breaking. Once equipment broke, liabilities climbed, especially if anyone were injured. I held the solution to these problems.

Not long after I approached the city, there was an inaugural networking meeting put together by a national association for women business owners, to help forge better relationships between the city and female business owners. I was one of many who attended. As the event wound down, I found myself near a man who was dressed down and who had not spoken to many. I approached him to find out what he did. From my days in the military and in recruiting, I had developed a natural curiosity for what people do. It's fascinating, really, what we all do to stay alive and take care of our families.

He ran the city's motor pool. I thought that was awesome. From my days in the army, I knew motor pools were a great place to gain information. We discussed the types of broken equipment he saw, and there was plenty. Some were dangerous to drivers and other citizens alike if left unchecked. When I asked if he would receive enough replacements for the next year, he laughed. He had been advised to expect less, not more, of what he needed in the coming year.

I asked more questions. Over time, he and I developed a list of equipment lifespans and cost-to-cures. I worked up the difference between what he wanted and what he needed. When we looked at the numbers and saw the possibilities in my solution of leasing equipment, I asked who in the city administration would listen. We agreed that it would be the accountant and the department head that ran the networking meeting where we had met. He assured me that he was not comfortable making the presentation, so I scheduled the meeting and arrived by myself.

I designed spreadsheets and an interactive presentation that impressed the department head and accountant. When I finished, the department head said, "This is why we held the women's networking

Undeterred

meeting–to find new and interesting ideas." I was excited to be of service, but both assured me that they did not lease and had no plans to start leasing. I needed to speak to the city's chief financial officer.

Traction! I thought, and made the appointment with their blessings.

The Finance Officer proved cautious. I proposed a specific lease type and lender, which would cost less over time. The Finance Officer agreed to have another call with me in several weeks. At that time, he only had a few questions that I was able to answer readily. He made no official requests for anyone else to provide this service. I earned the business, having created an opportunity for the city to save money.

The Finance Officer agreed to move forward. It was a great win for my company and for me. He accepted my thanks and assigned a young assistant finance officer named Jashon Dudish to the leasing project.

During my first meeting in 2009 with Jashon and another man that I never saw again, they asked me a number of personal questions. "Are you pregnant?" Jashon thought that was hilarious. "How old is your youngest child, about a year and a half?" More laughter.

He asked about my troubles with the law, but I had not had any. He assured me that I did and that I would. "You just don't know it yet." This, unbeknownst to me, was a reference to the paper I had signed years before in Wisconsin. Being in shock about that still, I did not fully understand their comments, so I rationalized it like someone with my illness would: I chalked up their laughter and inappropriate questions as being due to their youth.

Jashon asserted familiarity with Jock and his hotel project, and I conceded that it had failed. Jashon informed me that Jock worked for "us," but, knowing Jock's disdain for government, I doubted that we spoke of the same man. Jashon was amused by my response.

Their rudeness was geared toward dissuading me from continuing with the lucrative leasing project, but I was eager to discuss the transaction. Given that the city had not structured a lease before, I asked if Jashon had ever worked on a lease. He said no. I acknowledged that there are variations and suggested that we exchange knowledge regarding financing. I had researched the city's vehicle needs, and perhaps he could teach me something that he knew from a different angle.

He looked at the other guy disbelievingly and chuckled. They had not run me off after all.

Jashon needed help understanding the numbers that I had gathered. I had given him a locked spreadsheet and offered to answer his questions. He suggested we might add fire trucks and engines to the list, which would raise the number of transactions. I was thrilled.

I answered his questions readily, especially about the calculating software. I was happy to help, since that was an important part of many engineering assignments I had done at West Point. My work in these spreadsheets powered our projections and conversations, and I walked him through them a few times over the phone. He wanted to know the formulas for the spreadsheet, so I told him how he could duplicate them.

Several days later, Jashon demanded the spreadsheet password, saying that he was going to brief the mayor. I was uncomfortable sharing it with him and offered to work whatever calculation he was attempting. He had no interest. He just demanded the password, telling me that if I did not share it, I would lose the contract. I gave him the password, and he hung up.

When I next heard from Jashon, he assured me that the city would not use my company again after all. When I asked why, he said they wanted finance contractors closer to the "organization" to continue with the work. The KKK "organization" had reared its head again.

Toni on Jashon's Decision

I explained my position to a senior Indianapolis business owner named Toni, and she empathized. "I tell everyone who will listen that our state, including Indianapolis, puts black women out of business by inviting them to die on the vine. It's happening to you now. You have a big, beautiful brain, but it still is happening to you."

We sat in her office, rich with cool colors and great art and floral arrangements. Toni was a handsome woman who readily gave of her time to many women trying to reach her status.

"Do you have advice for me?" I asked, still frustrated.

"You've done it, Tracey," she smiled. When I did not understand, she explained, "You started a company and did your job helping them save money. That's what you were supposed to do. The problem is that they would rather hear your ideas from someone other than you. To you, you did your job well, but to them, someone like you cannot get the credit.

"Tracey, don't internalize it," she continued. "It's not you. It's us," she paused. "It's not you. That may not help you feel better."

"You sound like a boyfriend I've never had: 'it's not you, it's me.'" We laughed. "Is there a solution?"

She thought through my options. "If you can market yourself outside of Indiana, you might have a shot. It's the white men here. The white women sometimes ignore it because they get somewhat better treatment, but I fight to change things every day. It's a huge struggle."

I hugged her. Toni smelled amazing and was always dressed for a camera. She impressed the senses. As I walked out, I realized that my own clothes were as aged as my car, and yet it was my new idea that had enabled "the boys" to save some money. Instead of calculating the income I would miss, I gathered pride in what I had accomplished, and resolved to move forward. I knew Indiana is not color-blind, but time would tell just how color-sighted Indianapolis was.

Mentor I, 2010

Another woman business leader suggested that I work with a friend of hers, a lobbyist to negotiate with the city on my behalf, so I called my mentor to get a second opinion. He deemed mine to be the only true minority-owned company in the area doing what I did. The other one in Indianapolis, according to him, was really run by a Caucasian guy, a millionaire that owned a large leasing company that, off the books, controlled a black-owned company in order to use diversity credit.

"He soaks up the diversity business. Plus 'they' like him," my mentor explained.

"They like the black guy?" I wondered.

"No, 'they' like the white guy, Matt Frogged. He's theirs. They are using the black guy to get minority business. They tip the black guy and keep the lion's share of the money for themselves," he educated me. "They don't like the black guy. He is just there."

"The fact that you needed neither a lobbyist nor a rich employee to succeed makes you unfavorable to them."

"Does this happen to everyone?" I wondered.

"To many. They approached other diversity companies in other specialties too. Nothing happening to you is a secret. It's easier for them to work with someone who will ask fewer questions. You surely will ask more once your commission is shared. Moreover you are stumbling onto a situation that will cost you more than you think with that lobbyist. Her involvement is not free."

"Thank you, I guess."

"Keep your head up. It's tough out there."

"It's tough in here." We laughed.

"You're smart enough to make it. Don't give up."

When I requested more information about why the city would not work with me after all, the Finance Officer refused to meet with me, and the department head and accountant began referring me to Jashon. When the transaction ended, everyone, including my team, was paid, except for me. Jashon had de-authorized my pay.

The city lawyer assured me that I could sue. The case would take two years or so.

My minority mentor advised differently. "You are a single mother who doesn't have the financial option to sue. They know your income. They have your tax information. The information is a phone call away. Sign the contract. And Tracey . . ." he trailed off, and I waited for him to finish. "Jashon is going to cut you loose and give this project to 'them.' Be prepared. Keep your head up. You did a good job, but they want to make money without you."

When I called Jashon to tell him that I had signed, he told me to "expect the story to change in the future." I did not understand.

"We did not need you to come up with this, and when you try to say you did, you are going to find another version of everything. For example, *you* volunteered your password. We had already started working on this. There were several bids. Just wait."

I wondered how Jashon would demonstrate that, given the computer data. "It won't be a problem, since it will take you ten years to remember," he jabbed. Generally, others cannot guess that a person has PTSD, but the KKK knew my illness well, using it to taunt me for years.

"There will be plenty of proof, and no one who will vouch for you," warned Jashon.

It's worth repetition: it takes money to maintain a separate reality from truth. If he and whoever backed him could create the proof on a server, I, a regular person, enjoyed little hope.

"*We* have the transaction now. Quite honestly, many of us have seen enough of you, way too much of you, if you know what I mean. We know all about you." He hinted again that I had legal problems, and suggested that I had a domestic abuse case that only need be filed.

Mentor II, 2010

"You did a good job, Trace," my mentor reminded me. "You are from Indiana, but you do not know how some business is done in Indiana. Now you know. They want to make this money amongst themselves. It does not involve you anymore."

You can never say that the owner of a project does nothing: he or she selects, approves, and funds the ideas. Still, properly recognizing a vendor for spearheading an idea that saved millions legitimizes the vendor's work.

I brought the initial research, ideas, calculations, and Excel skills, and Jashon brought the revenue and volume changes as envisioned. The decision was made to use someone closer to "the organization," which was not me. A different ending would have meant a great deal for my small business and family. I carried on.

Mommy, 2012

"Knock, knock." I smiled and blew a kiss at my mother as I entered her "office" once again.

"Sit yourself down," Mommy ordered while hugging me. "Talking about 'knock, knock' on a Walmart bench." We laughed.

"Well, I know you have other patients," I joked, knowing full well that I was my mother's most frequent "patient," if not her only one. The VA had been helping me for twelve years with PTSD and dissociative amnesia. Mommy had been helping me with everything else for forty-plus years. Whenever I experienced prejudice, I talked to her about it.

I had started working at a mortgage company and discovered that my manager was blatantly running minorities and women out of the company. A few guys on our team openly bragged that I was next. Needing the job, I stood up to the manager, the clash from which drew the attention of our entire chain of command. They would all eventually lecture him until blue in the face, but in that moment, a delicate stalemate existed, as our superiors balanced the need to protect a tenured manager and keep a brilliant contributor.

After I updated my mother on the situation, she took a drag on her cigarette. "When an execution is arbitrary, statistics rarely save one offender in a group,"

"Why?"

"It doesn't matter who the executioner picks next."

"So we're all guilty together?" I asked, confused.

"We're all terminated together," she clarified.

"I've been guilty a lot." We laughed.

Undeterred

She flicked ashes, expelling smoke into the air. "Now you are talking. Hey, it's a good thing you got healthier to deal with this yahoo. See what you would have missed?"

"What do you think is going to happen?" I was serious.

"*Make* something happen. Find another team in the company and announce that you are moving. When you get to that team, sell your toes off so he'll miss you."

"Own it, basically."

"Yes, Ma'am. You are over a quarter of his paycheck, honey, but he's acting like he doesn't like paychecks." She raised a hand to block the sun, while studying a helicopter overhead. "Tracey, you don't *have* to be a quarter of anyone's paycheck. You have options."

"I know," I said, thinking. "I am going to look into selling my house, just in case this job goes south."

Mommy shook her head. "Do your homework, and do what I said: dump your team. The only move you may need to make is internal. As far as that house, Papa would tell you to 'stand still.'"

Kritz's Threat, 2012

I listed my house on the market in 2012, not long after being accepted to dual business schools. Despite my sales, I was unsure about the job with the mortgage company. The company's vice president, my admitted fan, could not solve the problem of my lack of support from my manager. I decided to protect against potential losses by selling my house.

One Sunday, I drove through my neighborhood and found a random realtor performing an open house for a neighbor. A stranger to me, he agreed to drop by my place when he finished the open house.

Nothing about him indicated that he was a Klansman, but my face or name assured him that I was a preferred target of the Klan. It was his lucky day. He, therefore, approached me as an enemy, jabbering of Klan supremacy in Indiana and taking credit for their crimes. He planned to compromise me.

Tall with short, dark hair and a heart-shaped head, Kritz Hillograss wore khakis, a tie, and a medium-weight dark jacket, despite the warm spring weather. He sold for a RE/MAX office in southern Indianapolis at the time, but later opened his own brokering office. When he came by my house, we sat at the dining room table with his back to a window. I sat next to him, facing the kitchen island and refrigerator.

"What do you do for a living?" he asked without a smile.

I told him I was a mortgage originator for a company and I also owned a small leasing business. My Chihuahua, Hector, barreled down the stairs and took an instant dislike to Kritz, who said nothing more until I picked up the small dog, allowing him to stand on my lap.

"We don't need originators. We have our own."

The statement struck me as odd because I was not seeking employment.

"What does your personal business do?" Kritz continued, though he already knew. He already knew me. He was fishing, because that is what Klansmen do.

"I'm a lease originator for corporations and municipalities."

"Is business good?" he wanted to know.

"I am taking a break from leasing right now to focus on my mortgage job and dual master's degrees in business and international business."

"Where have you had business dealings?" Kritz asked. These seemed like odd questions for someone whom I thought would be more interested in my house.

"The City of Indianapolis. I originated a lease program at the city–"

"We know that," he cut me off, apparently bored by the discussion. "You were going to use that deal to start a political career. We cannot have that."

"I'm not a politician. The deal was my idea. It was not a political deal. It was a smart decision."

"And we have it now." Kritz was nonchalant in his response. Hector calmed enough to sit still on my lap.

"Have what?"

Undeterred

"Your good idea. We have it." He took no notes and rarely lost eye contact with me. "Were you grateful we let you keep that first deal with the city?"

"I am grateful I pursued it from a different angle. I enlisted the motor pool–"

He cut me off again, asking what was the biggest deal I had worked on in Indianapolis. More fishing.

I answered, "A deal with a medical facility. I won a big request for business."

"Did you get paid?" His eyebrows raised; he knew the answer. The deal was shut down. No one was paid. "Of course you didn't, right?"

"I beat out my competition," I pointed out. My only competition was Puttnam Industries, the Klan's answer to diversity leasing.

Kritz cleared his throat. "You made no money on the victory. That would have been different, had we won." I was not sure if they could have kept the contract or not. I knew for a fact that I won the proposal and did not get the contract.

That moment would have been the perfect time for my brain to kick in and realize that I was sitting in my dining room with someone who was against me, my son, and our livelihood. Nothing kicked in. "What does that mean?" I asked instead.

"Well, the *organization* is beating you everywhere else in Indiana. Leasing in Indiana is ours. Diversity leasing is ours, too. With your municipal idea, which is also now ours, we have made a killing."

I should have asked who owned the diversity company of which he spoke. I assumed the owner was a woman, since diversity business is set aside for companies that are owned by minorities, women, veterans, or gays, lesbians, bisexuals or transgenders. I should have realized that if Kritz spoke of a woman, I would have already met her through a women's business group. I didn't make the connections.

"How long have you had the diversity business?" I asked. At that point, my brain defaulted to believing that the owner had to be a white woman that I had not met.

"Since long before you came on the scene. We want to get more diversity business, but leasing is low-hanging fruit. We got that." He let that sink in.

Had Jashon passed Indianapolis' leasing to the Klan on his way to Chief of Staff of the City? How did Kritz and his compatriots own diversity leasing?

"Well, I have a new idea to help me prepare to compete better. I will try it after graduate school."

Kritz dropped his pen on the floor, and when he bent to fish it out from under the table, Hector objected mightily to Kritz's changed position.

"Our motto is: we get everything after the first sale. We are all well-connected. We will turn your idea against you without a second thought. We do not have to run the company in order to *infect* it. We will take any idea we want in our state."

I did not know how to take that. Another person would have drawn quicker conclusions, but Kritz only seemed cocky to me. I was facing the refrigerator and sink, thinking that I wanted a cold drink, something to quench my thirst as the room heated up, but I didn't want to offer anything to Kritz.

"Have you looked into Detroit?"

I could hear the TV growing louder in the family room behind me. "No," I said.

"You may want to."

"Why?" Audio advertisements for a morning show blared.

"You'll get better consideration in Detroit."

I stood with Hector to turn down the TV. "Why should I go to Detroit?"

"Because we have Indiana. We do not want you entertaining thoughts of a political career here. After we voted to set you up with Jock, we decided that we had enough on you. You can live here, but you cannot move inside of Indianapolis proper."

Indiana is a fried egg, sunny side up. The conservative egg whites surround a more liberal yolk in Indianapolis. To complete its influence

Undeterred

in the state, the Klan has to solve the problem of that center piece. It scrambles Indy with criminal activities and institutes itself wherever possible. Theirs is a labor of hate and self-love.

"You know Jock had a longtime girlfriend." He checked my face for a response.

I was surprised that he knew Jock, but I should have been surprised that he knew that *I* knew Jock. Kritz continued, relishing his role, "Jock and his girlfriend were together when you met. We forced him to date you. He didn't want to. You cannot remember right now, but you will. Trust me, you will." His words meant more to him than to me.

Kritz's tone begged me to recall events that I was still in shock over. The only thing I could remember was Jock's body, because it was one of the last things I saw before going in shock. Many a heterosexual women would pass on dating him upon learning his secret. I recalled the embarrassed grimace on his face when he showed me. Kritz probably did not know Jock's secret, and I had no reason to tell him. I just sat reminiscing over the distortion on Jock's face, the grimace. If his girlfriend was happy, I was happy for them both. I tend not to wish people malice.

"You'll remember," Kritz promised. "You're *slow* like that. It's in your best interest to keep your mouth shut. Know what I mean?" He shook a paternal finger and scowled at me as if I were a child.

"I'm not slow." His declaration was offensive to anyone, mentally ill or not.

"We voted to stop targeting you after Jock," Kritz continued, not responding to my comment. "We know we have the upper hand. Jock does not want to be humiliated anymore either, so keep your mouth shut about us. Jock has paid enough for not squaring up that loan he had with us before his bankruptcy. No one files bankruptcy on us. No one."

For Kritz and people like him, control means having something demeaning or humiliating hanging over another person's head. To them, such a person should know better than to stand up for themselves. Perhaps the real story is not what you dangle over another's head, but their response, their decision to agree and disagree. My doctor said that no one cares what the KKK says; that's why they hide. If given a chance to publicly stand by his threat, would Kritz hide or run?

The references to Jock did not wake me from shock. Nothing would.

More on Insurance

Berk, my first insurance man, explained the insurance process clearly: struggling businessmen do dishonorable work to unloose the creditor's hold around their neck if the creditor is a long-armed, organized criminal unit like the KKK. The insurance men commit assigned crimes to threaten a target and downplay the KKK's involvement. Insurance men are also victims, forced to become a perpetrator to eliminate their debt. Their nonmember status encourages others to disbelieve the victim, despite a KKK message or threat to harm.

Outsiders will ask, "How could a Catholic do this?" in Jock's case, or "Why would someone married to an Hispanic do that?" in Berk's case. The cops will say, "He has no record." Observers claim to have known him for years: "He's helped the Little League team." In unison, "This cannot be true." Thus, this kind of "insurance" promises the ready disbelief of others. The insurance man occupies a single square of the chessboard as both a KKK multiplier and societal divider. He helps the KKK and hurts a fellow citizen simultaneously, while thinning the average citizens' ranks to save himself.

Meanwhile, the KKK castles.

On the other hand, consider the KKK's position on the game board. They love only themselves. Using a distressed businessman to hurt an enemy player is a way of sitting back and resting while watching your enemies destroy each other. The castled Klansman uses terror to force his opponent into self-annihilation for mere entertainment. The Klansman can win and leave many enemy pieces standing. His insurance man is left to checkers-like tactics, often pushing a fellow citizen around until extinct.

Insurance men do not dare speak without orders. Theirs is a position of sworn secrecy, since they lose their victim status upon doling that same victim status to others. Meanwhile, regular people occupy most squares around us, not defining themselves as combatants at all. Theirs is a carefree day in oblivion, their own brand of shock or ignorance. Cruel actions carried out quietly force the victim to question the very nature of peace.

Jock had been bragging lately of his financial comeback, and I was happy for him. When I first met him, he was stressed with financial pressures and drowned his nerves in scotch. I knew that he was under a lot of pressure, but I assumed he would get back on his feet with the Bloomington property that he tried to hold on to.

Jock had repeatedly tried to coach me out of shock over the years. He once remarked, "These shit heads are taking over everything." When I questioned whom he spoke of, he shook his head and said that they were men from his golf club. He asked if Bloomington doctors operated on me. I answered no. He whispered, "You may say that these fuckers ruined your life, and they are trying to say she dated someone." When I asked whom he spoke of, he again shook his head and reached for scotch.

Nothing could bring me out of shock about Jock, not even Jock. Kritz, a man I had just met, certainly couldn't. The longer I dwelled on Jock though, the more I was ignoring the ongoing conversation with Kritz.

Kritz' Privilege, 2012

"What other states have you thought of living in?" Kritz asked.

I listed states that I had thought might suffice. Kritz glanced away and ran through my list of states in his mind, concluding that my selections were all growing, popular hot spots for "them."

"Again, I would look into Detroit if I were you."

Finally, I asked who were the "we" and "them" of which he spoke.

With a long blank stare, Kritz said, "The organization," that oft-repeated code word for the KKK that I had been hearing, yet not recognizing, for years.

Clueless, I asked, "What is the organization called?"

Kritz paused and studied me, not fully believing my question, given my history. I studied the ceramic cookie jar shaped like a maiden on the shelf above my refrigerator. It had originally been my grandmother's and I forgot that I had it in my possession. The inevitable clicking of the ceramic halves tattled on anyone lifting its lid. It took skill to open that ceramic maiden clandestinely.

I asked Kritz again, "Seriously, what is this network called?"

"Think about it." As I thought about it, I heard the TV volume creep back up to annoyance. I did not know.

Not believing that I, of all people, asked what his organization was called, Kritz asked, "How do you *feel* right now?"

Truth be known, Kritz irritated me, especially his bragging about his friendship with my competition, which he claimed had locked me out of a deal that I'd rightfully won. "I feel fine."

"Are you in shock?" Only a Klansman or my doctors would ask that question. Only my mother could automatically tell just by looking at me.

"Well, that's a strange question to ask me." Asking a person with PTSD if they are in shock is both strange and useless, since we are the last ones to know.

I started talking about my competition: Timmy, the black guy who owned Puttnam, the only other diversity leasing business in the area that I knew of. When Kritz answered my questions about the company though, he spoke only of the white guy, Matt Frogged, who, according to many in the minority business community, actually controlled my competition and tipped the black guy for the use of his diversity status.

I focused on the cookie jar perched on the kitchen shelf, wanting to ask Kritz to stop tapping his finger on the table. "Well, what do you like about him?" I asked instead.

"Who?"

"What do you like about Timmy?"

"Nothing," he spit.

Undeterred

Kritz liked nothing about the owner of the company that was my primary competition, and yet he touted the company as great. My mentor had understood the situation, but I was having a tough time connecting the dots. My mentor had said, "They like the white guy, Tracey. He is a millionaire. He is theirs. Everybody knows it." My mentor chuckled. "Wake up, girl. You are in unfamiliar waters."

Mindful of my mental dilemmas, Kritz changed the subject: "There are plenty of good career paths in Indiana, but you will not find one. We have almost all the companies. We just won't carve a way for you. There are too many of us." Kritz's finger tapping continued until Hector's barking resumed. I wondered how long it would take the tiny dog to train him.

Dr. Kalen tried to push me toward a different career path in some sort of empirical science.

"We're not going to give you anything, as you can probably tell by now. I mean absolutely nothing."

I felt offended. I had not asked for anything from his company or his mysterious organization, so I could not imagine why he had said that. His bragging about diversity leasing business earlier also felt odd.

"Did I ask you for anything?" I asked. I was having increasing trouble keeping Hector on my lap, and I feared that, if loose, he would snip at Kritz's ankles. "I have good qualifications for many things. I did not ask you for anything. I will make a way for myself."

"Listen, I'm just saying…" he trailed off in thought. "Nothing you choose will be a good fit here." He shook his head. "Absolutely nothing. Not in employment. Not in business. We will take your ideas, everything. There is a selection process for every career path in Indiana. I'm just telling you that the likes of you will never be selected. There are too many of us." He continued to brag about how the best jobs in Indiana went to members of his organization.

Finally, he got to the point: "How much money do you need in order to move? Bottom line." He began tapping the dining room table with his pointer finger again, piquing Hector's interest to a growl until he stopped.

Kritz had not evaluated my house, had not even looked around, so I did not know how to take that question. "How do I know?"

"How much do you owe on it?"

"I want an answer based on the value," I told him firmly. The thought of working clearly irked him. He shifted his position in the chair, trying to find the words to explain to me that he intended only to tip me for the house and keep as much of my equity as possible.

Instead, he changed tactics again, asking, almost as an afterthought, "Can you write?"

"Sure, I have a good command of English. I wrote well in school and college. I wrote songs and poems coming out of the military. Do you need something written?"

Agitated that I did not understand his meaning, he held up a hand to stop me. "What do you write now?" he asked. "Books?"

Once again, the KKK was concerned with a possible book.

"I work every day."

He twirled his finger in the air to hurry my brain along. "In the future?"

"Grad school will have me writing something, I'm sure," I assured him. "I heard it's intensive."

Kritz abruptly demanded, "Are you writing a book or not?" Specifically, he wanted to know if I were writing a book about the KKK.

"Between work and starting school soon?" I postulated. "No, I am not writing a book." I couldn't imagine it.

His tapping began anew. Hector responded with a growl until I held him closer.

"Well, everyone from your case has moved on to bigger and better positions in the organization. No one wants to go through having to dodge reporters for you."

Curiously, I asked. "Do you dodge reporters, too?

He eyed me harder. A sufferer's face may not announce PTSD, but Kritz thought I was going into shock. "Do you feel tired?"

"No."

"Are you numb?" He knew my disease well.

"No."

He studied me as if in disbelief, and then hammered into a new topic. "How many security cameras do you have?"

"None."

"There is a security system on this house. Is it disabled?"

"Yes."

"We can see if a system like yours is really working when we enter." He nodded slowly, telling me to count on his words.

"Oh? Can you fix my security system?"

"No, we won't fix your security system! We can, however, test it and see if it works. If you are tricking us…" Kritz trailed off, unwilling or unable to finish the thought aloud. His concern was that I would tape the KKK going through my belongings while my house was up for sale. Such video could prove to be damaging. My concern was with getting my alarm fixed.

"Why bother with the test if you are not going to fix the alarm system?" I wondered. I was rewarded with a blank stare. He made no sense to me.

"There is an FBI office just inside Indy. Do you have friends there?" The KKK does not want to draw the FBI's attention.

"No."

"Classmates?"

"No."

"One of the first things we do in a house like this is scan for videos cameras. We have little boxes that blink red to alert us that you have a secret camera video taping us."

"Great." I did not know how that would help me, but I was okay with it. "Do you sell them?"

"Sell what?"

"Cameras. With all your organizational networking, maybe I can get a deal." He eyed me as if ready to spit. I was serious.

Kritz was loosing his patience. "No, we don't sell cameras," he snapped.

"Then why be experts at security systems if you're not helpful?"

"Listen," he scolded in a firm tone, "the organization will take you to task if this is a setup, Tracey."

"Setup? Are you setting up your own cameras here?"

"No!"

"Then why are you so obsessed with cameras? I'm confused," I confessed.

"Listen, this is serious."

"I hope so. I want some good offers."

He wore a blank stare.

Kritz's Walk-Through, 2012

I stood to escort Kritz through the house, glancing back at the ceramic maiden above the refrigerator. I smiled, happy to have rediscovered her.

Hector beat us up the stairs, where Kritz barely looked in my four bedrooms. Standing in my room, he declared that they would sweep everything for red dots. Hector and I watched as he held up his hand and waved an invisible, imaginary box around as if looking for red lights from cameras as he spoke. We were silent until Hector erupted in disapproval. I casually glanced at the carpet and considered getting it deep cleaned.

He faced me, pointing at my laptop. "How many computers do you have?" he demanded.

"Just one."

"This Mac right here?" He calculated that if I had a book about the KKK in the works, it would be on my Mac.

"Don't stare at it so long. I'm not letting it go with the house." I liked my joke. He didn't.

Though I had been the one to contact Kritz and ask him to come over, I could not understand him. We were standing alone in my house, having two separate conversations.

I had stolen countless cookies from the ceramic maiden cookie jar as a child. I insisted on having it from my grandmother's things for sentimental reasons. As I sat with Kritz, I did not discern his intent to steal as well. He did not want snacks or drinks, though; his appetite was electronic. My laptop was too irresistible to pass up if it housed a book about the KKK.

Don, 2012

Kritz would say that his tip about Detroit and his frank talk were nothing but kind gestures on his part. Still, it explained his next steps: peruse the numbers, come back for the paperwork, wait until she calls to ask you why you are not doing anything, and then float some suggestions to move her out of the house, and hopefully the state. It all made sense when I realized for whom his net was truly cast.

After nearly two months with no other visitors, a broker from Bloomington in Kritz's "sister RE/MAX office" came through my house. The day he came, Kritz asked again if I had installed new, functioning video cameras. I repeated that I had not, but when I asked if cameras were a selling point nowadays, he said that they were for this particular broker, identifying him as a camera expert. After the appointment, I was told that my house was "lackluster," and the broker had no interest in buying it. When I asked what the family, the real customer in my mind, said, the conversation was cut short. No family had come through my house.

The day of the broker visit, I waited down the street for the utility vehicle in my driveway to leave so I could get home. It seemed to not want to leave. I got impatient to get into my house and use the bathroom, so I drove closer. As I pulled up, I saw that the vehicle favored a locksmith truck. Of course, Kritz already had my keys, so I wasn't sure why the truck was there. There were several ladders of different sizes on both sides of the truck. I couldn't imagine what a broker needs to reach when viewing a house; high places for video feeds did not occur to me.

I raised my garage door, hoping to stir the broker to leave. In my opinion, he had been there too long. A white man with a dark newsboy cap walked out quickly, carrying a large CD holder. It was sloppily stuffed full of CDs that slipped out, making the case hard for him to close. He did not carry even one piece of paper. Perhaps he had memorized the house listing or stuffed it in his pocket?

The CDs indicated that he had copied information from my computer. I did not think to accuse him of copying my hard drive to search for a book that, as of that moment, I had not written nor even conceived yet. When you are rummaging for a find, you leave no stone unturned.

As I passed him, we exchanged pleasantries. It was Don, though my brain refused to recognize him.

"Well, this is awkward, isn't it?" he asked, breathing heavily. I ignored him and kept moving toward the back door through the garage.

He asked incredulously, "You don't even remember me?"

I stopped and stared at him blankly.

"Come on! Really?" he prodded.

I stood in the garage with one hand on the door.

"Well, you're not getting any better, I see. You are just getting worse. What a pity! We should have killed you back then. It did no good leaving you alive."

"Excuse me?"

"I should kill you now. We stopped voting on you after Jock," he said, ascending his truck with a smile.

Thinking of nothing to say, I faced his truck, still sitting in my driveway, decked out with ladders and side compartments.

"Goodness!" he smiled and waved me off like an irritant at my own house.

A week or two later, Kritz told me that someone had made a low offer on my house to "help me out." Only the broker with ladders and side compartments who claimed to recognize me had visited. The realtor confirmed that the offer was from "the Bloomington office." I rejected the offer and took my house off the market.

Undeterred

The only company in Bloomington that is a "sister office" to the RE/MAX I used is run by none other than Don Fletcher, who had advanced from being Dr. Kalen's office manager/security guy, to being an important Bloomington real estate broker–thus the preoccupation with security system cameras.

I had walked past a convicted felon who had been camped out in my house alone for forty-five minutes or more and, until much later, I questioned nothing. I calmly walked past a man who had illegally entered my previous home, stolen business from me, and made every effort to ruin my life. Seeing Don at my house that day slowly ignited flashbacks from Bloomington–their hatred for me based on the fact that I am black, female, homosexual, and, most tantalizing of all, a West Pointer.

Growing up, I thought Klansmen weren't seen during the day. Today, Hoosiers do not have to look for them at all: they're everywhere. My mind needs a trigger to recall terror; they only require a trigger to deliver it. It's so slight of hand, you might miss it. It's so heavy a hand, it might kill you. It's arbitrary which might happen, and the outcome does not depend upon merit.

Kritz acted about as decently to me as his discipline allowed. Of course, he sat at my dining room table and announced that the Klan owned the diversity business that my company had repeatedly failed to secure. He also ushered in a broker to access and assess my living arrangements. Was his plug for Detroit a distant cry from Bloomington to get me out of state again, or a gentle reminder that their vision for the future United States involves painting borders by color?

Kritz did not taunt me as much as other KKK members had. His indifference countered the others' viciousness. Kritz simply wanted to cash a realtor's commission check, if possible. Is there a difference though, when the result is less consideration for your fellow citizens?

Some Klansmen suggested that my writing a book would only serve to express how great and powerful the Klan is in Indiana and the United States in general. How mentally ill does a group have to be to want to take credit for kicking a mentally ill person from their job and home, for luring young women into hotel rooms to satisfy their testosterone surges, for coercing signatures, for peering into people's bedrooms and baths, for threatening citizens to not write books, or for attempting to kill someone for doing their job? A land where Klan-like behavior prevails is lawless, both for those with white and brown skin.

Cheer

Because I know the challenges of my disease, I often root for myself. Even in a metaphorical empty stadium, I throw up two hands and "woo woo" my prospects. I do not dwell on the past, and a given moment consumes my present, allowing me to make preparations for my future. That next idea is what fuels me. American citizens work hard to accomplish retirement and freedom. Many mentally ill people work hard simply to stave off homelessness and inequality. I have always seen myself succeeding--always, both before and after the drag of hatred and my disease. I find myself addicted to this simple mantra: I am worthy.

Part Four: Challenges

STRIFE, 2013-2016

For years I had ignored doctors telling me I had an iron problem. The inception of this advice dated back to when I moved to Indianapolis from Bloomington. My doctor had retired, but not before giving me iron pills, dietary advice, and guidance to underline the fact that something, somewhere was wrong with me. Every time she suggested a colonoscopy, I declined. The VA, not recognizing me as the disabled veteran that I am, would probably not cover it, so I avoided the exam.

My new doctor was African. Dr. Tuluo came with a thick accent and an intellectual presence that I can only describe as noteworthy. I listened to her because her voice drew me in to everything she said.

"Why are you ignoring all the warning signs," she asked with thick African intonation. She removed her stethoscope and placed it over her crossed legs. She was feminine, purposely healthy to demonstrate the theories that she preached. Her dreadlocks were as petite as her frame. I admired her wardrobe. She repeated herself, "Why are you ignoring the warning sign?"

I had no answer. It is embarrassing to say that you lack the funds to save your life.

"This is *the* ailment of your age group. You need the test."

Dr. Tuluo made good points, but she was haggling with someone who was unafraid to die. Shame prevented me from explaining that I could not afford the test. The only question that remained was, were my mother and son ready to watch me die? I imagined that they were not, which obligated me to try. I admitted to not being a documented disabled veteran, so I lacked the coverage I needed. She said we would work through that.

I underwent multiple ultrasounds for my OB/GYN to understand other ailments. A week later my OB/GYN wanted to see me in his office, where he drew pictures and painted scenarios, explaining why he needed to operate and explore. The results from the ultrasounds were questionable. He gave me less than twelve hours to prepare for exploratory surgery on the same day as my scheduled colonoscopy. When I asked why the urgency, he admitted that something dwelled inside me that did not like being captured on film.

I lay on a gurney with Mommy in tow, grateful that she was willing to sit through a one-hour surgery with me. I thought about leaving because the cost of the surgery might tank me.

"Tracey," Mommy said, "your doctor wants you here. Lay back down."

As I waited to be taken down to the OR for the surgery, a lady from finance entered my room. "Hon, have you ever applied for your disability?"

I informed her that I would be denied, explaining what had happened with my medical records. With a gentle hand on my shoulder, she said that if my records were not available, I could make my case through letters from eyewitnesses who supported my claim. No one had ever told me that before. I asked if I should postpone my surgery, and she smiled and asked, "Can you get the letters?"

I had never tried, but I felt that I could make a go of it. Seeing that I was shaken by the possibility, she asked me to rest. She would mail instructions on how to apply and provide more guidance if I needed it.

The operating room was like an icebox, but we were rocking to "Born in the USA." A few people joked with me. The anesthesiologist asked my

Undeterred

name. Before I could finish telling him my address, everything disappeared, or maybe I disappeared. I no longer heard the music's beats.

I awoke to four doctors staring down at me, a beautiful team to awaken the sleeping. They wore green and white, leaning in as if ready to pounce. Folks had never looked better!

I slept the rest of the day. My OB/GYN came in again the following morning. "Tracey, how do you feel?"

"Fine."

"A little sore?"

"Yes."

"You will be very sore now, but it will get better."

I assured him that I was fine.

"Tracey, I spent five and a half hours with you yesterday on what we thought would be a one-hour surgery." He paused to let me think that through.

"I am not sure I have seen a tumor that large before. It was much larger, much more pervasive than anything we imagined. What concerns me though is that when I asked you how you were doing before the surgery, you repeatedly said 'fine.' I find it hard to believe that you were fine with a tumor that size consuming your reserves. It covered every organ, everywhere. You had to be tired, run down. I can assure you that you had that tumor for many, many years."

I did not know what to say.

"Are you constantly in the habit of telling people that you are fine when you aren't?"

"Maybe."

"How was your energy before?"

"Fine."

"Did you feel sluggish?"

I did not remember. "Sir, what is sluggish? You just get used to fighting. It's like being in a ring. To fight something, you just keep swinging."

"What you are saying is that you don't know what a good day feels like," he observed thoughtfully.

I considered that. "Maybe not," I confessed. I had certainly felt like I had good days with family and friends, but I could not describe them then. *Had my disease numbed me for too long?*

Taking several breaths and searching for a response, he averted his gaze. "Well, bursts of energy line your future, young lady. I expect you to leap with exuberance once your pain goes away."

"Okay."

"Bless you, Tracey. Get ready to feel great again."

"Thank you."

Jobs and Race

With new energy for my dual master's degrees, I traveled to Peru and South Africa as part of my regional studies. The international component of my degrees insists that students think globally. Latin America, Africa, Asia, and Eastern Europe are in a race to receive manufacturing jobs and heal poverty within. The stereotypes that these areas are not ready for investments are fallacies. These regions are prepared to work and sustain themselves.

The question is, where are the jobs? South Africa is the most poignant example. When the work force approximated slave labor, international businesses flocked to the country, happy to bring jobs that paid next to nothing, keeping their labor costs down. When Apartheid ended and fair employment became available, international investments dwindled. Johannesburg appears to be a ghost town in places now; the world does not seem to be interested in helping South Africans to their feet.

The example of Peru is different. Eighty percent of Peruvians are impoverished and either poorly educated or entirely uneducated, while a thin middle class separates the masses from the rich. An educated workforce attracts international investment, bringing jobs. Peru enjoys a robust economy and it could educate its workforce, but it shows sluggishness or a convenient confusion in accomplishing that mission.

In my opinion, this is due to a failure to define people as equal to one another, a persistent problem throughout the Latin American region. It

Undeterred

is a vital societal piece of the puzzle that prefaces international investments and bringing in jobs. When people are deemed equal, society educates everyone equally. If there is a question of worth, historically, a society fails to educate its people. It happened right here in the US with slaves. Equality begets the opportunity for education, humane treatment, better investment, and results.

I hate this example, but it resonates. My grandparents and I fished a lot. For years, Papa would put the worm on my hook for me because I detested the task. With time, I grew tired of asking for help, and I took the worm and ran the hook through the "eye," as Papa called it, though science calls it the *clitellum*. The worm writhed because its nervous system felt the blow. Both sides of the worm curled up, and I hooked the longest side several times, leaving the smaller side free to wiggle on my line. Not once did I cry for the worm, because the worm was not human. I have killed hundreds of worms in my lifetime while fishing.

Nineteenth-century Southern relics depict alligators hunting black babies, which were used by white men as lure for onshore traps. When you do not define someone as human or as equal, your treatment of him or her does not need to be equal. Using the black babies as bait meant nothing to the hunters.

Degan preached to me once that the KKK believes that nothing of value has dark skin. White men ranked first, and then their women. Black men were grossly inferior, and their women were necessarily even lower than that. I joked that the little black dog I found behind an office had value. Degan sneered that he had white skin with black hair. In her mind, this made him more valuable than the very few animals bearing dark skin, along with every person who had a non-white complexion. The emphasis on skin, more than on any other organ in the body, like the heart or the brain, serves only to fuel hatred.

Minorities, Degan argued, along with some women, gays, and people of different religions, can be treated without compunction when they are not defined as equal. You can use them for bait without tears. At times, the KKK may have to work with an "inferior" minority male like

Timmy, but there was never a reason to conjure that same respect for a minority woman. In their minds, there is rarely a reason to listen to minority females, even if we are smart and articulate.

Degan's insistence that minorities were beneath her made it nearly intolerable for her to set eyes on minority drug reps, especially women. She believes that she deserves better, and those sales representatives strolling in and out of the office that she felt trapped in, with bright futures ahead of them, turned her stomach. Her hope was always that the other Klanspeople would agree to expel them.

Degan indicated that most Indiana Klansmen lack the ability to control their disdain for smart, minority females. Consumed with hate, they were unable to metabolize or quench their rage upon the sight of such women. The Klansman sees in her a worm writhing. The woman sees a monster drinking hate to the point of drunkenness.

Earthworms earned equal disrespect from me. I lectured them on what was important to me: I wanted a big fish. I never discussed the future of their offspring. I did not care about their prospects, other than to bring me a big fish. Should the worm survive my fishing exploits, I tossed it to the side, just as a psychopath tosses aside one victim for another.

When I left Bloomington, Tohm took out the insurance against me to protect his reputation. Everyone I met deemed me an idiot who was good only for chastisement. The KKK has no remorse for its treatment of nonmembers. The national database dictates those they love and those they hate. They deem anyone who is not fighting in their ranks to be a slithery worm worthy of the degradation, of baiting death's hook.

We have to ask ourselves as a nation if that is okay. As a nation, we have to ask ourselves, *Are we equal?* The collective answer dictates our future.

Unrest

There are calls for civil unrest right here in the United States because we continue to trample on equality. Some say the government would win such a contest; others sincerely doubt that. I considered this as I stood in Nelson Mandela's first house in Johannesburg. There are bullet holes in the walls that you can feel with your fingertips. Authorities took a great number of shots at him. The paint covers little.

The first exhibit in the Mandela museum displays oversized ID badges that were used to identify a person's race and place in South African society. If there hadn't been a mixing of blood, would people need such cards? I looked into the eyes of the white people there and tried to imagine their detestation of my family and me.

Photo after photo detailed the horrors of an uprising between people who chose not to coexist. The rage in their eyes reminded me of those I'd known in the Bloomington doctors' offices. It's not worth experiencing a war of hate. Our soil supports too much and too many to brush aside equality.

Indianapolis is a place ripe for quiet, casual racism, but it prospers more through integration. When doctors band together to harm others, when businessmen find comfort in exclusion, when political representatives permit inequities based on KKK membership, that is when hate, long-standing, deep-seated hate, snakes through society's systems to establish itself as part of the institution. It's not everyone, of course, just a vocal, active, hateful few.

Ironically, the KKK is a national minority. Once upon a time, they used illegal means to prevent individuals from voting; now they can use money to get themselves to the top and have their ideas trickle down to the rest.

I'm only one person, an individual. What happened to the people who were less intelligent, less articulate, or more ill than I? Were they equally entertaining? Were their spirits broken? I muster the will. I stand. I speak. I write. I am.

Mommy, 2014

Mommy beat me to her office bench and I took a seat next to her. Fresh from graduation of both masters from Kelley School of Business (MBA) and Thunderbird School of Global Management (MGM), I radiated with dual-degree graduation bliss, while Mommy, needing open-heart surgery, barely eluded cardiac woes.

Her mission seemed more pertinent than mine.

I often drove her to her cardiology appointments and kept her chuckling about our lives, keeping her mind focused on the positive.

"These doctors make you wait so long," she lamented.

"Mommy, don't worry about the length of tomorrow's appointment. I can work around it."

"I have three appointments. That's a lot."

"I also see three doctors."

"For what?"

"Every PTSD patient should see a psychiatrist, a therapist, and a family practitioner as well."

"I wish that you still had Jewel. Jewel was there for you. Her eyes saw through your illness. She helped you so much."

"I hope that her retirement is delightful." Jewel and I had untangled a lot of webs together. We made a good team, and I missed her.

Our conversations on the bench never addressed retirement for my mother. She had been working and smoking since she was fourteen years old. She lost Mama to lupus, her sister to breast cancer, and Papa to a rare bone disease much like cancer. She appeared to enjoy considerable health, but had lost weight and developed an appetite for candy reminiscent of Mama's. I could see the changes that each year brought. My wish centered on her not dying in Walmart, that she be able to retire just like Jewel.

Her greatest value to me was as a sounding board. Our times in her office afforded me the opportunity to rethink my life, her life, and our relationship. With all the people stealing things from Walmart, the only thing I wanted from the Walton family business was my mother. To keep her from working to death, I'd be willing to steal her myself.

Revering Home, 2015

I'm not Paula Revere. The redcoats are not coming, and the white coats, be they the KKK or just their doctors, claim they've always been here. This book is not a Mr. Microphone warning of a looming, foreboding war. But it's strange to exit the army and be hunted by other citizens. We want to think that other Americans are not our adversaries; that our real enemies are overseas, not nestled within the borders of the country we promised to protect.

Groupthink has shaped history and wars. If you take a homogeneous group of people and allow them make decisions both for themselves and others outside the group, they will make decisions favoring just themselves almost every time. The belief that they are absolutely right only compounds the results, because they reassure each other. It is possible for good things to arise from groupthink, but preventing prejudice may be all but impossible, even when existing laws should prevent it. The majority may not want to follow a given law, so they institute a new one. Democracy is threatened by groupthink when what the majority wants lies outside the laws of a nation.

My team at work suffered from groupthink. I stopped being a quarter of an unappreciative man's paycheck when I left his team. The VP disbanded that group within months, deeming their prejudice a poison for current and incoming employees. One member of that group was put on final disciplinary action for joking about black women's vaginas and the inferiority of minorities. Ironically, he was a white man married to a black woman. The pressure to fit in with bigoted guys was so great that he disparaged his own wife to save face. He wouldn't be allowed to join the KKK.

Not everyone hails the KKK, but in Indiana the number warrants national recognition, as does the fervor. They are proud of their illegalities, but afraid of being named. They are affluent men sitting in khakis and ties at desks, watching crimes they ordered on camera. It's entertainment at the expense of others, more interesting than mainstream TV. What may be tasteless to most citizens delights these men when perpetuated against those they hate. They not only harm the person, they strongly reject the idea that he or she has potential, inviting them to believe that subjugating a fellow American is perfectly acceptable. It is arbitrary, unjust, and no way to run a civilization.

Indiana quietly vacillates on inclusion, and not always in a forward direction. The KKK identifies talent outside of its ranks and doggedly erases that talent through intimidation. They swear theirs is not fear, yet they shudder at certain voices not of their own ranks.

I'm not an expert on rapists, white supremacists, or psychopaths. I have simply watched them laugh, sneer, and applaud what they believed to be my fall or death. My history relates post-traumatic stress disorder and crimes of hate. Jayns and the KKK practiced deceit, secured with the notion that my illness might conceal their actions. But ultimately, PTSD protects the sufferer, not the perpetrator.

Only I could withstand the death threats, the murder attempts, and persist with this brain. I have lingered long enough to see men thirst with hate, long for energetic action, feel empowered to hurt others, and possess a willingness to kill. They hunt and kill in groups. I've witnessed the excitement and applause.

Still, I feel myself undeterred. Much may be at risk with this writing, but more may be at risk without it. What if others are targeted? The

Undeterred

KKK's efforts are quiet, steady, unchecked, and unspoken–a colossal rotation of individuals' Civil Rights backwards.

A nation asleep is a nation in danger. Life shakes us in order to wake us. I've seen hate interwoven throughout the fabric of medicine, politics, education, and business in Indiana.

The KKK's rule of law is incongruous with the law of the United States. They follow a dictator, such as a grand dragon. Members forfeit their rights as American citizens to a man that can order them dead, either of his own accord or with an electronic vote that he reserves the right to reverse. Imagine the fear and compliance invoked in a believer and, indeed, even for a nonbeliever among his troops.

Despite my PTSD, I've never cried about the rapes–not the physical mistreatment during West Point, nor the electronic molestation from Bloomington. God said, "Cast not your pearls to swine," and in the disabled, the Lord conceals sacred jewels unappreciated by those blind to divine intentions. I do not give more to those who value me so little.

Sometimes when I drive and I take in the sun's warmth or admire the clouds, I shed a tear for my grandparents. I can never stop giving to my mother and my grandparents, who always recognized my value.

Mommy, 2016

One February morning, I went to the VA to pick up a copy of my disability paperwork. The Department of Defense awarded me military disability status for the rest of my life. I only had to collect one letter for the board to review my case.

Elaine, my current doctor, congratulated me and chuckled that the process couldn't have ended sooner. Hers was sarcasm and jest.

"Why do you think I was the last to understand the KKK?"

"That's your disease, Tracey."

"PTSD with dissociative amnesia is a dangerous disease," I confessed. She only nodded.

"Why do you think the KKK strangely evil to the point of shear obliviousness?"

Elaine smiled. Though Caucasian, she knew that her life and the lives of her husband and children would diminish in quality considerably under the arbitrary rules of prejudice. She did not answer my question.

"To live in a world where hate rules," I explained. "You have to create a different reality from that which is real. Anyone different from you is naturally witless. If they are educated, they are wrongfully so. When they laugh and joke, they are not as charming as you. In fact, they are probably being belligerent. Supremacists believe there should be punishment for that."

Elaine looked up to search for a response. "That's *their* disease, Tracey. We *treat* people like the ones you have met..."

"Only if they ask for help, though," I interrupted.

"Only if," she agreed. "And that does not happen often. Still, people do not care what the KKK think. That's why the KKK covers their faces from the world; so that the rest of us won't ignore their hateful rhetoric or worse, judge them for it."

She faced me squarely and asked, "What kept you going?"

"When I was little we drove all over this state finding places to fish. Whenever we began to cross a covered bridge my grandmother would begin the prayers asking the Lord to keep us safe. The car darkened once we entered our jaunt and I feared the rickety road beneath our tires. I closed my eyes and thanked God that I was with my grandparents, but I peeked ahead to find a welcomed, constant light. There was always hope ahead. The experiences taught me to never give up. The light is before you, a command from above to never give up."

She smiled having been on a few wobbly bridges herself. "You have survived with passion."

"I was predestined to stare fear in the face and take treatment from hideous characters, to live and shine light on exactly what we are doing to each other," I observed. "Mine was a different fate.

With a nod, she handed me the printout of my records, and I headed for the garage to find my car.

I drive a convertible. Sometimes global warming allows me to drive with the top down in February. The car choice was at first a reluctant experiment at the suggestion of my son, but I have learned to appreciate how close it leaves me to my grandparents. I imagine them hovering on clouds, just over my right shoulder.

Later that afternoon, I picked my mother up from her "office" to visit a cardiologist. We made light talk in the car, because she was worried about the appointment. When we arrived, I let her out at the door because a light rain had begun. I found a parking spot and joined her inside.

As we sat in the sparsely crowded waiting room, Mommy, an avid reader, set aside her book and removed her reading glasses to think aloud, "My sister knew that she would die from breast cancer. I know," she affirmed with a nod, "that I'll die from heart problems."

I kissed my mother but could not tell her that we had something in common: I may die from a hate crime. Hate crimes transpire from heart problems, albeit someone else's.

Rest in Peace, Mommy
You motivate me.

Nancy Ellen Brame
September 1945 - September 2016

Originally from Indianapolis, Tracey Brame graduated from the US Military Academy at West Point with a degree in political science. Since then, she has earned dual masters degrees from the Kelley School of Business and the Thunderbird School of Global Management. She is the owner of West Point Financing, an equipment leasing company, and has devoted her life to exposing the modern, coercive methods of the Ku Klux Klan in the United States.

Endnotes

1. Helpguide.org, Emotional and Psychological Trauma http://www.helpguide.org/articles/ptsd-trauma/emotional-and-psychological-trauma.htm

www.ingramcontent.com/pod-product-compliance
Lightning Source LLC
Chambersburg PA
CBHW071259110426
42743CB00042B/1107